IMAGES
*of America*

# HOLLY SPRINGS

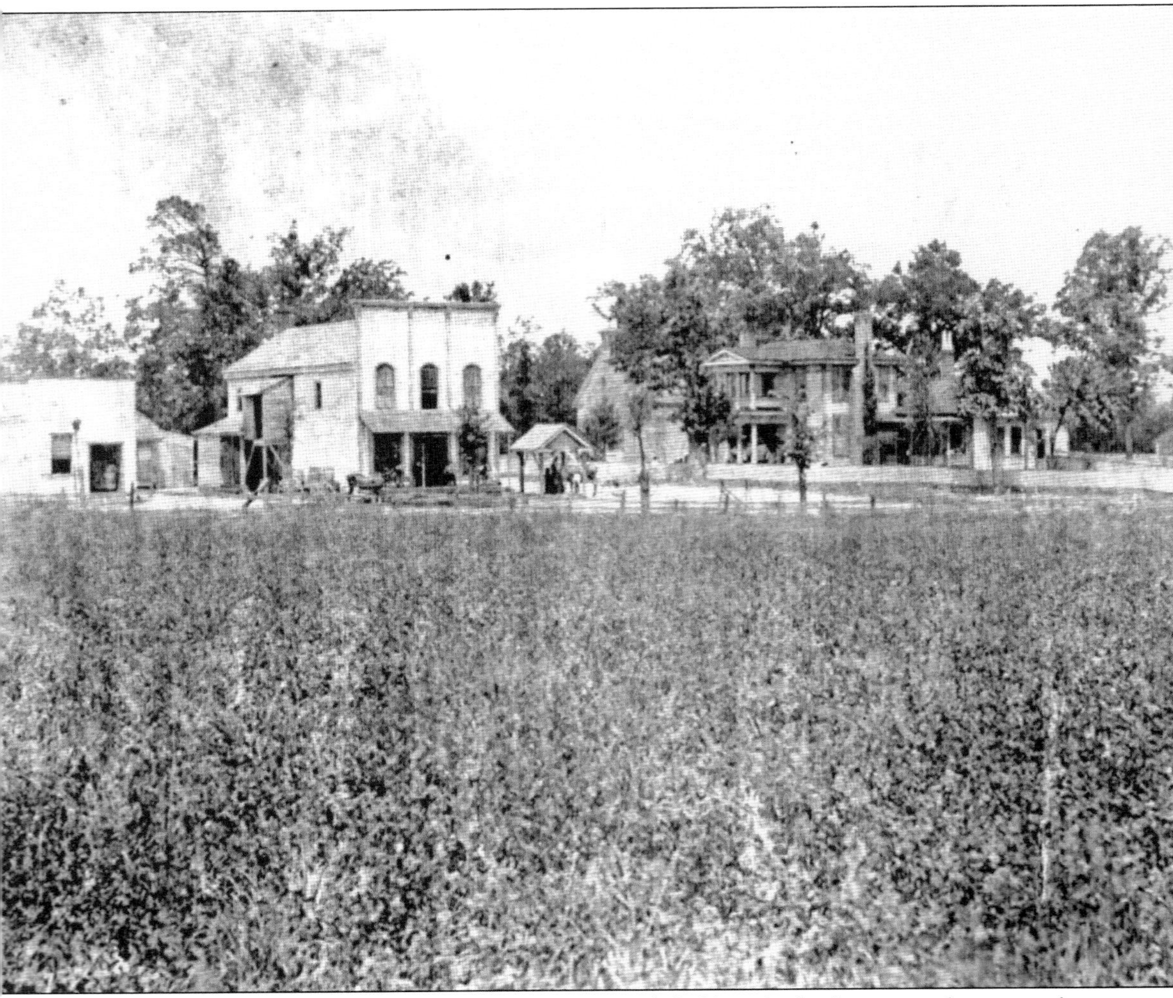

Upon arriving in Holly Springs around 1817, Archibald Leslie built a general mercantile store and established a tailoring business near the intersection of Avent Ferry Road and Center Street. Old-timers say the Western Sun Masonic Lodge No. 72 may have met on the second story of the building from 1818 to 1828. Lumber receipts state that the manor house was built about 1840. Leslie sold the manor, store, and surrounding acreage to George Benton Alford after the end of the Civil War. It is thought that Alford encouraged his good friend Thomas B. Holt, fellow Middle Creek resident and merchant, to relocate to Holly Springs as well. Chances are they ran the old Leslie General Store as partners. Fire consumed the old building before 1876, and soon thereafter, each businessman opened his own separate general store serving the community: Alford's on the corner of Main and Center Streets and Holt's near his house on Main Street near Earp Street. (Wright collection.)

**ON THE COVER:** Billy and Janet Stephens pose for their father, R. W. Stephens, staff reporter for Raleigh, North Carolina's *News and Observer* newspaper in this photograph taken in 1949. (Wright collection.)

IMAGES
*of America*

# HOLLY SPRINGS

Town of Holly Springs

ARCADIA
PUBLISHING

ISBN 978-0-7385-5441-9

Published by Arcadia Publishing
Charleston, South Carolina

Printed in the United States of America

Library of Congress Control Number: 2008924519

For all general information contact Arcadia Publishing at:
Telephone 843-853-2070
Fax 843-853-0044
E-mail sales@arcadiapublishing.com
For customer service and orders:
Toll-Free 1-888-313-2665

Visit us on the Internet at www.arcadiapublishing.com

*This book is dedicated to all the people born and reared in Holly Springs who have, with true-to-form Southern hospitality, watched their little sleepy town grow in population from 600 to more than 20,000 in 20 short years. With the influx of new arrivals, their community was acknowledged as the Fastest Growing Community in North Carolina in 2000, and in August 2007,* Money *magazine ranked the town No. 22 on its list of 100 "Best Places to Live" in America. Quiet little Holly Springs is neither quiet nor little any longer!*

# Contents

# ACKNOWLEDGMENTS

The Town of Holly Springs would like to thank a number of people who have helped in the preparation of this book. The publication of this collection would not have been possible without the tireless efforts of Holly Springs town historian Barbara Koblich. It was her idea, and she followed through, completing the project on behalf of the town with much enthusiasm, dedication, hard work, attention to detail, and a commitment to the historical truths and the people who are featured in these pages.

We also express appreciation to our contributors. Most of the photographs in this book came from the personal collections of longtime Holly Springs residents David Adams, Sylvian Brooks, Fred Burt, LaVerne Cofield, Evelyn and Bremen Dewar, Christine Epps, Vada Fiegler, Jean Goodwin, Jimmy H. Hancock, Drew Holland, Jerry Holland, Gerald W. Holleman, the Holly Springs Masonic Lodge No. 115 AF&AM, Mary and Billy Holt, George and Kathy Huegerich, Ken Jarvis, Doris Jones, Jean Jones, Dorothy Lanier, Cora Mae Lassiter, Mary Macon, John McNeil, the Railway and Locomotive Historical Society, the estate of Mary Lee Johnson courtesy of Lori Stokes, Theresa Underwood, Christine Utley, Carolyn and Nathan Williams, and Jimmie Ann Wright.

Select photographs were provided courtesy of the North Carolina State Archives as credited in captions, with special thanks to Kenny and Druscie Simpson.

Special thanks go to Karen-Marie Allen, manager of the Olivia Raney Local History Library, for her technical support and to Elena Owens, librarian of the Wake County Branch Library in Holly Springs, for her editing assistance.

A special appreciation is expressed to Cynthia Ellison, Melissa and Eric Lindbeck, and William and Claire Rousseau of the Holly Springs Historical Preservation Society, Inc., for their support and efforts.

# INTRODUCTION

In the early days of North Carolina history, in the far southwestern corner of what is now Wake County, Colonial travelers would stop to refresh their livestock at the abundant freshwater springs surrounded by towering holly trees.

A community soon grew up around those deep aquifers and extended into the outlying areas of Buckhorn, Wilbon, Collins, and Holleman's Crossroads, becoming what we now know as Holly Springs. These first pioneers found the area appealing with its fertile, well-drained soil and ample sources of fresh water. Many of those pioneer families, with names such as Burt, Holland, Holleman, Norris, and Utley, still are familiar in Holly Springs today.

The first chapter of this book focuses on the early years of Holly Springs' history, beginning in the early 1800s, when the surrounding area was untamed and unexplored. Period photographic images portray the enterprising men and women who against odds settled the community and developed commercial as well as agricultural opportunities that would benefit the entire southern part of the county.

Holly Springs has a rich history marked by periods of vitality and prosperity, interspersed with economic recession, coinciding with the Civil War and World Wars I and II. The second chapter depicts scenes from the lives of residents after World War II, when our town, along with other towns across America, thrived and grew.

Other chapters take a look at the progression of the churches and educational institutions of Holly Springs. Early facilities for both of these had humble beginnings either in log cabins or in private homes. The ensuing images show the advancement and improvements made to both these foundations over the past 175 years.

The last chapter showcases the homes, fraternal organizations, and commercial buildings that have stood as silent witnesses to Holly Springs' history, and as the title "If Walls Could Talk" depicts, we look at the structures' history and quite possibly their secrets.

Although it is impractical for this book to depict every founder, every building, every organization, every business, or every person, we do hope that a good representation has been achieved. By taking a trip back in time to the days of simple farmhouses, country stores, one-room schoolhouses, and dirt roads, our goal is to bring the reader from the past to the near present using each chapter to show how the area has grown into a progressive community with a county-managed school system, picturesque churches, thriving businesses, and modern roads.

It is the author's hope that the historical facts and profiles contained within this book will provide those who are curious enough to examine its pages with a window into the past history of the town of Holly Springs.

—Barbara Koblich, Town Historian

*One*

# Holly Springs
## The Early Years
## 1800–1949

TOWN OF HOLLY SPRINGS
MAYOR'S OFFICE
HOLLY SPRINGS, N. C.

An Act to Incorporate the town of Holly Springs in the county of Wake.
Laws of 1876- Chapter LV.-"# 55.

Section 1. The General Assembly of North Carolina, do enact,
That the town of Holly Springs, in the County of Wake, be, and the same is hereby incorporated by the name and style of -the town of Holly Springs, and be subject to all the provisions contained in Chapter Three of Battle's Revisal and the act amending said chapter.
Section 2. That the corporate limits of said town shall be as follows,- Beginning at a point 227 Rods South West of J.P.Goodwin's residence,- Thence running North 320 Rods,- Thence East 320 Rods,- Thence South 320 Rods,- Thence West 320 Rods to the first station.
Section 3. This act shall be in force from and after its ratification.
Ratified the 26th day of January A.D. 1877.

An act of incorporation for the Town of Holly Springs was granted by the General Assembly of North Carolina on January 26, 1877. (Town Historical collection.)

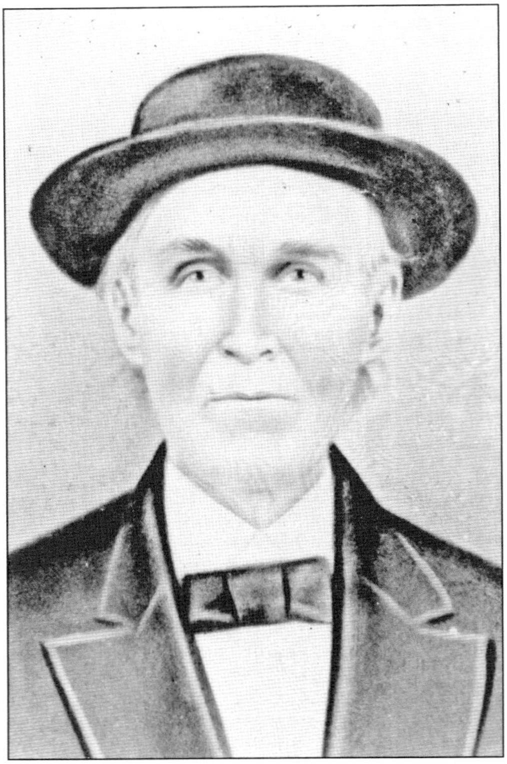

Archibald Leslie arrived in Holly Springs around 1817. He established a tailoring business and general store on a 180-acre holding. By the early 1840s, construction had started on an impressive two-story manor. The Leslies chose to leave Holly Springs after the Civil War; they did, however, give their emancipated slaves land along West Holly Springs Road. Many descendants of the freed Leslie slaves still live in Holly Springs today. (Town Historical collection.)

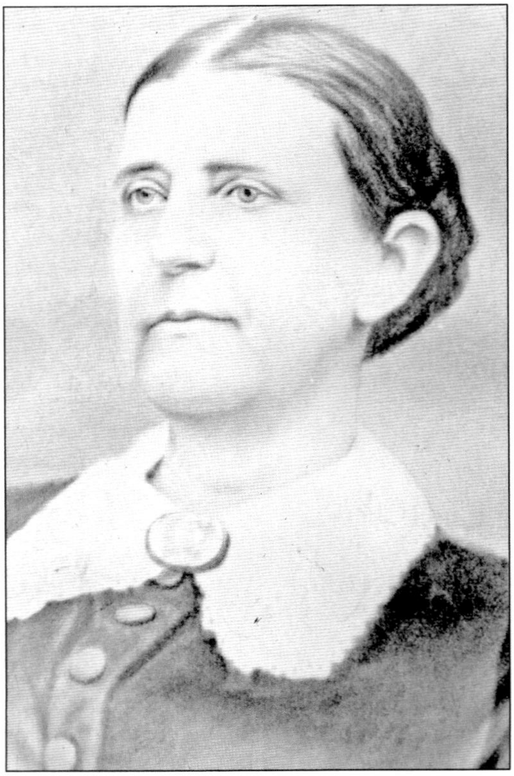

The daughter of a wealthy local family, Isabella (Rogers) Leslie was the epitome of a Southern belle. With boldness and bravery, she endured the occupation of her home by Union officers during the two-week encampment of Union troops in April 1865. Family lore tells that Isabella met the officers on the front steps of the manor, demanding that they "act like gentlemen" while they were in her home. (Town Historical collection.)

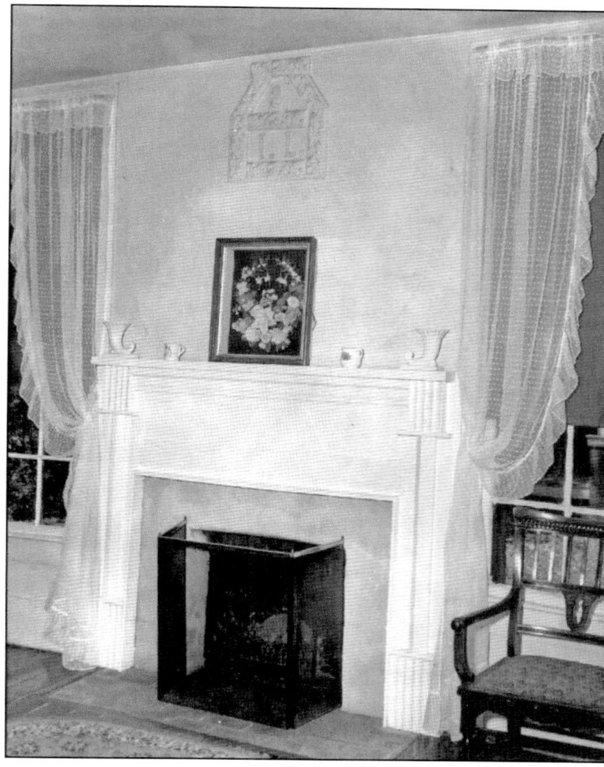

On the southwest side of the entry hall of the Leslie-Alford-Mims House is a ladies' parlor. Above the fireplace mantel are the initials "I. L." for Isabella Leslie, mistress of the manor. Opposite the ladies' parlor, on the southeast side of the entry hall, is the gentlemen's parlor. Using similar craftsmanship, "A. L.," the initials of Archibald Leslie, were placed over that parlor's mantel. Both parlors are done in the style of typical Greek Revival interiors popular in the 1840s. (Both, Wright collection.)

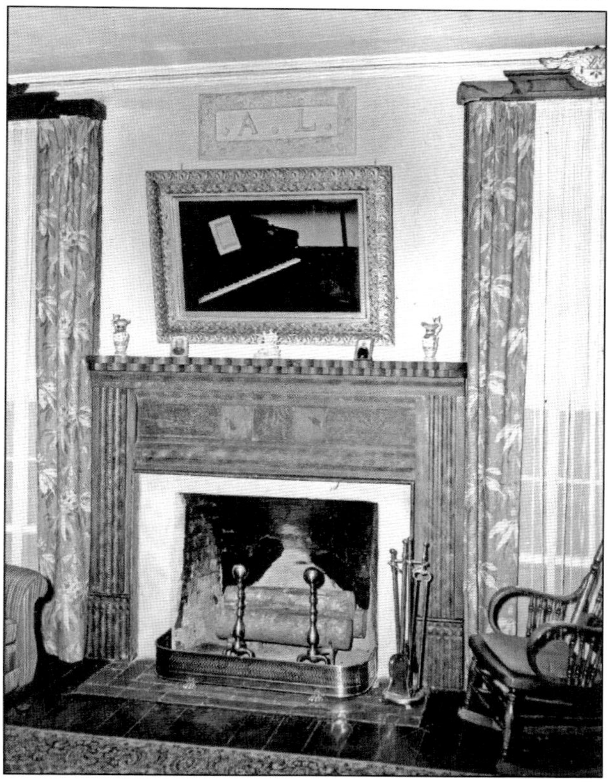

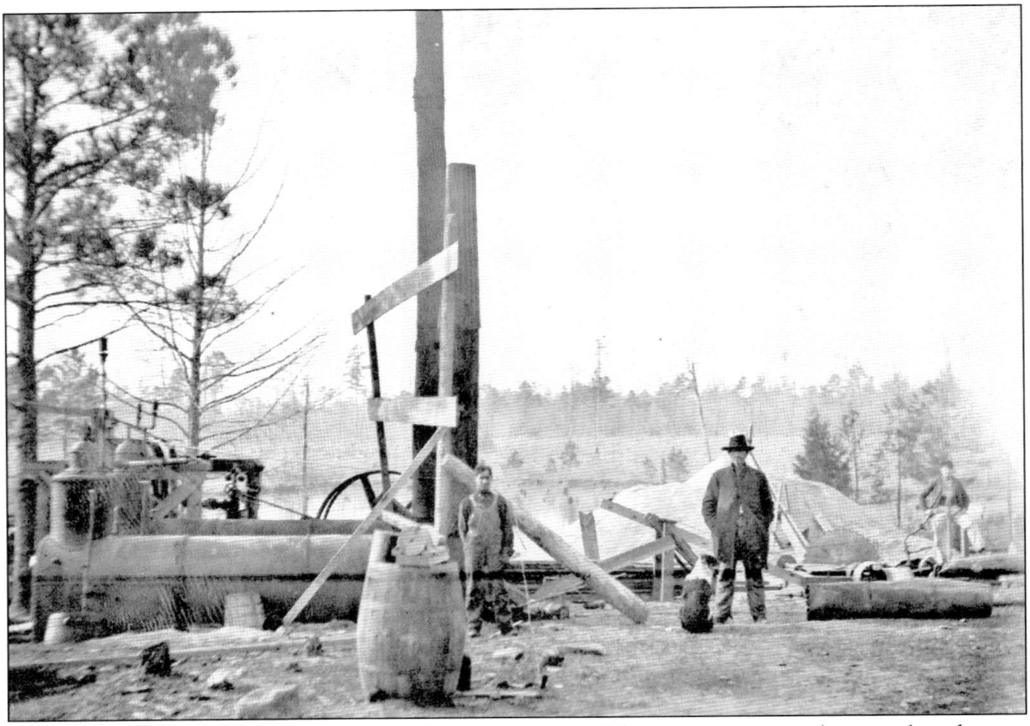

Lumber sawmills in the area were one of the mainstays of the community, as they employed many locals and utilized the region's natural bounty of longleaf pine trees. Shown here is a sawmill in the Holly Springs area. (Courtesy of Jerry Holland.)

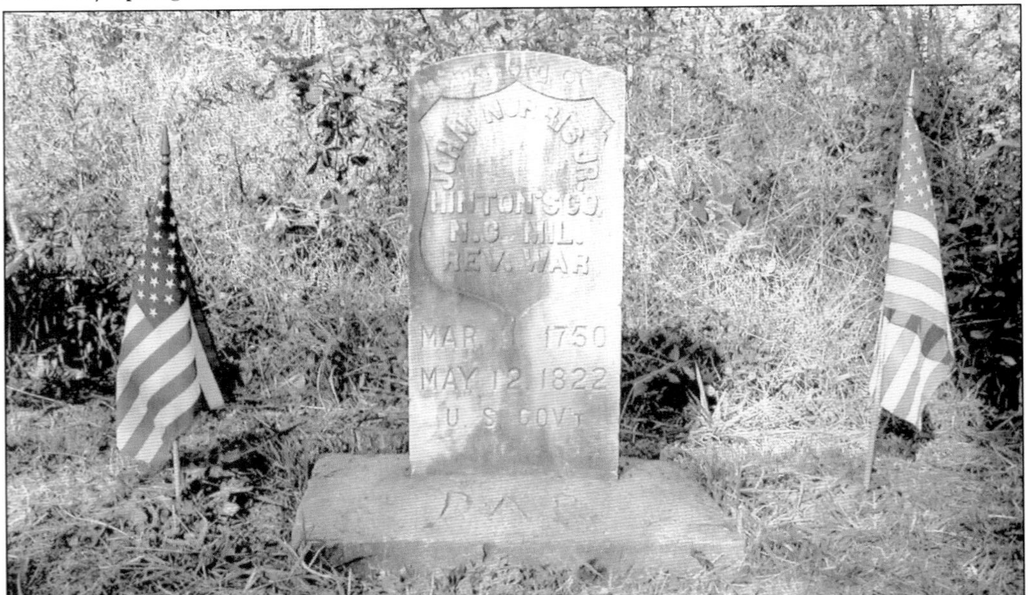


The Daughters of the American Revolution placed this marker honoring local patriot John Norris Jr., a Wake County militiaman who served under Col. John Hinton during the Revolutionary War. Norris is buried in a family plot near this marker, erected in the vicinity of his home between Holly Springs and Holleman's Crossroads. (Drew Holland collection.)

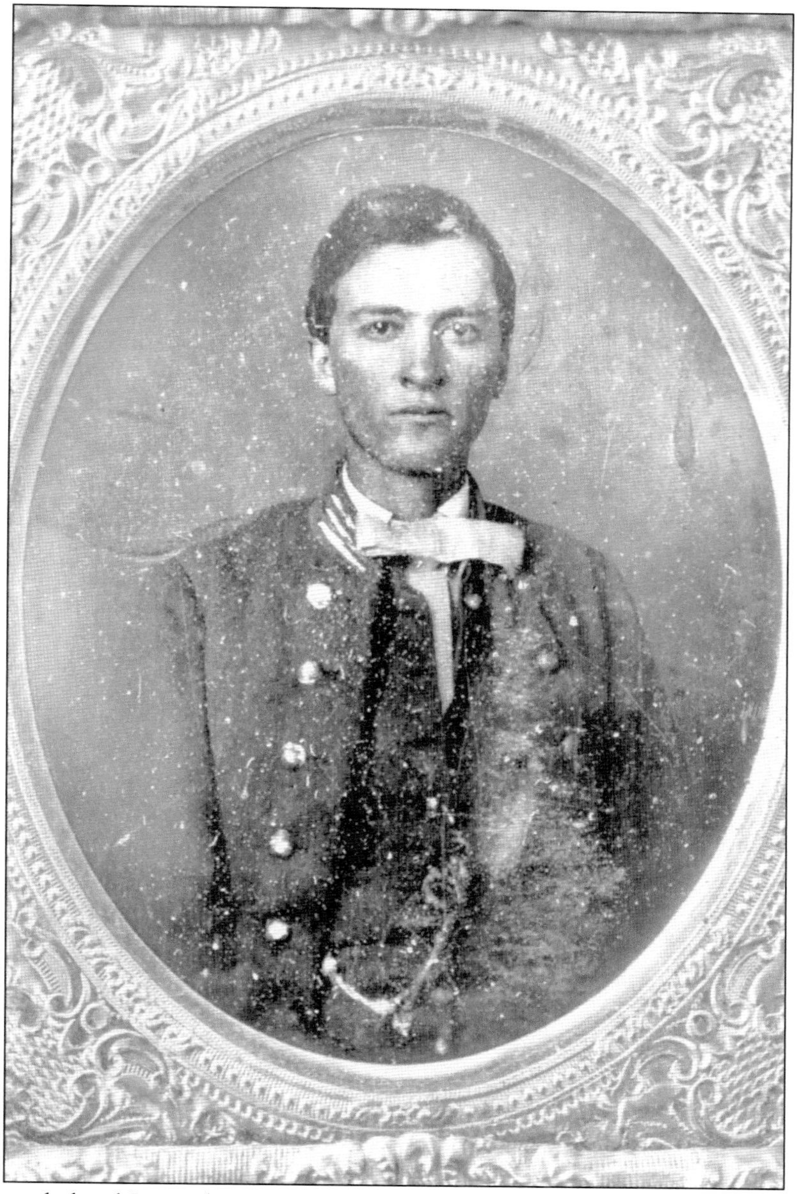

This photograph dated September 1863 was taken on the wedding day of James Theophilus Adams and Lucy Ann Beckwith. Upon enlistment in May 1861 at the age of 21, Adams was appointed second lieutenant of Company D of the 26th Regiment, North Carolina Troops. The regiment was organized from companies raised from the Holly Springs area and from the middle and western portions of North Carolina. Company D, known as the "Wake Guards," initially consisted of 60 men from the Holly Springs area. The average age of each soldier was 23 years old, with the oldest being 55 and the youngest a tender 15. The regiment fought gallantly in many famous battles of the war, such as New Bern, Malvern Hill, Gettysburg, the Wilderness, and Hatcher's Run among others. The regiment would forever have its name etched in the annals of history as holding the distinct honor of reaching the Confederate "high water" mark during the Pickett-Pettigrew Charge, as well as the tragic distinction of suffering the highest casualties of any unit, Confederate or Union, during the Battle of Gettysburg. (David Adams collection.)

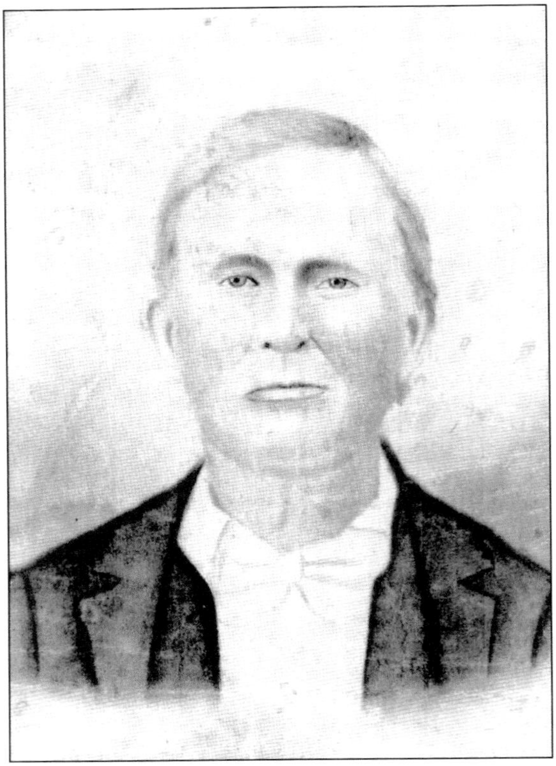

Simpson Washington Holland, son of Bennet and Patience (Norris) Holland, was born in 1826. Simpson's father, Bennet, was instrumental in the Holly Springs Masonic Lodge No. 115 and in the establishment of the Holly Springs Academy. Simpson inherited the homestead and farm of his uncle Needham Norris. Active in the Masonic Lodge himself, Simpson carved a wooden letter G, symbolic in the brotherhood, that still hangs in the lodge today. (Drew Holland collection.)

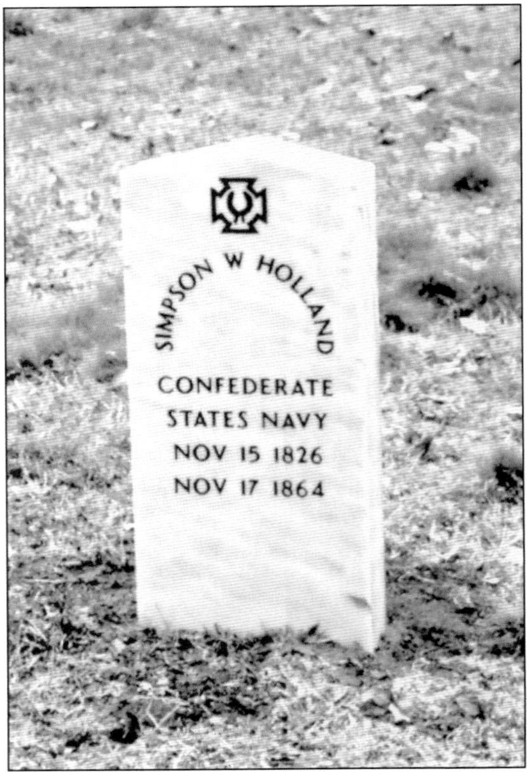


Simpson Washington Holland died in November 1864 near Richmond, Virginia. Cemetery records reflect he served in the Confederate navy. His cause of death is uncertain, and he was buried in an unmarked grave, a common practice during wartime. After 140 years, Holland finally received the recognition deserving any veteran. In 2007, Drew Holland paid tribute to his great-great-great-grandfather with the placement of a headstone on his grave. (Drew Holland collection.)

George Benton Alford, son of Green Haywood and Rebecca (Jones) Alford, was a successful and progressive businessman with a dream of making Holly Springs into an industrial city. Alford had numerous business interests: a general mercantile store, sawmill, cotton gin, turpentine works, and a brick kiln, even draining Sunset Lake to plant rice paddies. Starting the Holly Springs Land and Improvement Company, getting the town incorporated, and founding the Cape Fear News and Advertising Company were more of his many accomplishments. (Wright collection.)

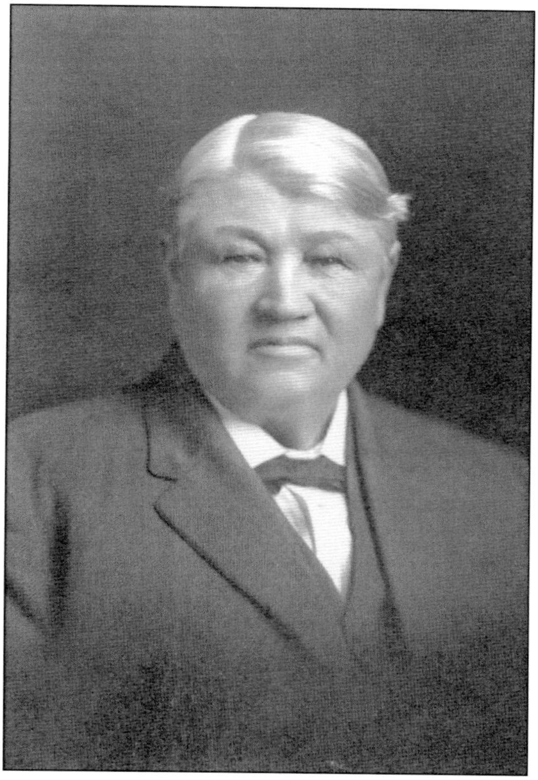

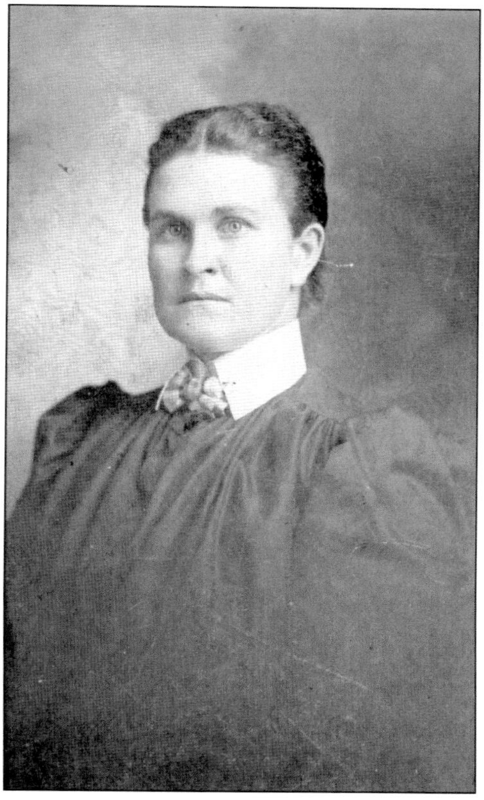

Texanna Ora Branch, widow of Walter Collins, was the second wife of George Benton Alford. Texanna had four children—Martin, Roger, Hubert, and Delcie—from her marriage to Walter Collins. Texanna brought her children into her marriage to George Benton Alford in 1899. Texanna was born July 14, 1865, died January 25, 1938, and is buried in the Alford family plot on the property. (Wright collection.)

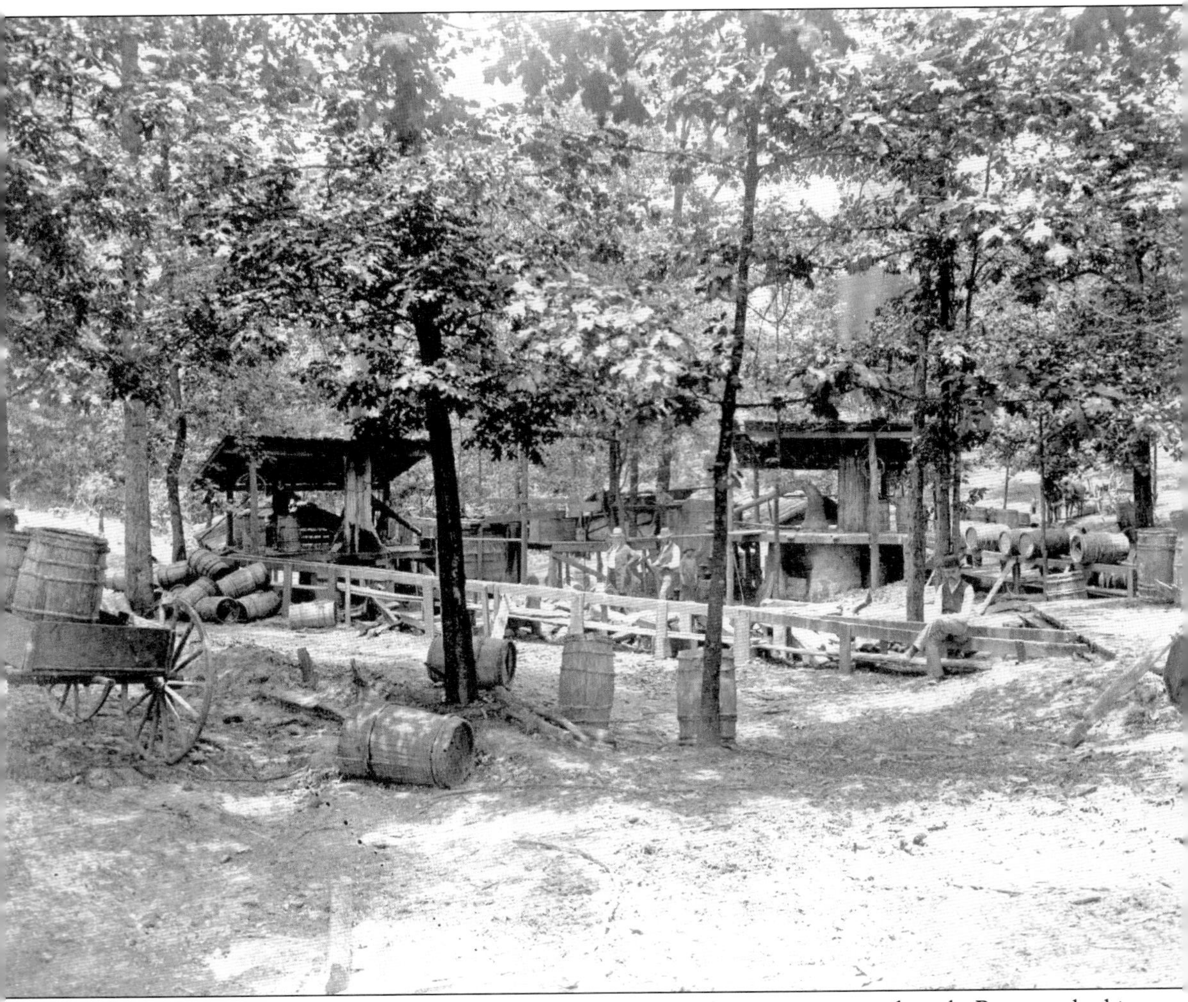

The abundant local pine forests provided a rich source for turpentine and pitch. Rope soaked in pine tar was used to caulk and seal the wood hulls of the ships used for commercial trade at that time. This turpentine distillery, built by George Benton Alford, was located just a few hundred yards behind his residence. (Wright collection.)

Mary-Ann (Matthews) Holland witnessed a period in American history that saw the best and the worst of human nature. Women such as Mary-Ann suffered wounds as deep as any battle infliction. Like so many other women after the Civil War, she raised her family without the benefit of her husband, Simpson, relying on her sons to fill their father's shoes. Her grave sits peacefully at Collins Grove Baptist Church Cemetery. (Drew Holland collection.)

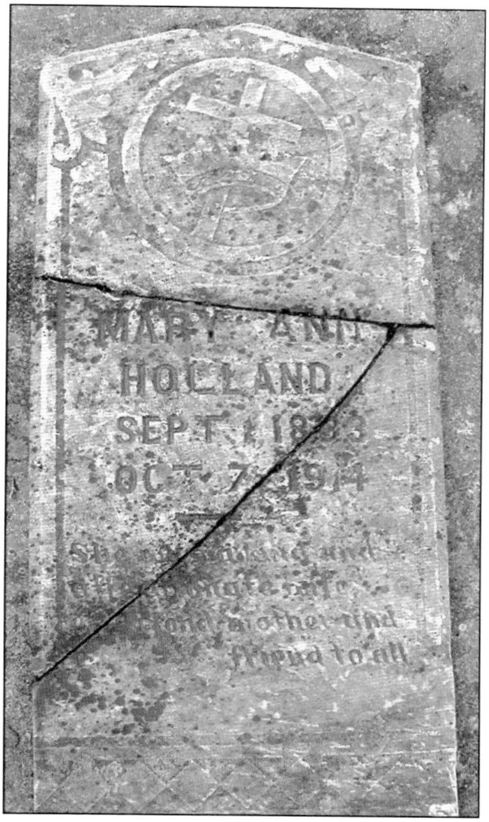


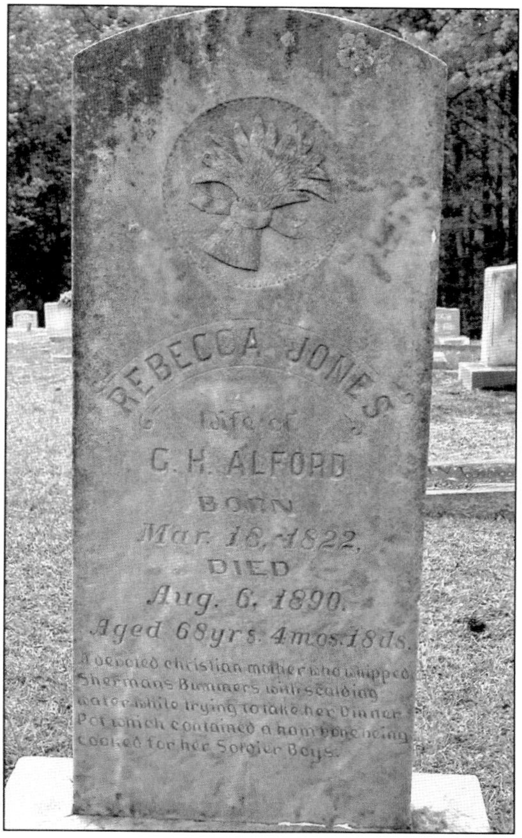


In April 1865, food was scarce in the war-ravished South. In the kitchen of Rebecca Alford, the aroma of a simmering pot of soup brought a scouting party of Yankee soldiers to her doorstep. Unknown to the Yankees, the soup was intended for a few Confederate "soldier boys" who were camped nearby. Rather than relinquish her soup pot, she scalded them with the boiling liquid. (Town Historical collection.)

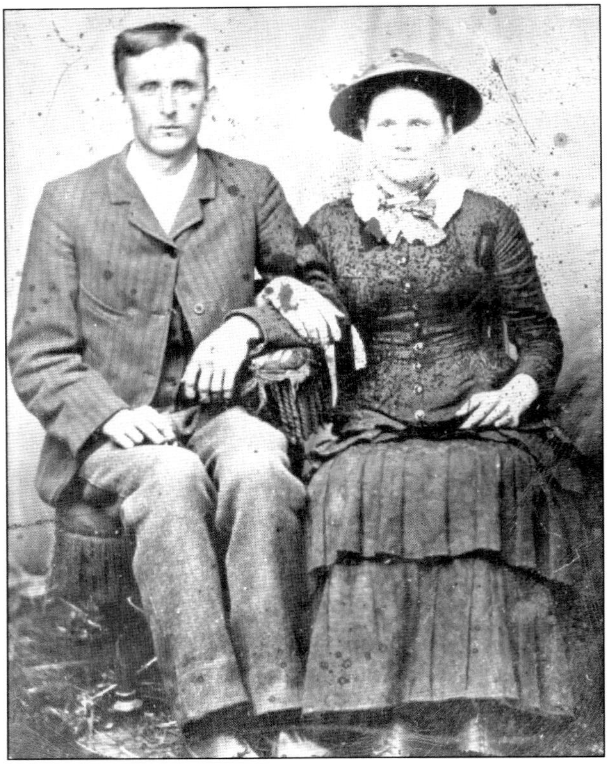

Arcavius "Cave" Burwell Utley and Savannah (Hare) Utley are pictured in this late-1800s photograph. As a boy attending Holly Springs Methodist Church, Cave felt preaching should be his life's work. Though he tried to turn a deaf ear to the call, it would not be silenced. For 26 years, he was a pastor and was satisfied that several hundred had been converted in meetings he held. (Faye and Tim Congleton collection.)

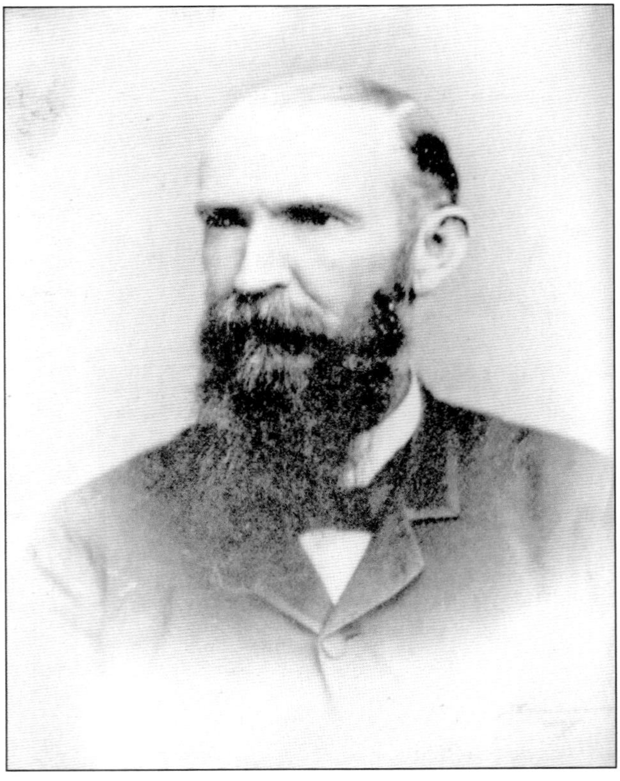

Dr. Britton Suggs Utley, pictured here, practiced medicine and had a drugstore on Raleigh Street near his home. Utley was appointed postmaster of the Holly Springs Post Office in February 1880. He also served as lodge master in 1869, 1870, 1873, 1889–1894, and 1897–1898. Utley is a direct descendant of William Utley, a planter born in Virginia who was among the first settlers in Wake County. (Courtesy of Holly Springs Masonic Lodge No. 115 AF&AM.)

The Burt family lives on land that was originally a portion of a land grant of several thousand acres given to their ancestors in the 1700s by the King of England. Shown here in an 1898 photograph are, from left to right, Raymond Archdale, Max Rollins, and their father, Joseph Judson Burt. As an adult, Raymond led a successful campaign to obtain a county high school in Holly Springs. (Fred Burt collection.)

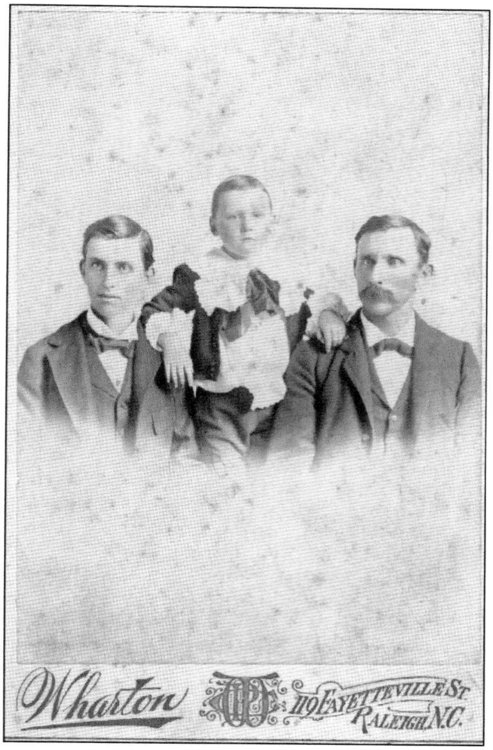


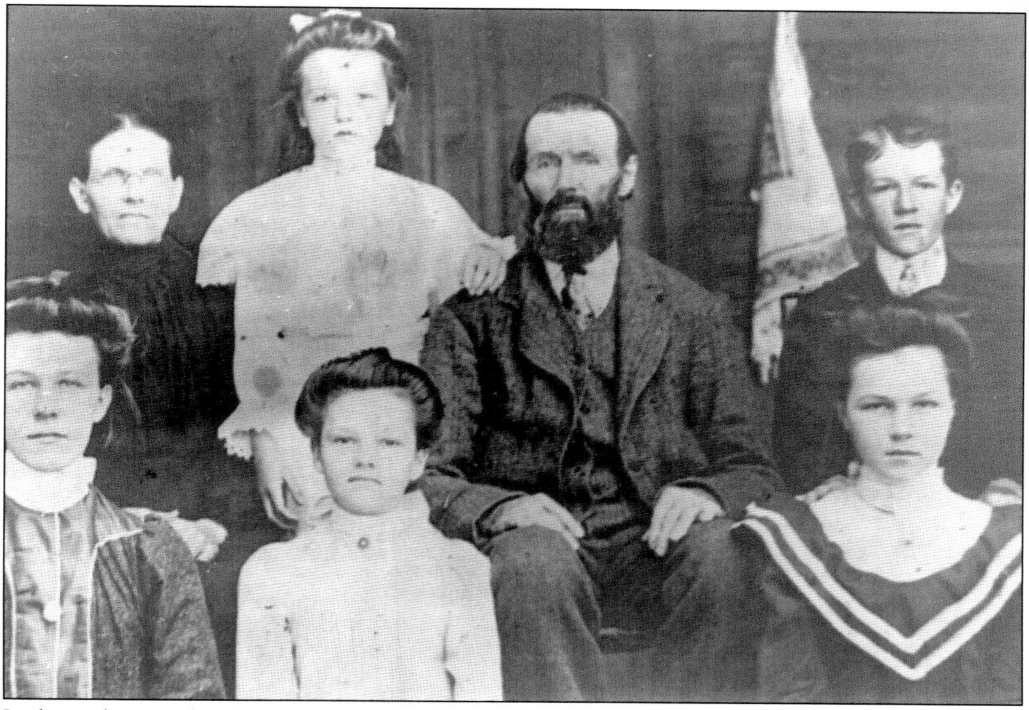

In this early 1900s family portrait, John Henry "Henderson" and Sarah Catherine (Whittington) Norris are pictured with their children. From left to right are (first row) Stella, Myrtle, and Pearl; (second row) Sarah Catherine, Halsey, John Henry, and Earnest. (Christine Norris-Epps collection.)

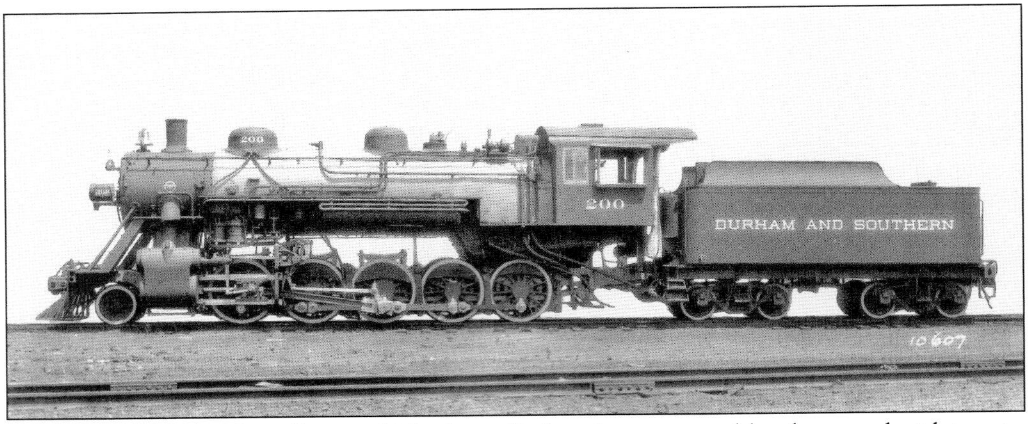


The charter for the Cape Fear and Northern Railroad was granted by the state legislature to George Benton Alford in 1892; however, construction on the railroad did not begin until July 1898. In later years, the line was extended to Durham when purchased by the Durham and Southern Railroad. The original depot building was supposedly destroyed by a fire set by two mischievous young boys attempting to steal gasoline. (Collection of the Railway and Locomotive Historical Society.)

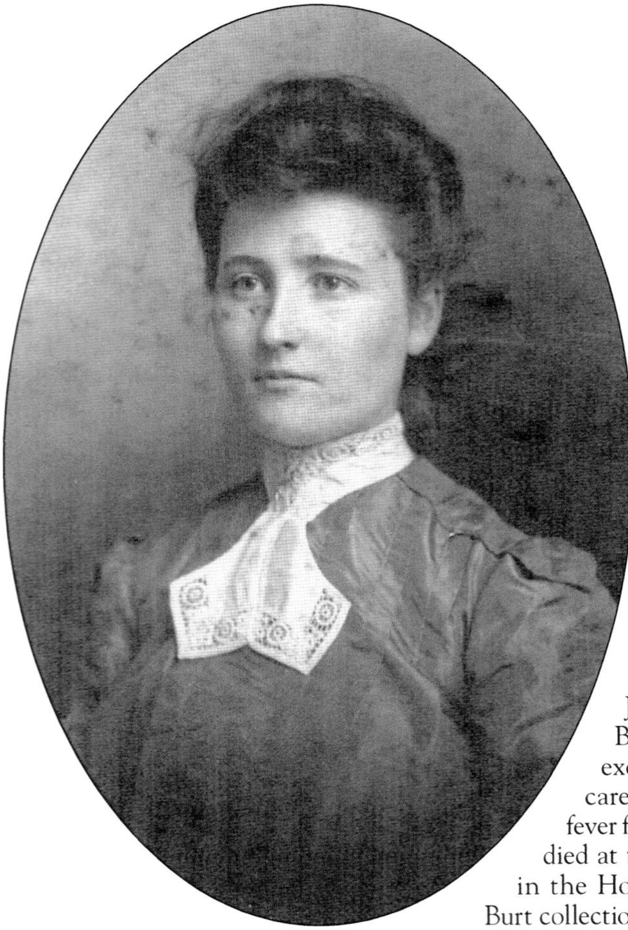

Stella Burt, daughter of Joseph Judson and Sarah "Annie" (Rollins) Burt, was full of anticipation and excitement to be starting her teaching career. Unfortunately, she caught scarlet fever from another teacher at the school and died at the tender age of 23. Stella is buried in the Holly Springs Town Cemetery. (Fred Burt collection.)

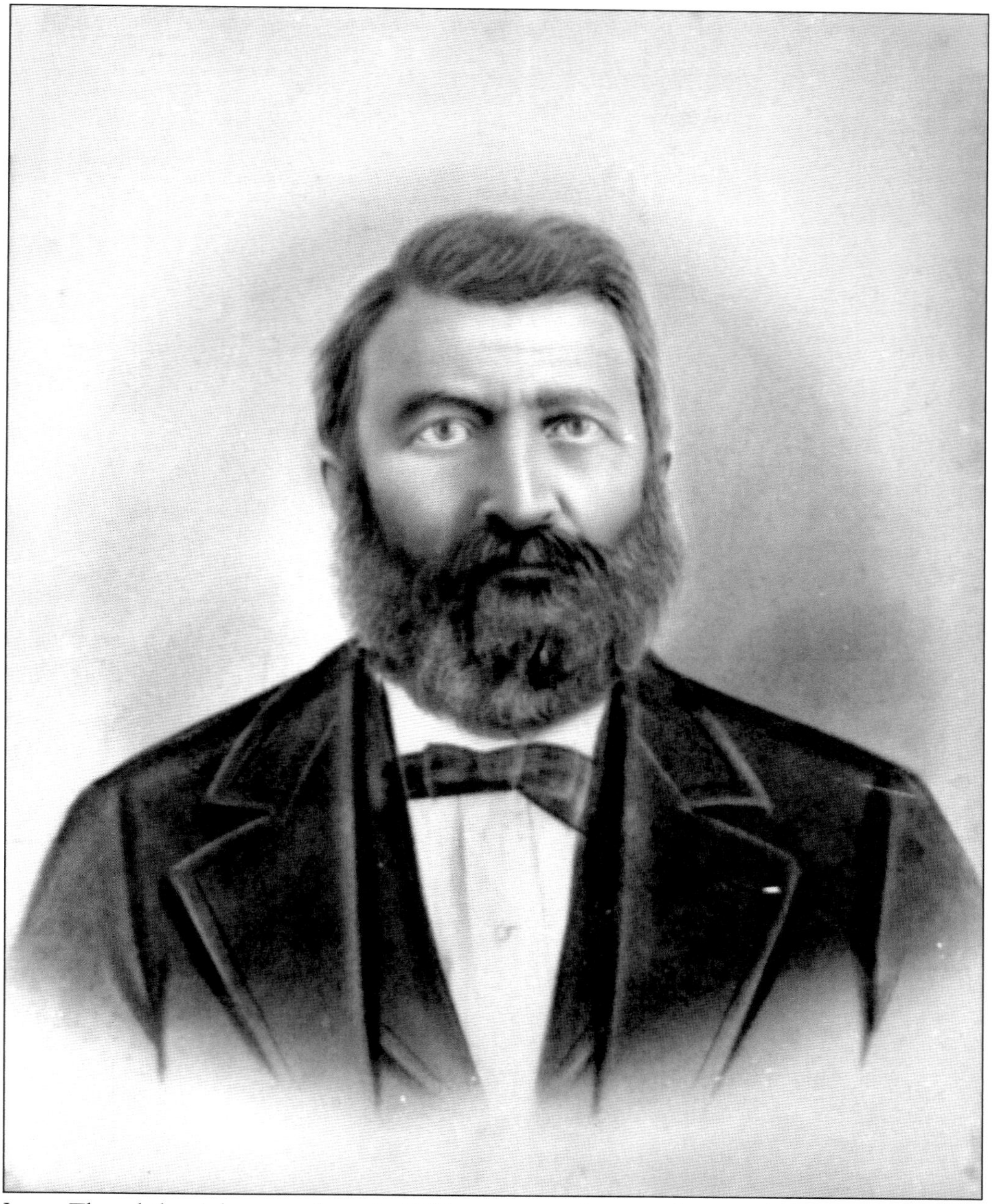

James Theophilus Adams was born in 1839 to parents who were farmers. A farmer himself, the 21-year-old Adams enlisted on May 29, 1861, into the 26th North Carolina Regiment and was appointed to second lieutenant the same day by Capt. Oscar Rand. Training at Camp Crabtree, the regiment left to help defend New Bern by September. Adams assumed the captaincy of Company D on April 21, 1862. Wounded at Gettysburg, he was promoted to major after that engagement and then to lieutenant colonel on May 6, 1864. Adams was in command of the regiment when it surrendered at Appomattox Court House, Virginia. Active in the Masonic Order, he served as lodge master during the following years: 1867, 1868, 1877–1879, 1899–1901, and 1908–1910. A postwar photograph of him, shown above, still hangs in the Masonic Lodge in a place of honor. (Courtesy of Holly Springs Masonic Lodge No. 115 AF&AM.)

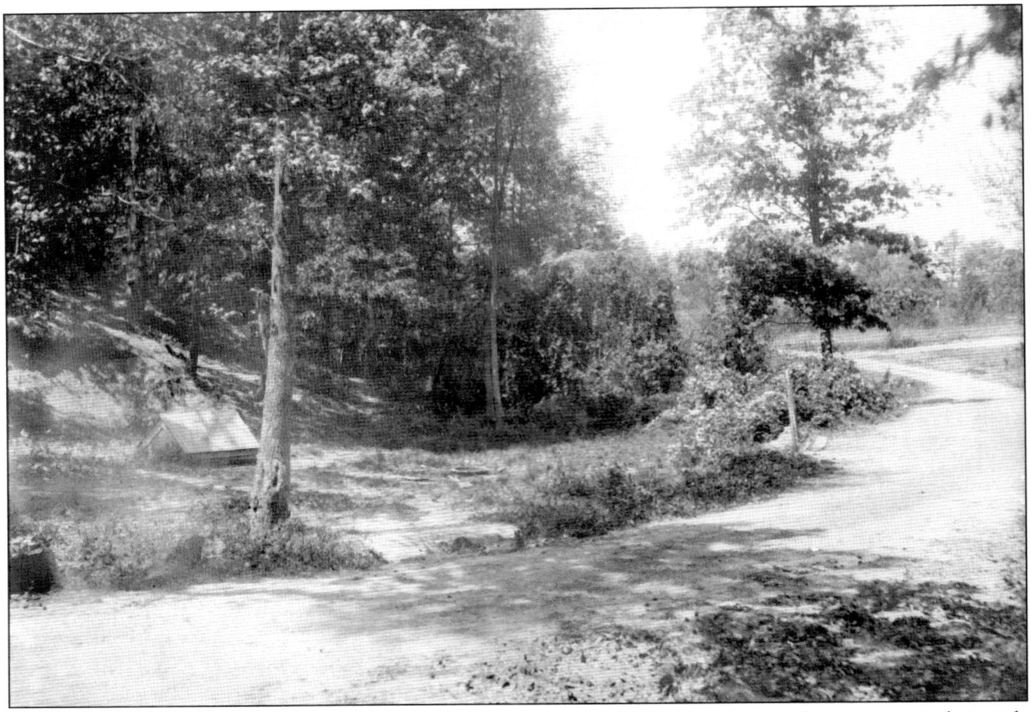

One of many freshwater springs in the area, these particular springs were the most popular with the local residents. The springs are shown here covered with a small "doghouse" to keep out leaves and debris. The dirt road to the springs began at Avent Ferry Road near what is now West Center Street. (Wright collection.)

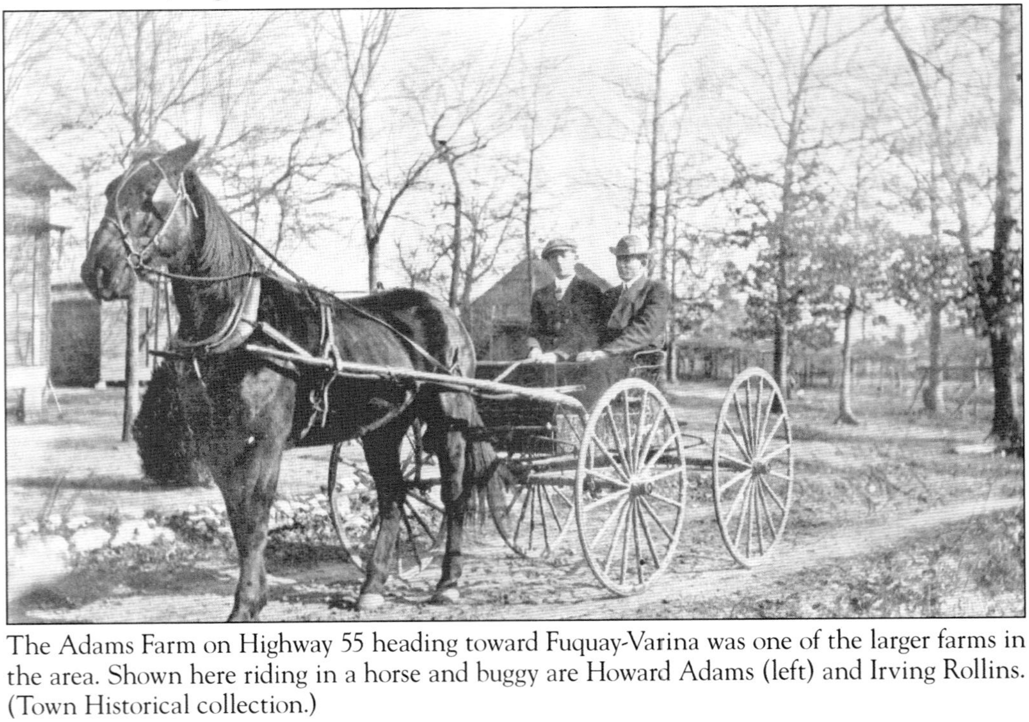

The Adams Farm on Highway 55 heading toward Fuquay-Varina was one of the larger farms in the area. Shown here riding in a horse and buggy are Howard Adams (left) and Irving Rollins. (Town Historical collection.)

Rev. Henry Wayland and Hersilia (Banks) Norris built their home on Avent Ferry Road in the mid-1880s. Norris, a graduate of Trinity College, now Duke University, was ordained at Collins Grove Baptist Church in 1879. Norris served the congregation from 1881 to 1884. (Ken Jarvis collection.)

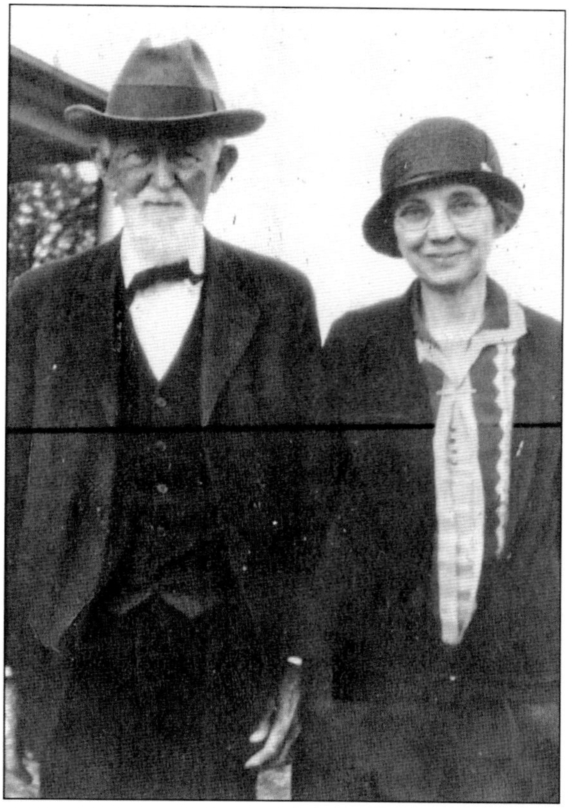

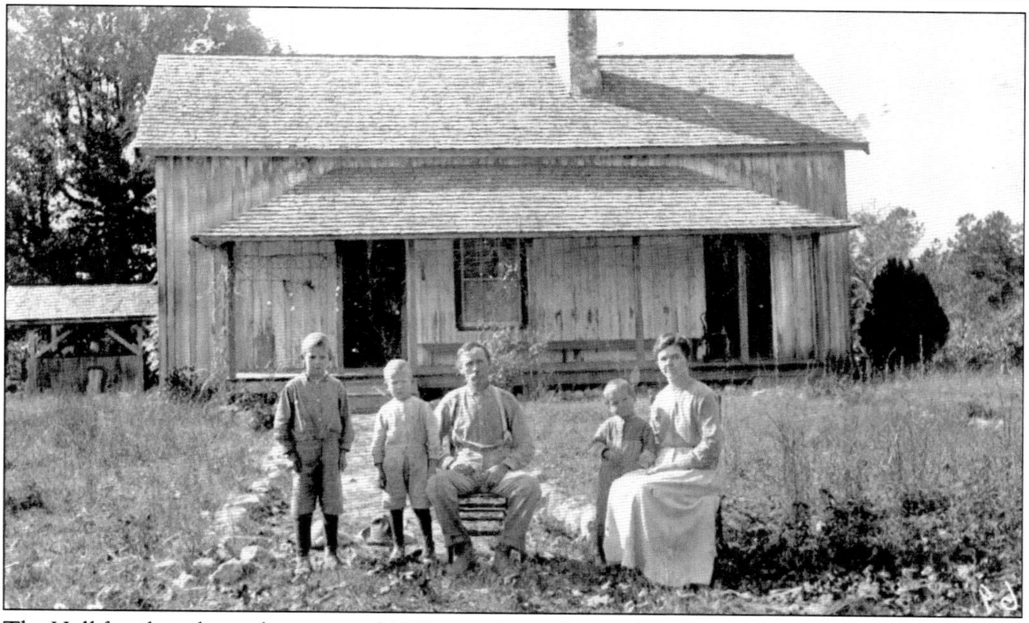

The Hall family is shown here around 1918 seated outside their home. A traveling photographer came by one day offering his services to the family. Pearl had been out digging potatoes and was distressed to find that she had a hole in the apron she was wearing. Pictured from left to right are Allen, Millard, George W., George H., and Pearl (Welch) Hall. (Nathan and Carolyn Williams collection.)

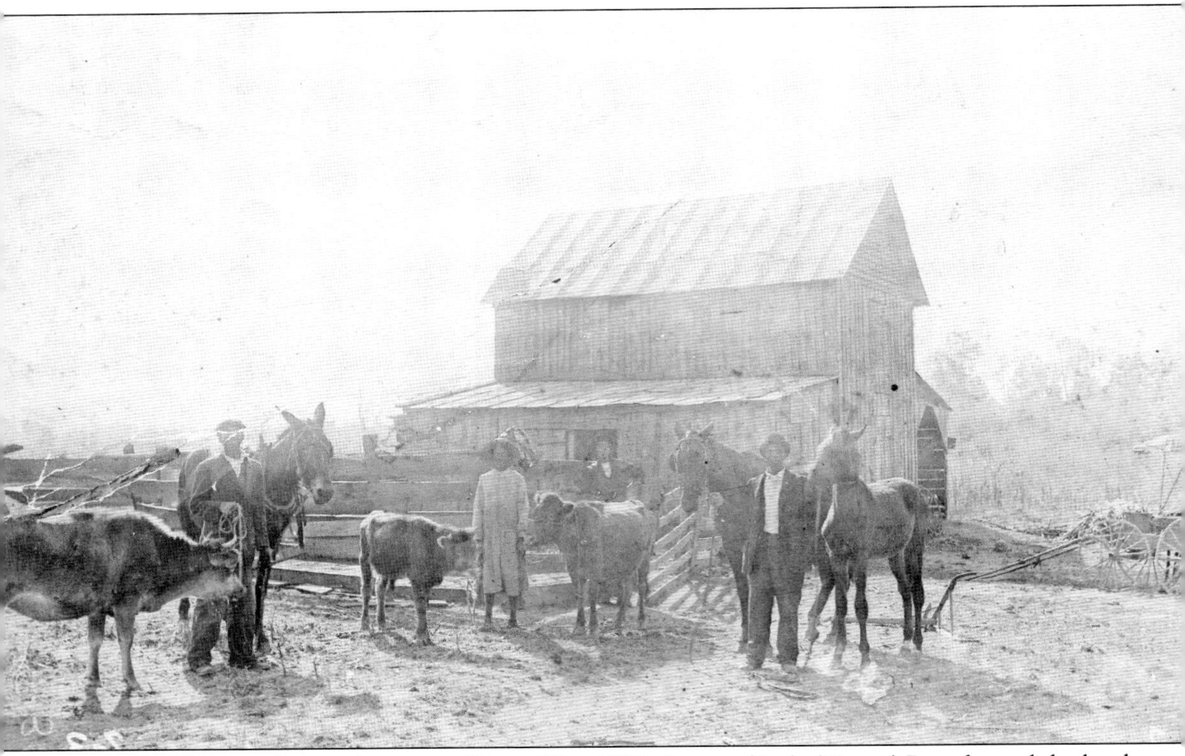

In Wilbon, in the area known as "Piney Wood," Herbert and Lula (Norris) Page farmed the land. In this *c.* 1918 photograph, standing in front of their barn, from left to right are Dewar Bunch (the Pages' nephew), his sister Annie Blanche Bunch (their niece), Lula, and Herbert. Cora Mae (Norris) Lassiter was also raised by her great-aunt Lula and great-uncle Herbert on this farm along with her cousins Dewar and Annie. (Courtesy of Cora Lassiter.)

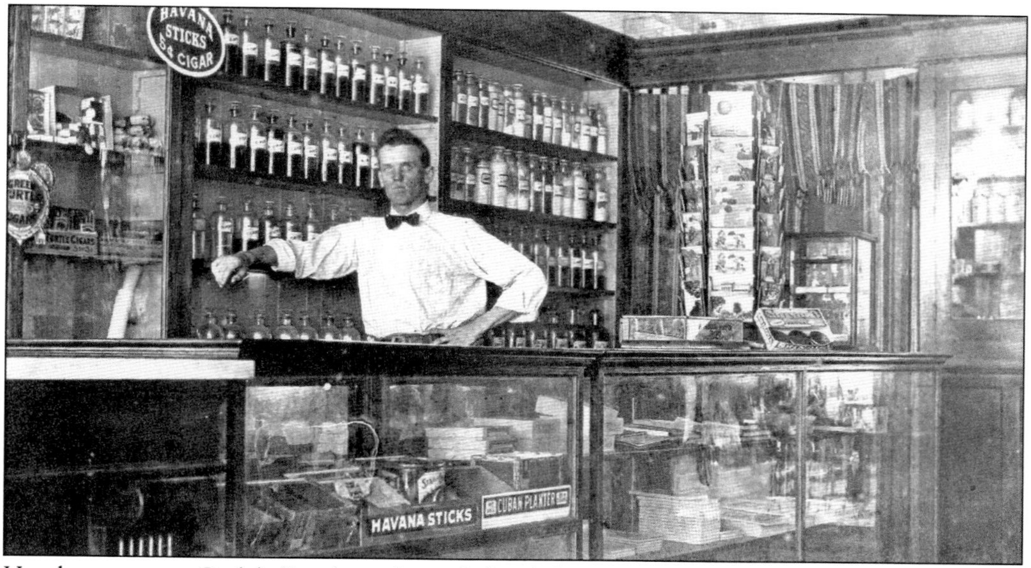

Handsome young Carlyle Brooks is shown behind the counter at Holly Springs Drug Company in this 1920s photograph. The drugstore sat at the corner of Center and Main Streets, or Apex Street, as Main was known back then. William Lonnie "Father" Price made caskets and had a blacksmith shop at the back of the drugstore. (Town Historical collection.)

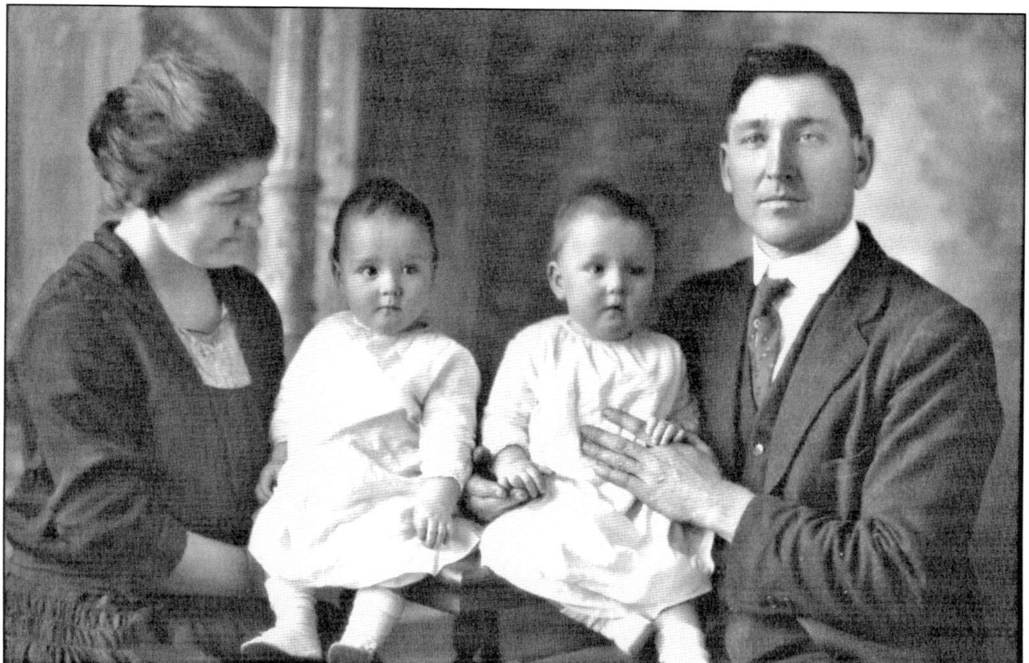
In this 1926 professional studio photograph of the Burt family, seated from left to right are Alla Mae (Fuquay), Roy and Elmer (twin boys), and Max Burt. (Fred Burt collection.)

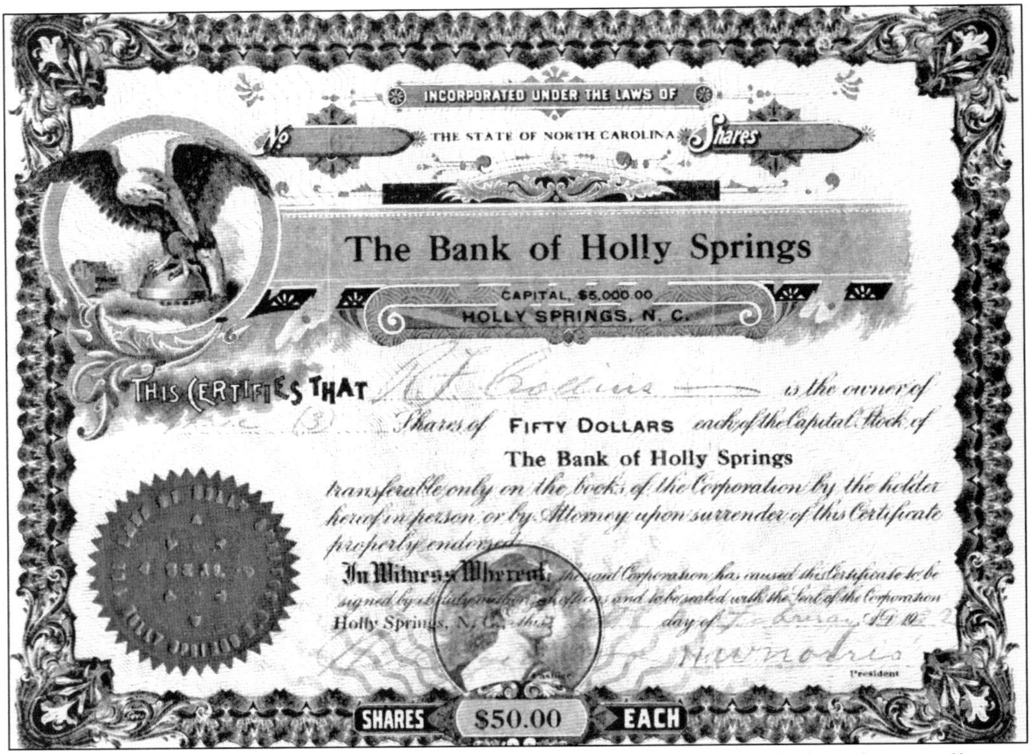
INCORPORATED UNDER THE LAWS OF
No THE STATE OF NORTH CAROLINA Shares

The Bank of Holly Springs

CAPITAL, $5,000.00
HOLLY SPRINGS, N. C.

This Certifies that _______ is the owner of (3) Shares of FIFTY DOLLARS each of the Capital Stock of

The Bank of Holly Springs

transferable only on the books of the Corporation by the holder hereof in person or by Attorney upon surrender of this Certificate properly endorsed.

In Witness Whereof, the said Corporation has caused this Certificate to be signed by its duly authorized officers and to be sealed with the Seal of the Corporation Holly Springs, N. C. this ___ day of February 1922

Cashier President

SHARES $50.00 EACH

A Bank of Holly Springs stock Certificate is dated February 1, 1922. Definitely a small town in 1922, Holly Springs was just beginning to enjoy "modern amenities." At first, electricity was available to residents only in the evening until 11:00 and on Thursday afternoons so the women could do their weekly ironing. (Courtesy of Jerry Holland.)

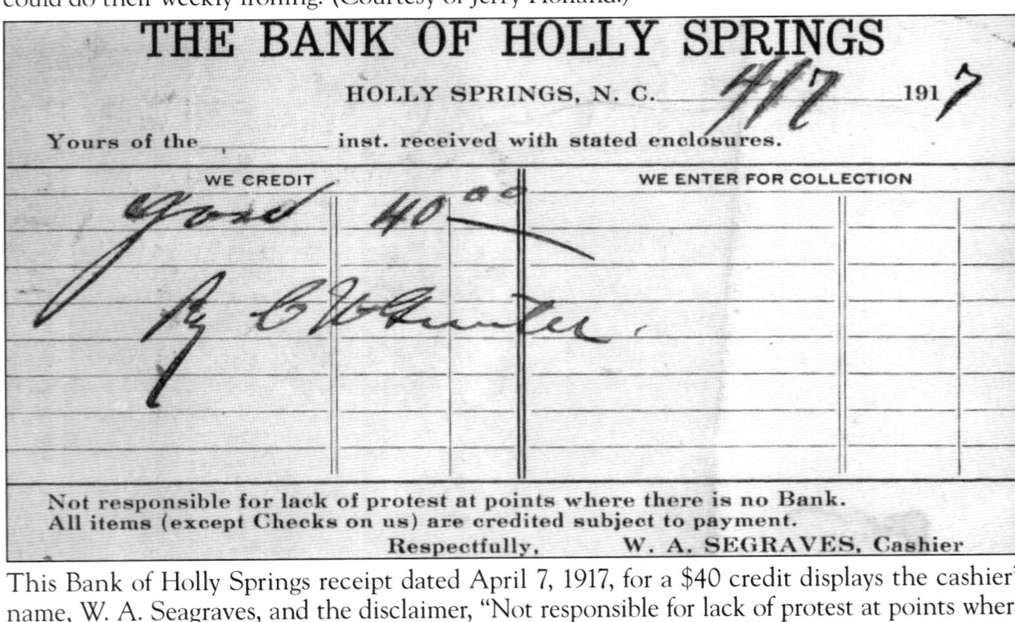
THE BANK OF HOLLY SPRINGS

HOLLY SPRINGS, N. C. 4/7 1917

Yours of the ______ inst. received with stated enclosures.

| WE CREDIT | | WE ENTER FOR COLLECTION | |
| --- | --- | --- | --- |
| Good | 40.00 | | |

Not responsible for lack of protest at points where there is no Bank.
All items (except Checks on us) are credited subject to payment.

Respectfully, W. A. SEGRAVES, Cashier

This Bank of Holly Springs receipt dated April 7, 1917, for a $40 credit displays the cashier's name, W. A. Seagraves, and the disclaimer, "Not responsible for lack of protest at points where there is no Bank. All items (except Checks on us) are credited subject to payment." (Courtesy of Jerry Holland.)

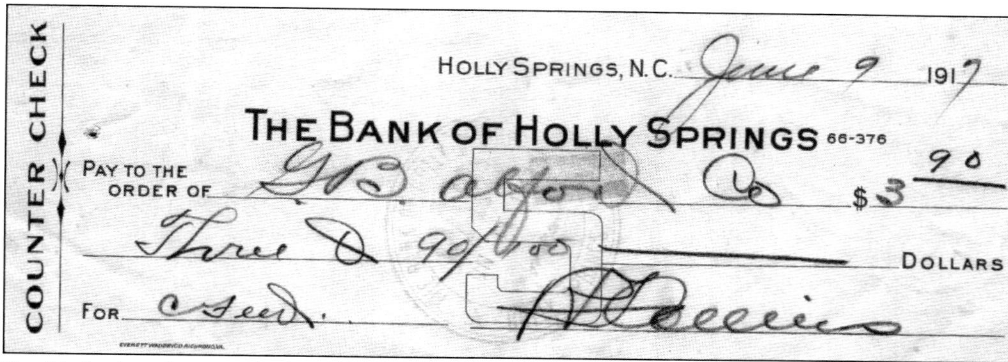


Established in the years before the dawn of the 20th century, the bank was a symbol of the town's prosperity and promise. Here is a counter check from the Bank of Holly Springs issued on June 9, 1917, made payable to G. B. Alford Company for $3.90 for "c feed." The counter check was signed by R. Collins, who was coincidentally Alford's stepson. (Courtesy of Jerry Holland.)

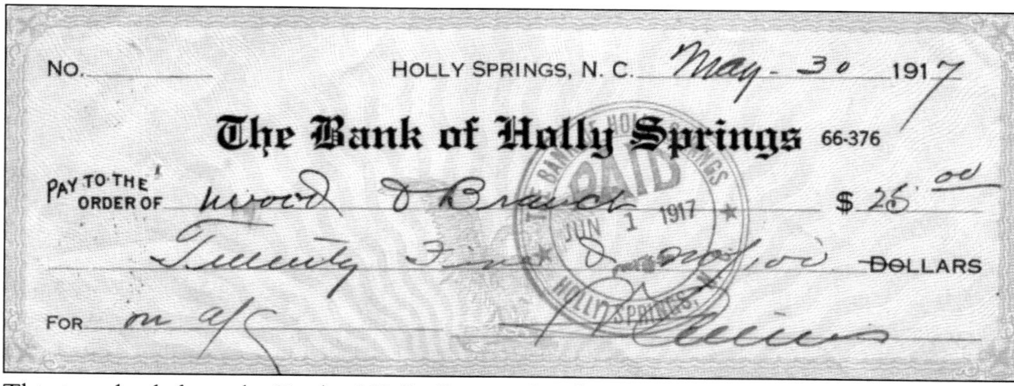


This is a check from the Bank of Holly Springs dated May 30, 1917, and payable to Wood and Branch for $25. The bank failed in 1924. It was the first bank to do so in North Carolina before the Depression. The life savings of many people were lost forever. Local speculation has it that an unwise stock investment or a misappropriation of funds was the cause of the collapse. (Courtesy of Jerry Holland.)

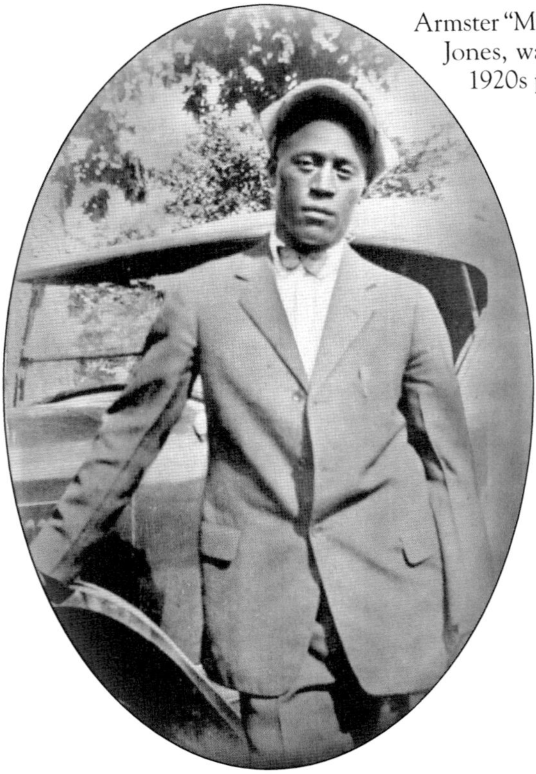

Armster "Man" Jones, the son of Alfred and Nancy (Spence) Jones, was born around 1902 and is shown here in a 1920s photograph. (Courtesy of Jean Jones.)

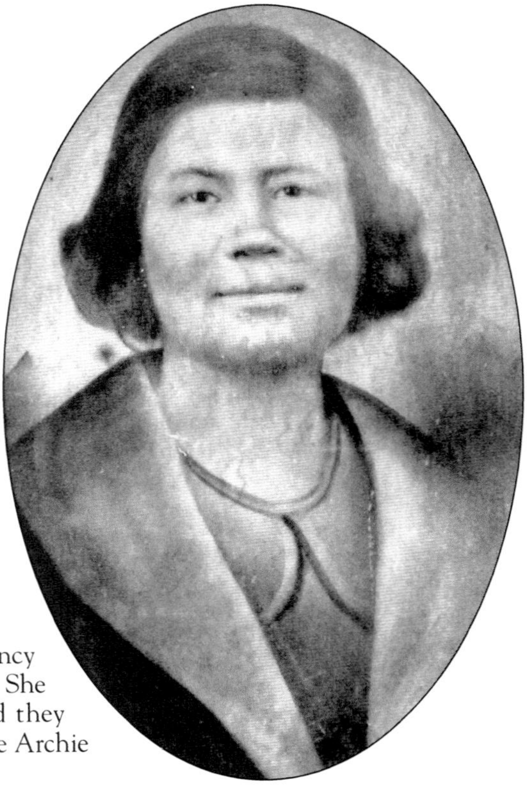

Nealie Richardson, daughter of Neal and Nancy (Mitchell) Richardson, was born around 1904. She married Armster "Man" Jones in 1925, and they had three children: Nancy, George, and Willie Archie "Monk." (Courtesy of Jean Jones.)

Proud parents Marcus and Delcie (Collins) Mims snapped this *c.* 1926 memory of their toddler, Ivan "Ike" Mims, shown here at the age of three. (Nathan and Carolyn Williams collection.)

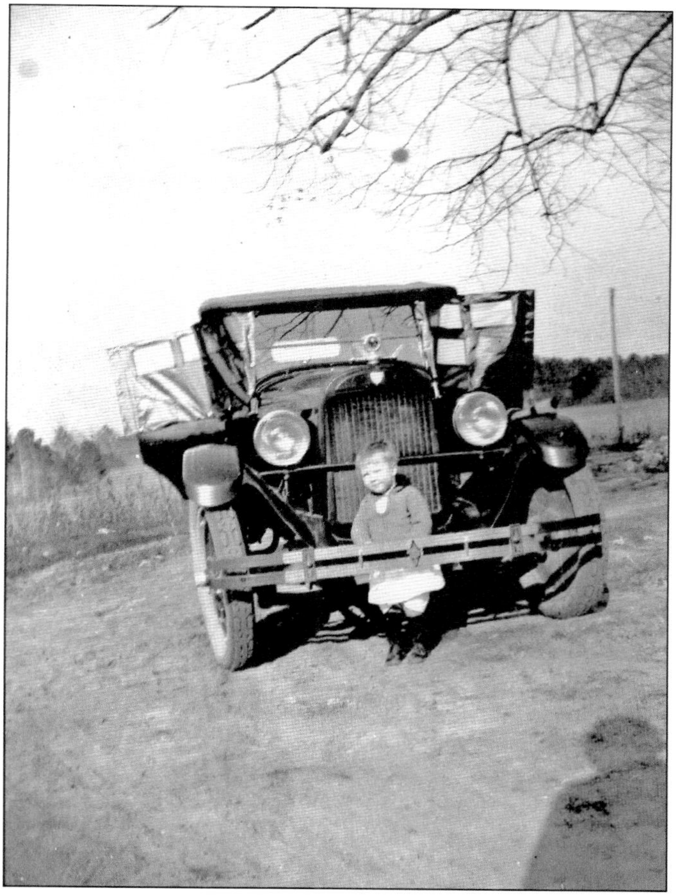

Standing from left to right are sisters Mary Lee and Lillie Mae Utley, who shared this bicycle no doubt (below) as they grew up in rural Holly Springs in the early 1920s. (Mary Lee Johnson collection, courtesy of Lori Stokes.)

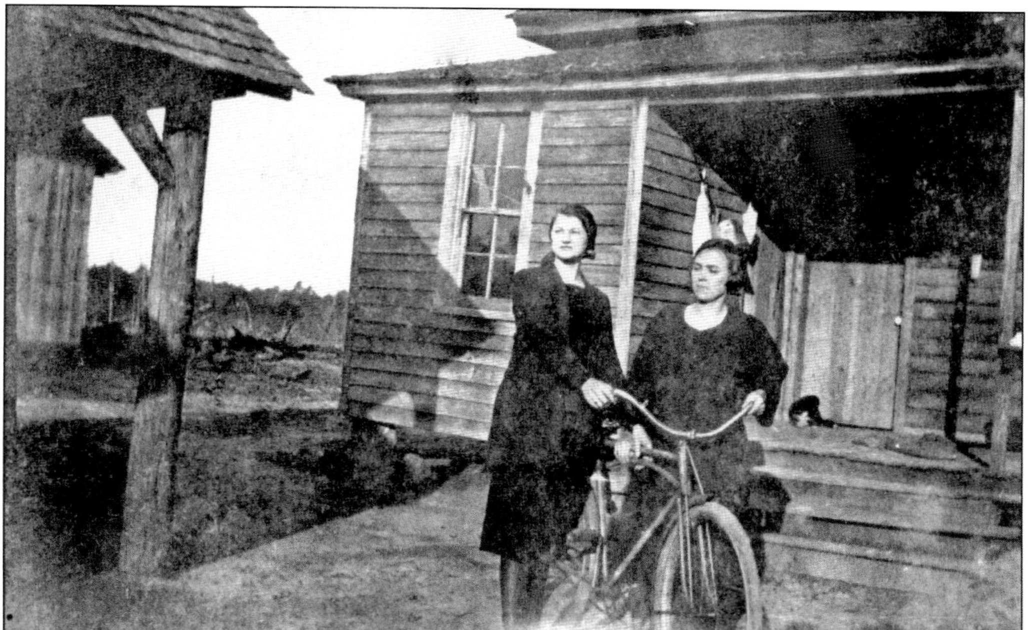

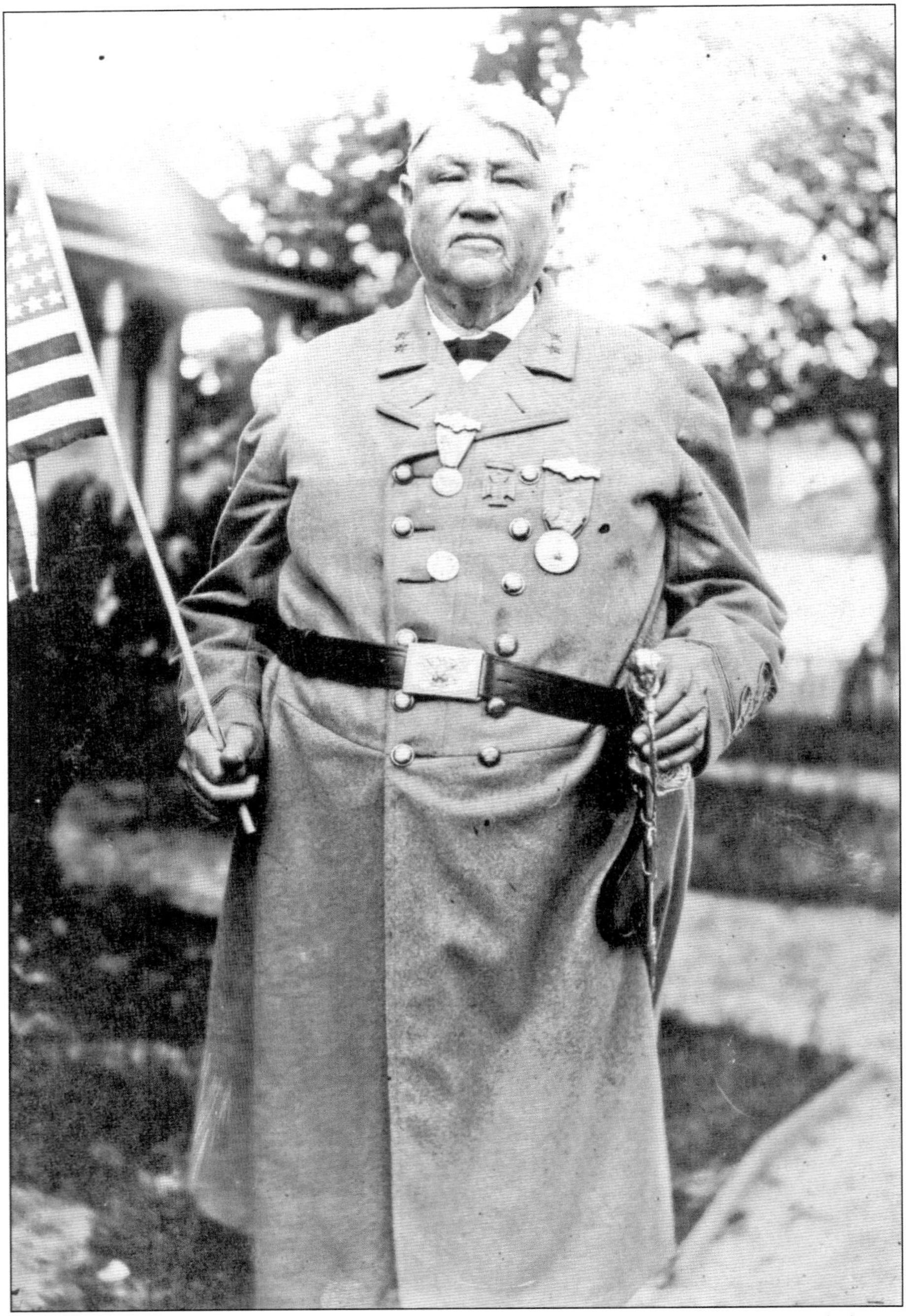

George Benton Alford's military service began in the fall of 1864 when he joined the cavalry brigade. He was with his company at Petersburg and Dinwiddie Courthouse. Taken ill with typhoid fever, he was sent to the hospital to recover. Upon his recovery, he was ordered back to his regiment. Before he reached the front, Richmond fell and the war was over. At the surrender, as at his enlistment, he was a private. In later years, Alford was honored by his comrades by election to the position of commander of the camp of United Confederate Veterans and given the honorary title of colonel. (Wright collection.)

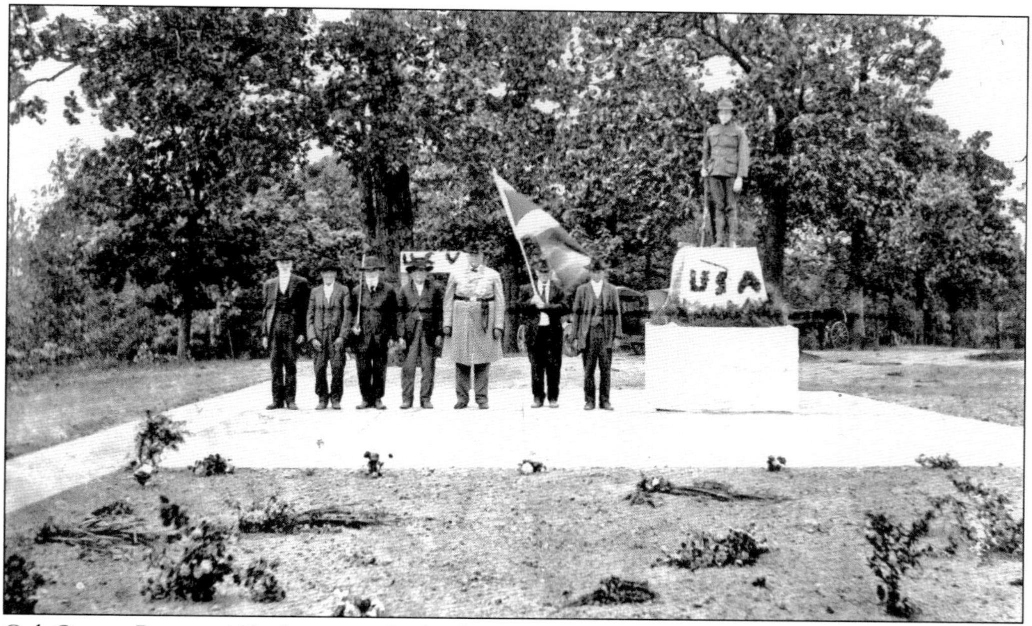


Col. George Benton Alford organized a fund-raising campaign to generate interest in a monument to commemorate local soldiers who served during the Civil War. In this picture, a person is standing on a platform to symbolize the Confederate Infantryman whose likeness would be placed atop the monument. Standing head and shoulders above his fellow veterans, Alford is shown here third from the right. The monument was dedicated in 1923 with an impressive ceremony attended by dignitaries from across the state. Alford's name tops the list of those honored on the monument: "41st Regiment, Col. G. B. Alford, Commander." The ladies, not to be surpassed, are shown (below) supporting the cause as well. The monument stands in front of the Leslie-Alford-Mims House on West Center Street. (Both, Wright collection.)

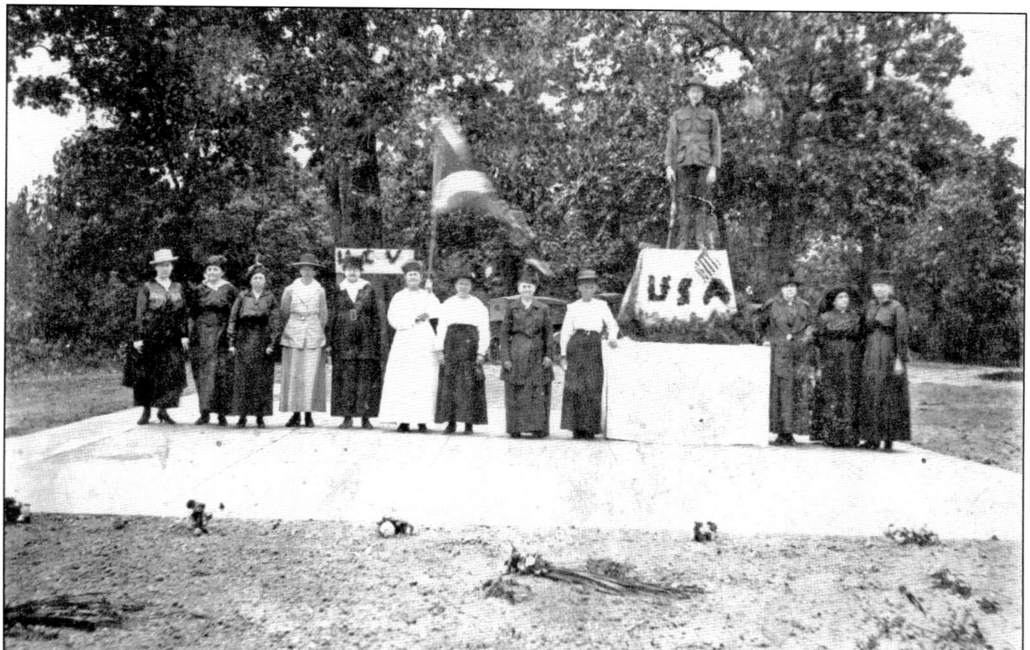

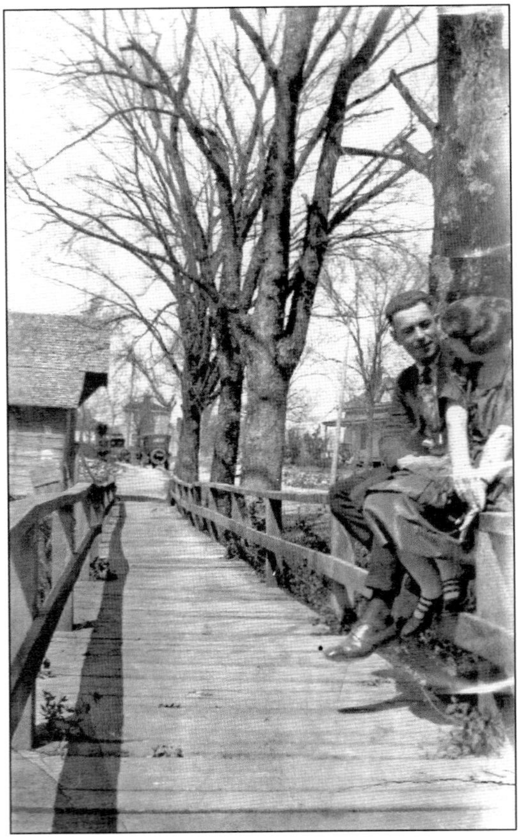

In this 1920s photograph, William Tally Price and an unidentified young lady sit on a footbridge located across from David Baker's Store, predecessor of Paul Cummings Store on Main Street, or Apex Street as it was called then. On the left is the edge of what was known then as the Guard House, and in the background are the Nathan Burns House and the Brown-Holloway House. (Doris Jones collection.)

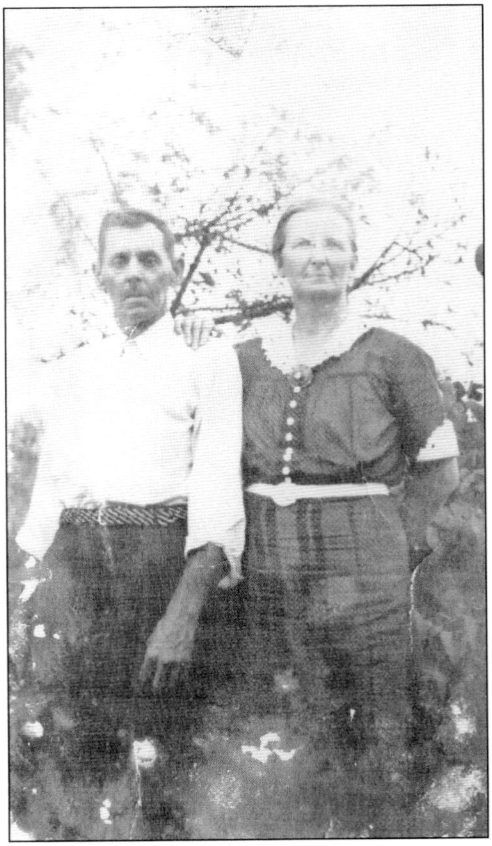

Linda (Utley) and Carl Burch "Burt" Holland were married in 1907, and they set up housekeeping and made their livelihood on their farm on land where Harris Lake Park is currently located. By 1938, Linda had inherited one-half of her parents' farm on Avent Ferry Road, and she and Burt relocated to the Utley family homestead and lived out their lives on this farm. (Courtesy of Gerald W. Holleman.)

Delcie (Collins) Mims, daughter of Texanna (Branch) Alford by her first husband, Joseph Collins, acquired the Alford estate when her mother passed away in 1938. She and her husband, Marcus Edward Mims, had one daughter, Margaret, and three sons, Joseph Howard, Hubert Edwin "Ed," and Ivan Collins. Hubert Edwin "Ed" Mims would take ownership of the manor, willing it to his sister's son James Bethel Wright. (Town Historical collection.)

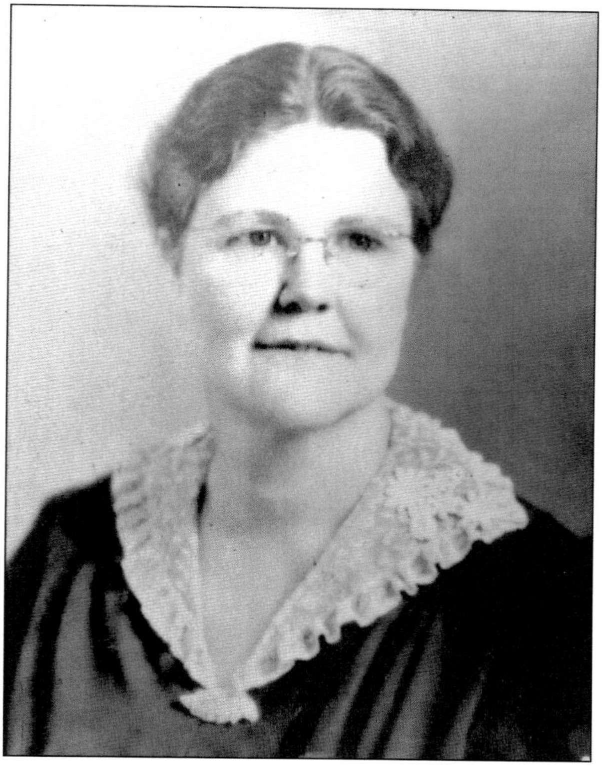

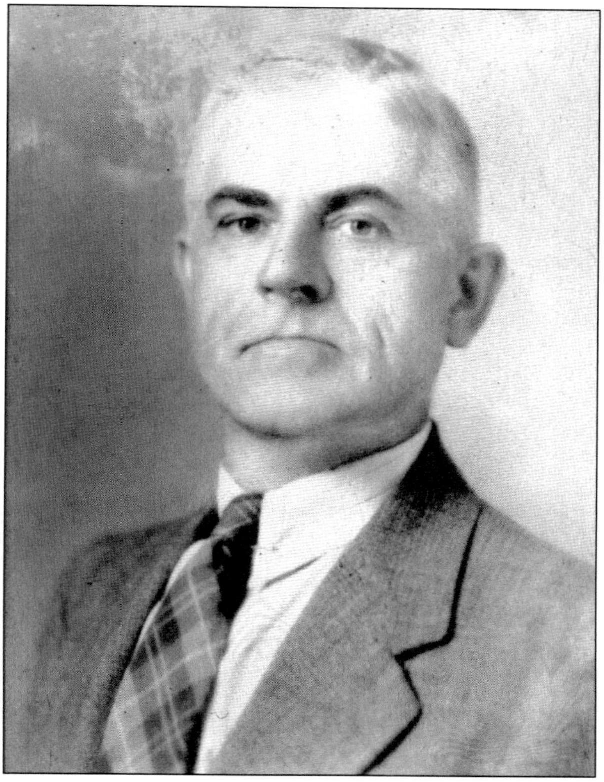

When Marcus Edward Mims married Delcie Collins, he became part of the extended Alford family. Mims served as a town commissioner from 1927 to 1929 and was again elected to serve from 1931 to 1935, a total of three terms. (Town Historical collection.)

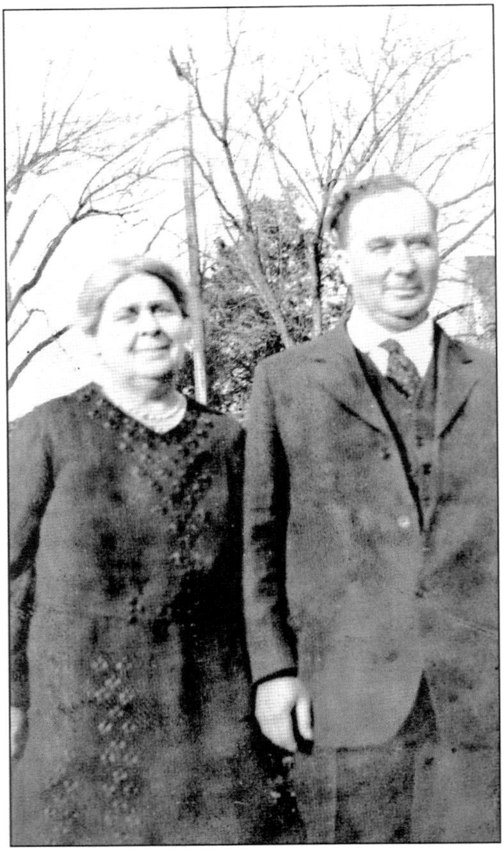

William Lonnie "Father" Price and his wife, Della Frances, are pictured here in a late-1930s photograph. Price owned the drugstore building at the corner of Center and Main Street for many years, also utilizing the back of the building to manufacture caskets and to operate a blacksmith shop. (Doris Jones collection.)

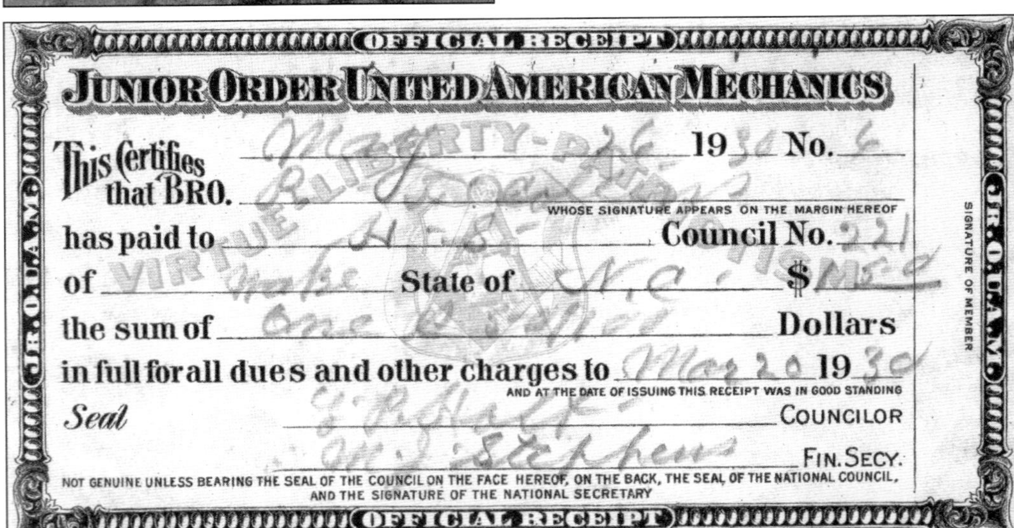

OFFICIAL RECEIPT

JUNIOR ORDER UNITED AMERICAN MECHANICS

This Certifies that BRO. ____ 19__ No. ____

WHOSE SIGNATURE APPEARS ON THE MARGIN HEREOF

has paid to ____ Council No. ____

of ____ State of ____ $ ____

the sum of ____ Dollars

in full for all dues and other charges to ____ 19__

AND AT THE DATE OF ISSUING THIS RECEIPT WAS IN GOOD STANDING

Seal ____ COUNCILOR

____ FIN. SECY.

NOT GENUINE UNLESS BEARING THE SEAL OF THE COUNCIL ON THE FACE HEREOF, ON THE BACK, THE SEAL OF THE NATIONAL COUNCIL, AND THE SIGNATURE OF THE NATIONAL SECRETARY

JR. O. U. A. M.

SIGNATURE OF MEMBER

OFFICIAL RECEIPT

The Council No. 221 Junior Order United American Mechanics had its lodge building on Main Street located where the Clothes Closet is now situated. This receipt dated May 26, 1930, from Roger F. Collins was for dues. The order rented out the bottom floor of their building to the town to use as a meeting place. The original building was sold to the town in 1941 and razed in 1946. (Courtesy of Jerry Holland.)

Eunice (Cotton) Holleman, her mother, Gilly (Utley) Cotton, and Eunice's son Gerald Holleman make up the three generations in this 1937 family picture. (Courtesy of Gerald W. Holleman.)

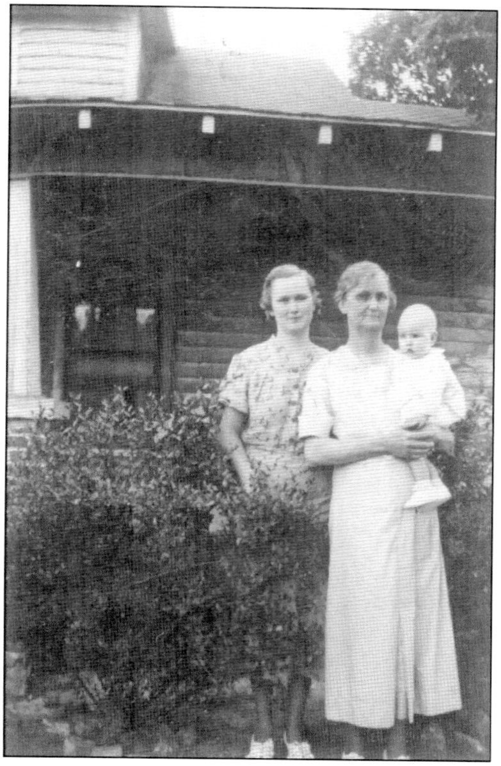

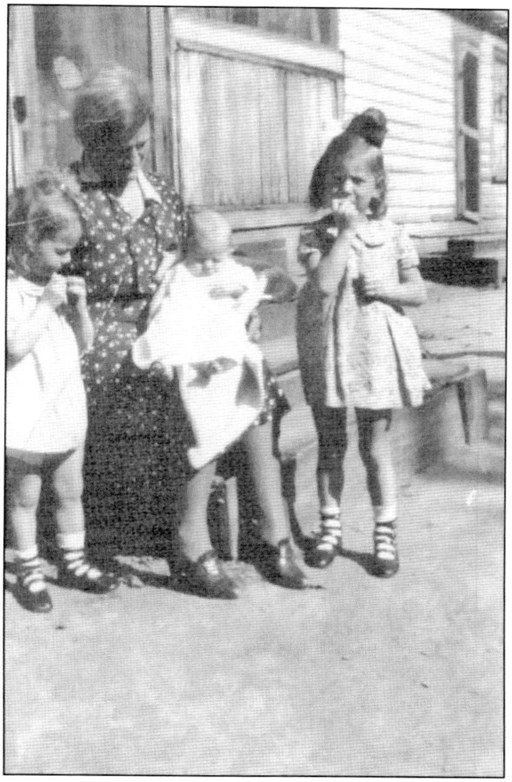

This picture taken in October 1937 shows the Creech girls with their beloved aunt Laura Templeton in the yard of the Templeton home place on Main Street. Standing by the back porch are, from left to right, Georgie Creech, Laura Templeton and infant Mary Creech, and Kitty Creech. (Billy and Mary Holt collection.)

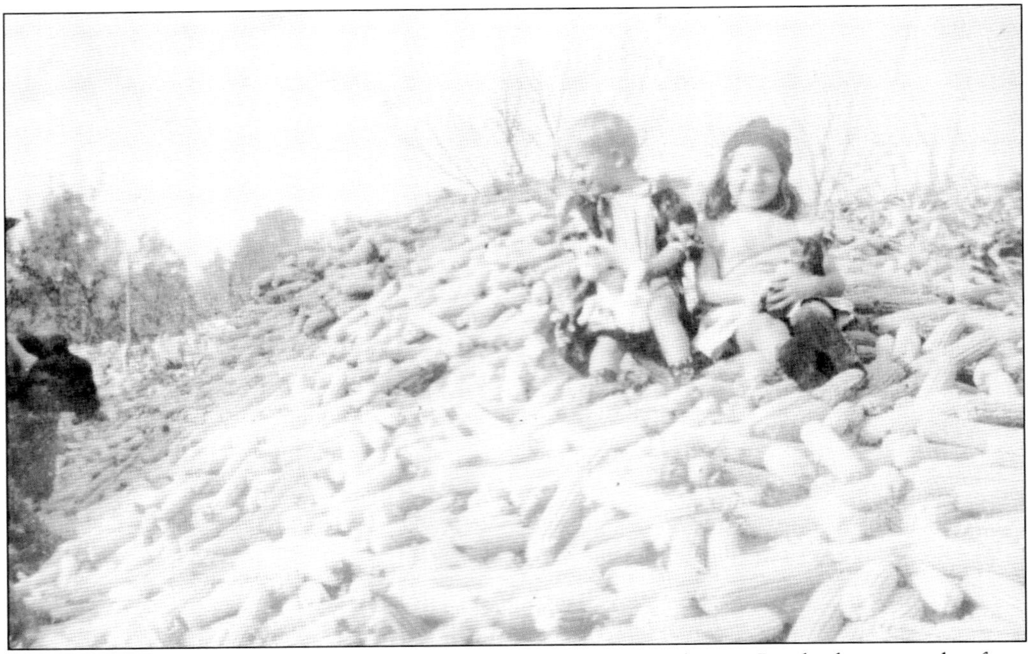

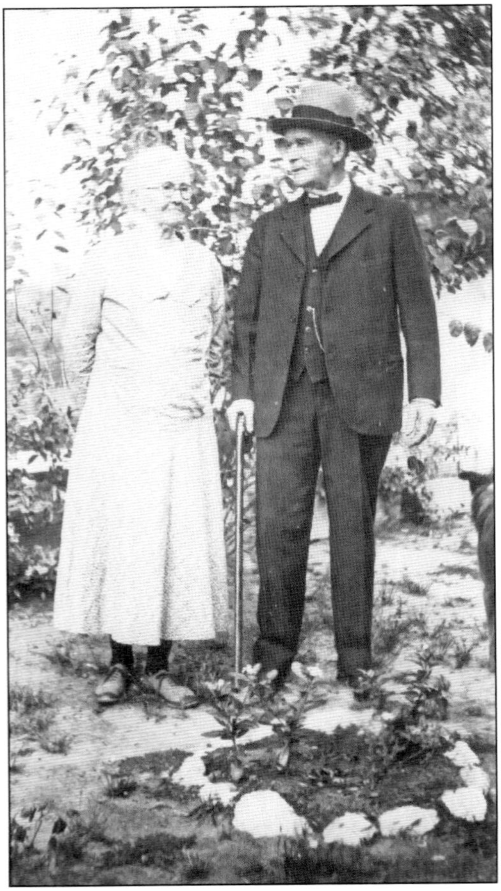

That is a lot of corn! Perched atop a pile of freshly shucked ears of corn are Mary (left) and Georgie (right) Creech. This photograph, taken in 1939, shows the girls on their parents' farm, which was located where the Oak Hall Shopping Center on Main Street is now. (Billy and Mary Holt collection.)

Born in 1859, Cornelia was the daughter of Simpson and Mary-Ann (Matthews) Holland. She was a small child when her family's home was used as a field hospital by Union troops encamped in the area in April 1865. She and her mother and siblings were charter members of the Collins Grove Baptist Church. She is shown here with John Marshall Hare, whom she married in 1879. (Mary Macon collection.)

In 1939, Sylvian Knowles was a young teacher recruited by George Cullipher, principal of Holly Springs School, to teach fourth grade, but after only two days, he added the third grade to her job duties. Sylvian married Claire Brooks, and they had one son, Bill. Sylvian taught school for 27 years, was the principal at A. V. Baucom Elementary for nine years, and served as the mayor of Holly Springs from 1981 to 1983. (Sylvian Brooks collection.)

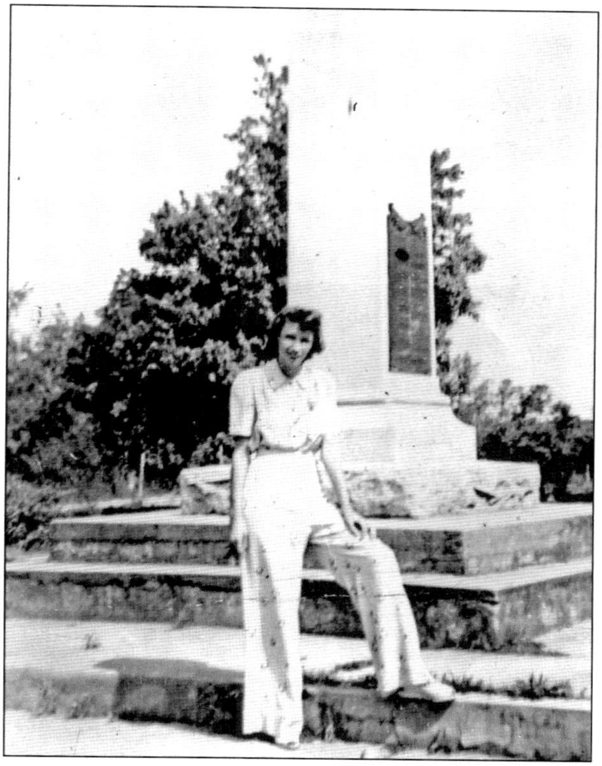

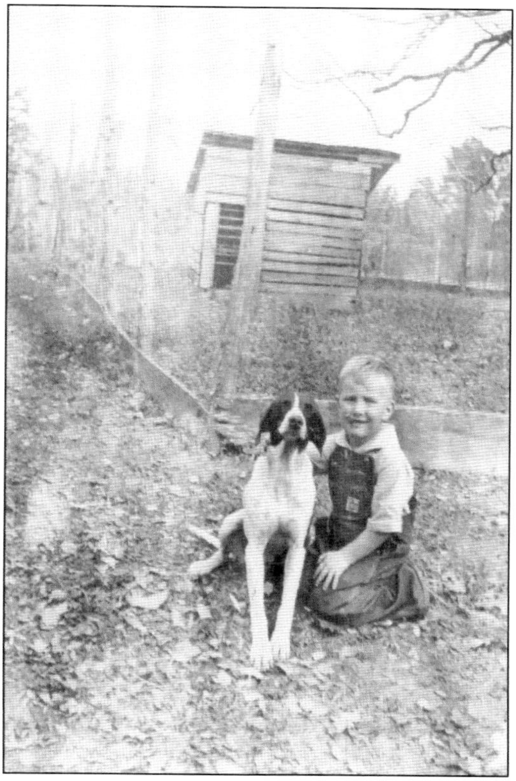

A young Gerald Holleman and his faithful canine buddy Mack are pictured in this 1940 photograph taken on his grandfather and grandmother Utley's farm on Avent Ferry Road. (Courtesy of Gerald W. Holleman.)

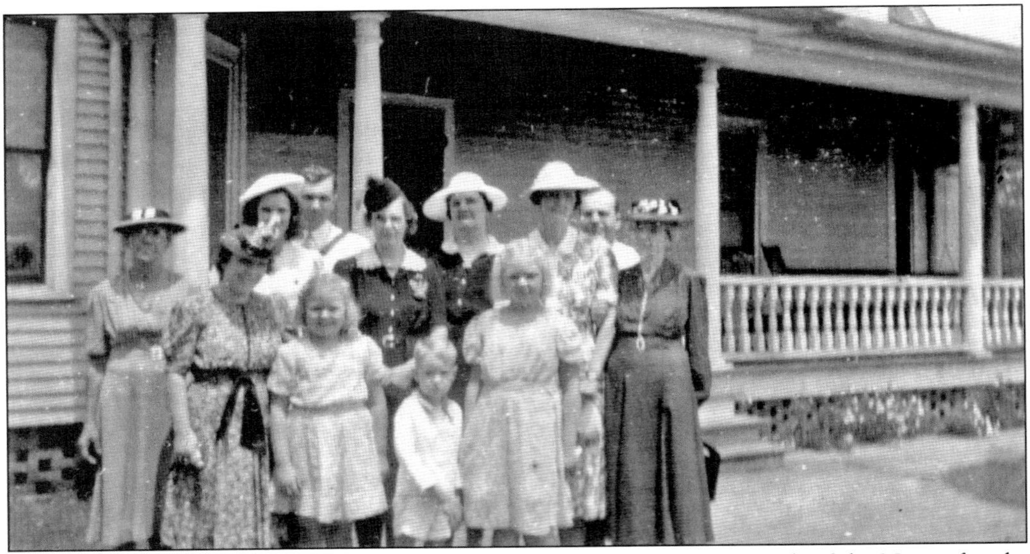

A family gathering was the perfect opportunity for this *c.* 1941 photograph of the Norris family. Standing in front of the house on Avent Ferry Road are, from left to right, Pearl (Oldham) Jones, Sue Norris, Henry Thomas Norris Jr., Nancy Norris, Maggie Oldham, Frances (Adams) Norris, unidentified, Ruth (Ufford) Norris, May Adams, Inda Collins, Hersilia (Banks) Norris, and Walter Jarvis Adams. (Ken Jarvis collection.)

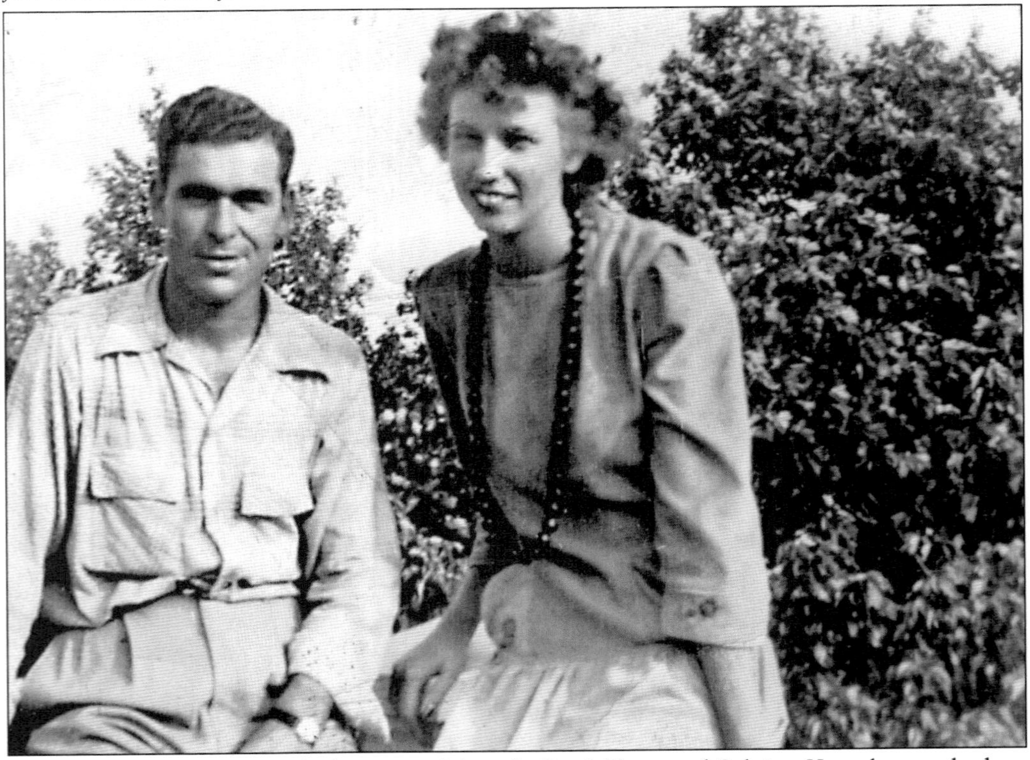

This early-1940s photograph shows good friends Cecil Shaw and Sylvian Knowles perched on top of the Leslie-Alford-Mims House. Access from the third floor out to the widow's walk gave them a bird's-eye view of Holly Springs. (Sylvian Brooks collection.)

Paul Cummings took over his father-in-law David Baker's convenience store/gas station in 1943. Pictured in this *c.* 1940 photograph are Mary Lou Royal and an unidentified man in front of the store. When Main Street was widened, the store was razed, as the store itself and the gas pumps were in the right-of-way. The current convenience store was built farther away from the street. (Vada Fiegler collection.)

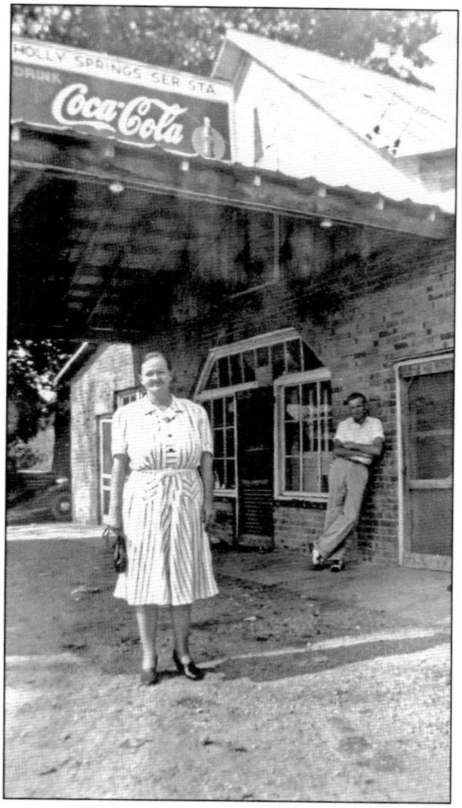


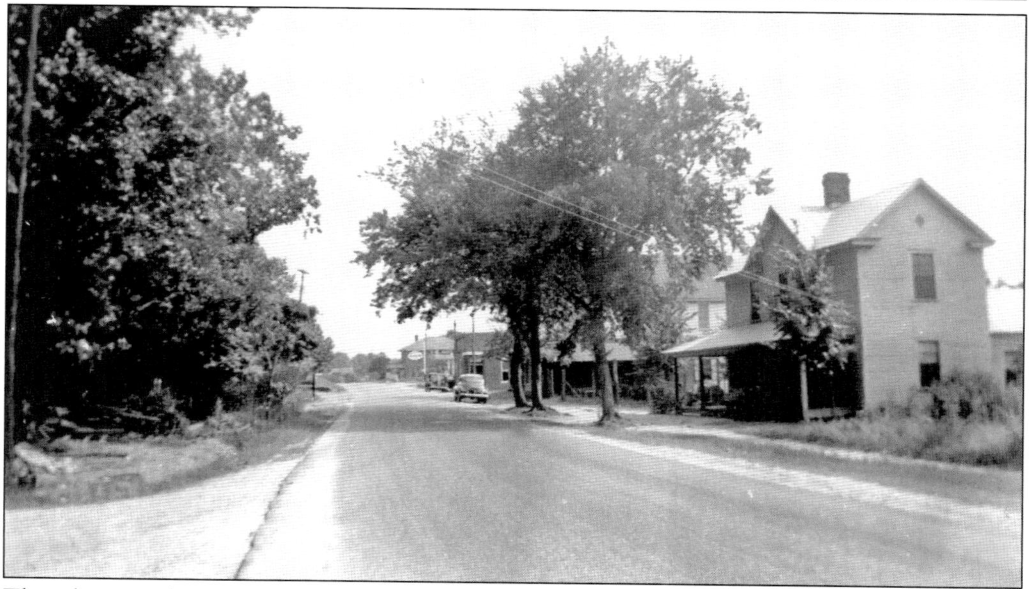

This photograph was taken in the 1940s on Main Street looking from Cummings Store toward Center Street. The house on the right was the Hare House, which burned down in the mid- to late 1950s. Next door was Lashley's Store, and on the opposite corner was the post office, which took the place of the failed bank. An Esso station sat between the post office and Seagraves Hotel. (Vada Fiegler collection.)

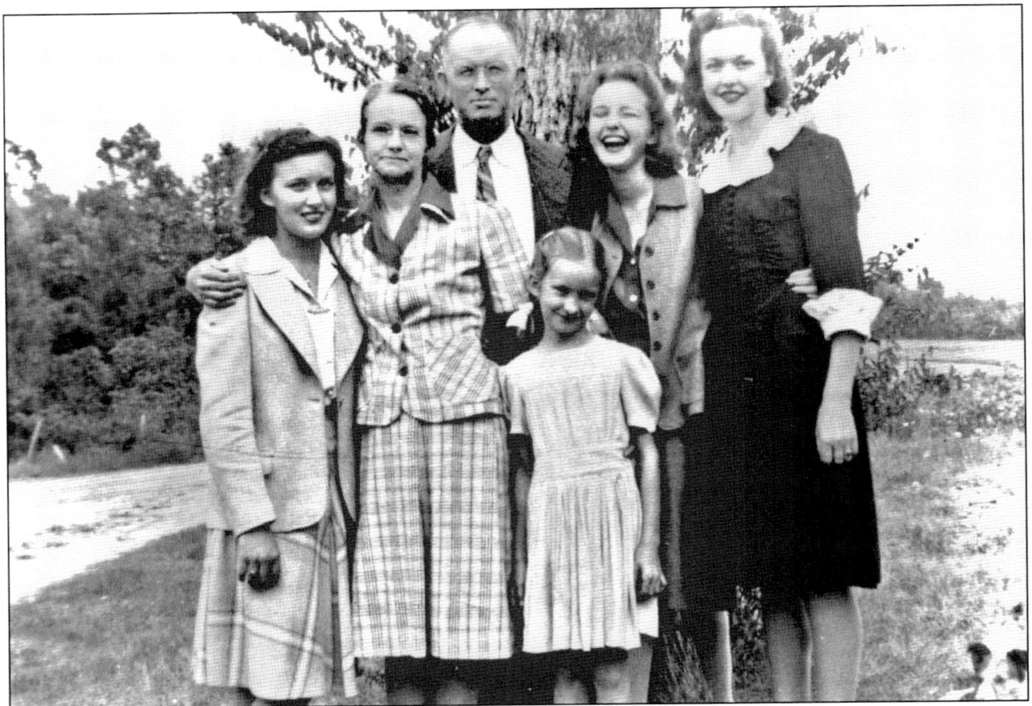

The Exum Hare family gathers for their traditional, annual Thanksgiving Day photograph in 1943. Standing by a tree in the yard are, from left to right, Rubelle, Ella, Exum, Jean, Martha, Mary, and Ted the dog. (Jean Goodwin collection.)

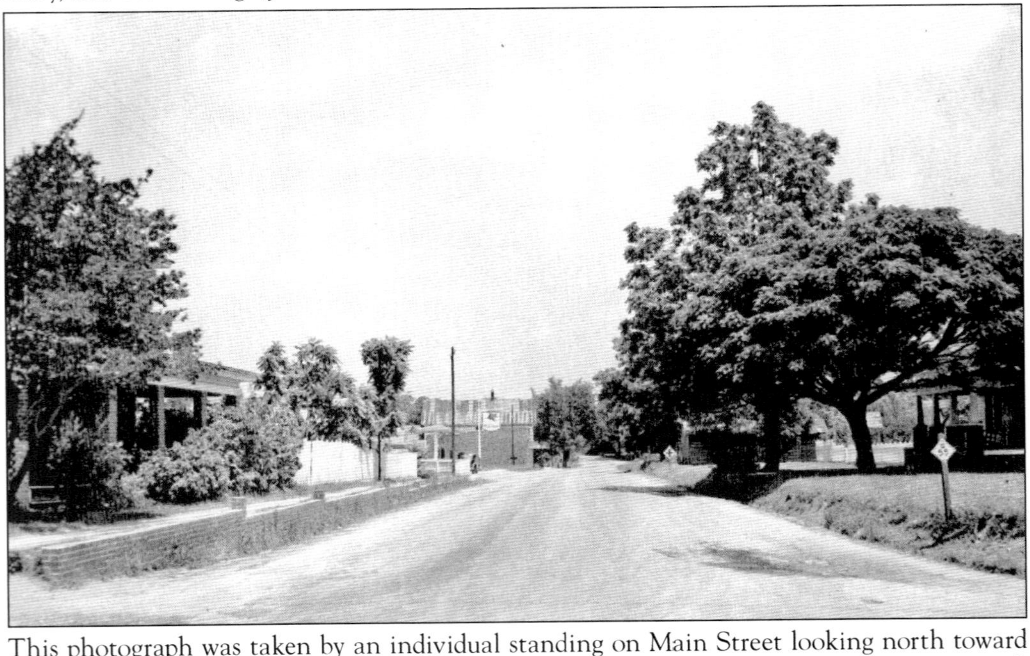

This photograph was taken by an individual standing on Main Street looking north toward Center Street before it was paved. On the left side of the picture are the old Seagraves Hotel, a Sunoco gas station, and Tom Lashley's store. On the right side of the picture are the Harold Brewer House and the John Fabius Jones House. (Wright collection.)

Shown here in a late-1940s photograph is Lynn Adams Jr., the son of Lynn and Jennie Belle (Minter) Adams. The Adams family raised tobacco and had a large farm on Holly Springs Road. Lynn is pictured here standing between the barn and tractor. (Christine Adams-Utley collection.)

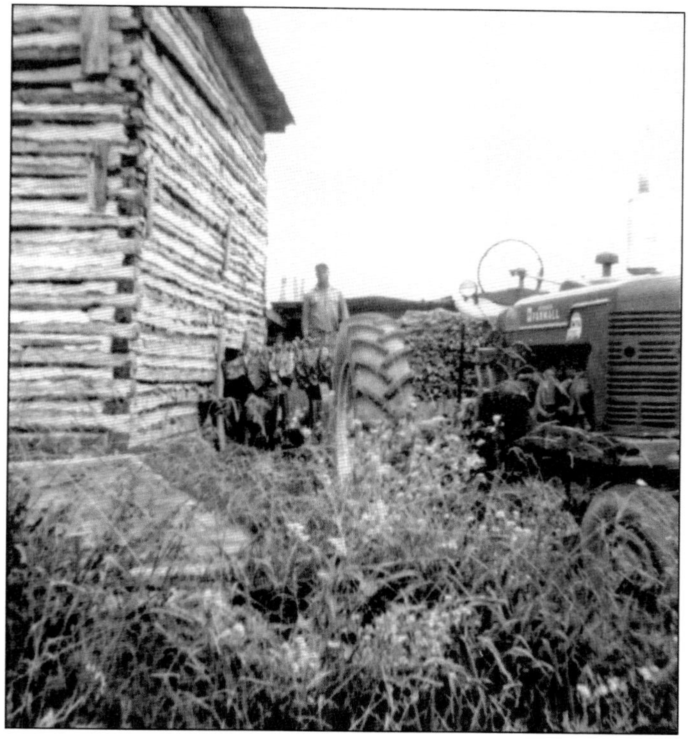

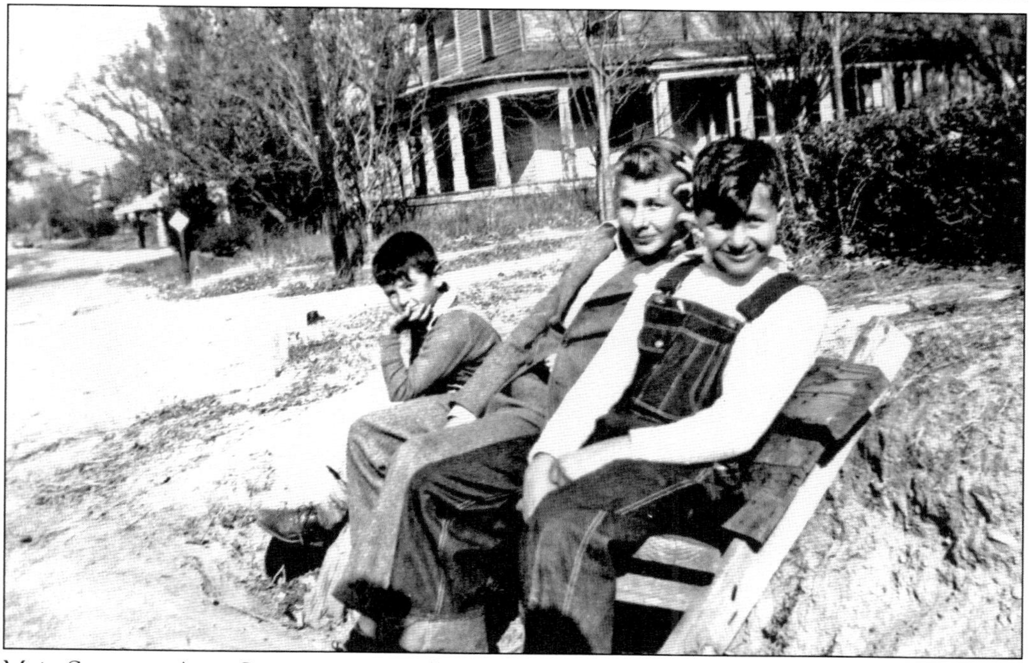

Main Street, or Apex Street as it was called at the time, was unpaved, giving the village a rustic feeling. Parents felt comfortable allowing their children to ride their bicycles or walk through town. Seated on a bench are, from left to right, ? Brewer, Glen Earp, and Billy Calvin Brewer. In the background is the David Aimon Baker House, which stood where Fidelity Bank is now. (Doris Jones collection.)

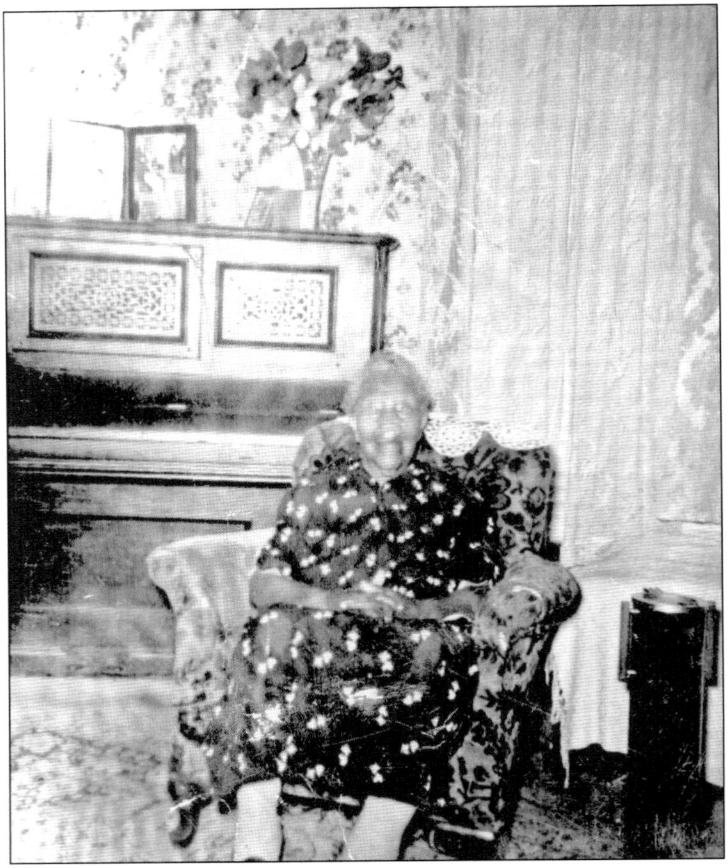

Shown in this 1940s photograph is Molly Minter, who was born around 1864. She married Eli Minter around 1904 and had six children and 11 grandchildren. (Christine Adams-Utley collection.)

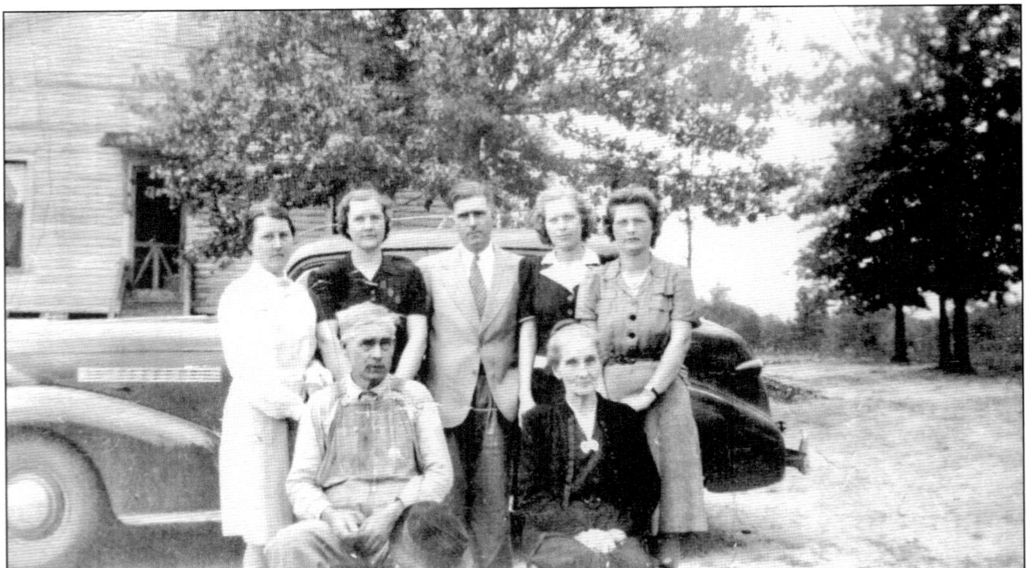

Posing by the family car in this 1940s photograph are, from left to right, (first row) Fred and Hester (Rollins) Utley; (second row) Lillie Mae Utley, Ida Utley, Lattie Utley, Myrtle Utley, and Mary Lee Utley. (Mary Lee Johnson collection, courtesy of Lori Stokes.)

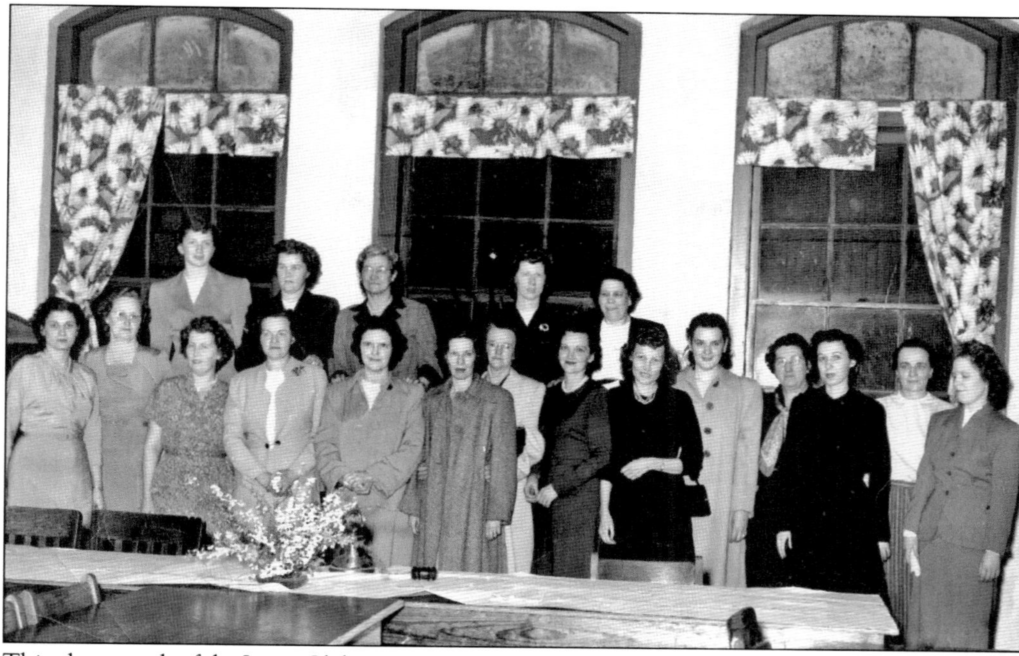

This photograph of the Lions Club meeting was taken at Holly Springs High School cafeteria around 1948. Club members are, from left to right, (first row) Rosa Lee Cotton, Eunice Holleman, May Womble, unidentified, Clair Brewer, Ann Hall, Ella Hare, Neva Earp, Evelyn Belton, Dot Stephens, Grace Baker, Mary Lee Woodhouse, Blonza Smith, and Mattie Morton; (second row) Mable Holland, Dot Holland, Mary Johnson, Kathryn Cummings, and Pearl Jones. (Vada Fiegler collection.)

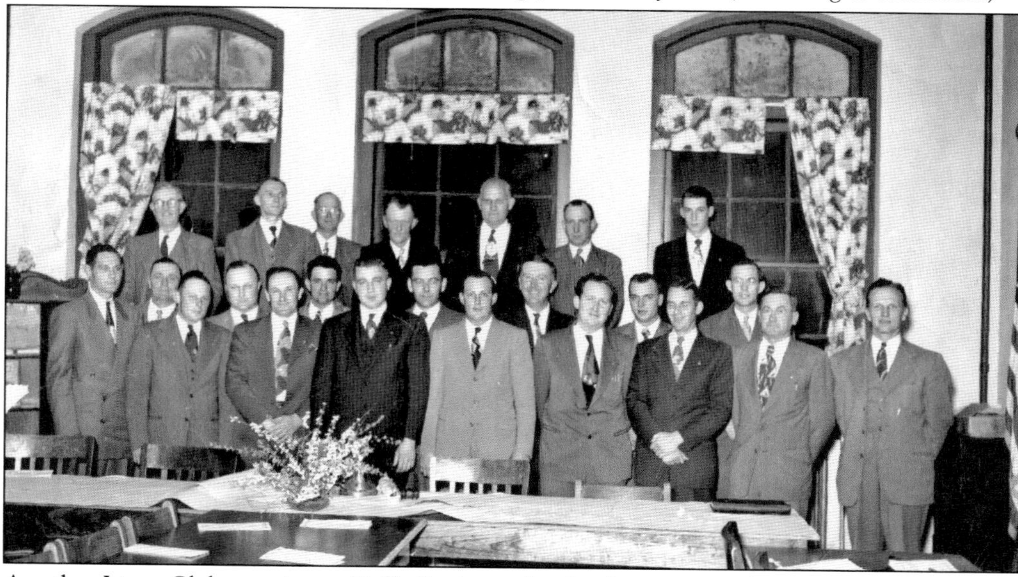

Another Lions Club meeting at Holly Springs school cafeteria around 1948 included members, from left to right, (first row) Burnie Holland, unidentified, Paul Cummings, Wick Holland, Charles Cross, Charlie Woodhouse, Ed Belton, and Howard Earp; (second row) Elmer Brewer, Sherrod Holleman, Reggie Cotton, unidentified, George Hall, Earl Smith, Graham Wood, and Marvin Morton; (third row) Thurman Johnson, Harold Brewer, Exum Hare, Coy Baker, Ernie Brewer, Jack Stephens, and Glenn Adams. (Vada Fiegler collection.)

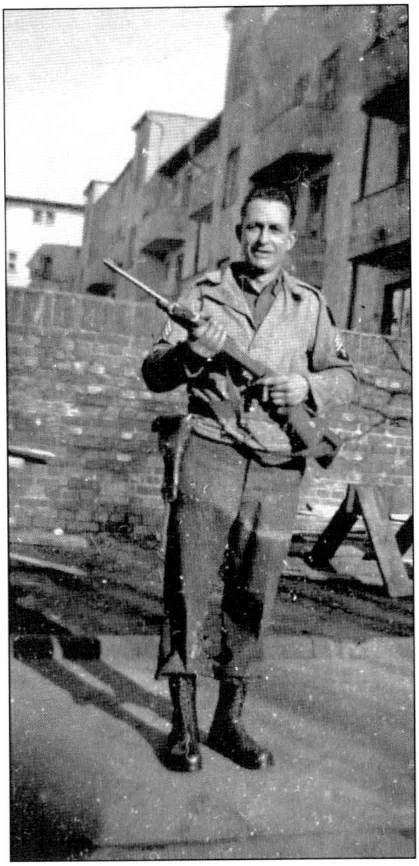

From the American Revolution to Operation Iraqi Freedom, Holly Springs has been honorably represented by its brave young men. Native son Sgt. Rupert Johnson is proudly pictured here in his World War II army fatigues. (Mary Lee Johnson collection, courtesy of Lori Stokes.)

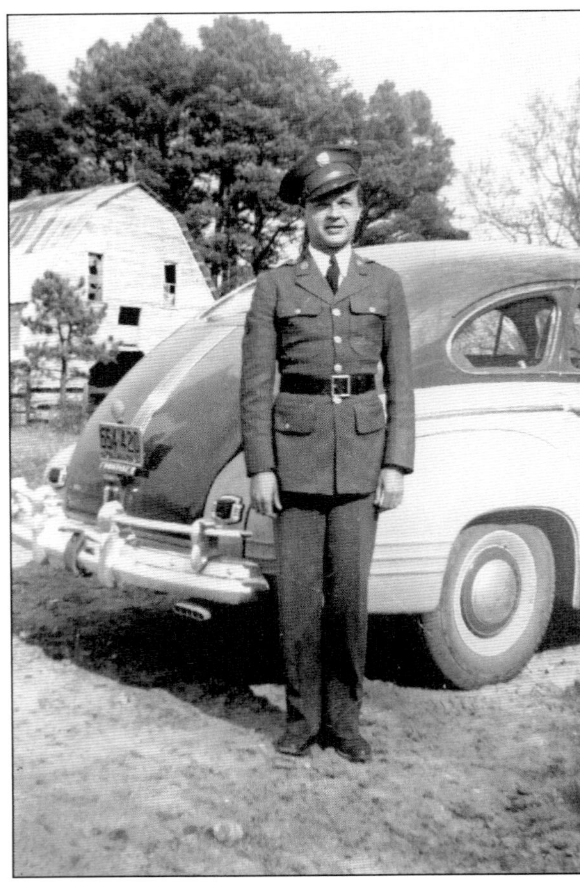

Charles B. Earp, son of J. Oscar and Challie Earp, stands proud for his commitment to his country in his World War II uniform. (Mary Lee Johnson collection, courtesy of Lori Stokes.)

Shown here in his World War II uniform is Reggie Cotton, son of Lonnie and Gilly (Utley) Cotton. Pictured here with his siblings, from left to right, are Reggie, Thelma, Homer, and Eunice Cotton. After the war, Cotton returned home and purchased the Esso gas station from Wray Hare. The gas station was located on Main Street between the Seagraves Hotel and the old bank/post office building. (Courtesy of Gerald W. Holleman.)

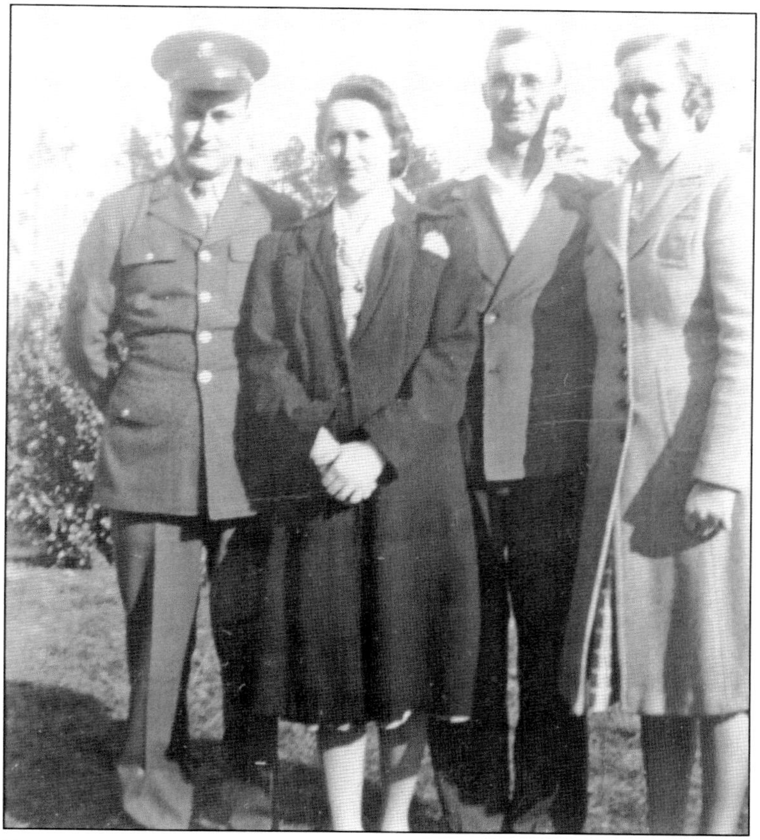

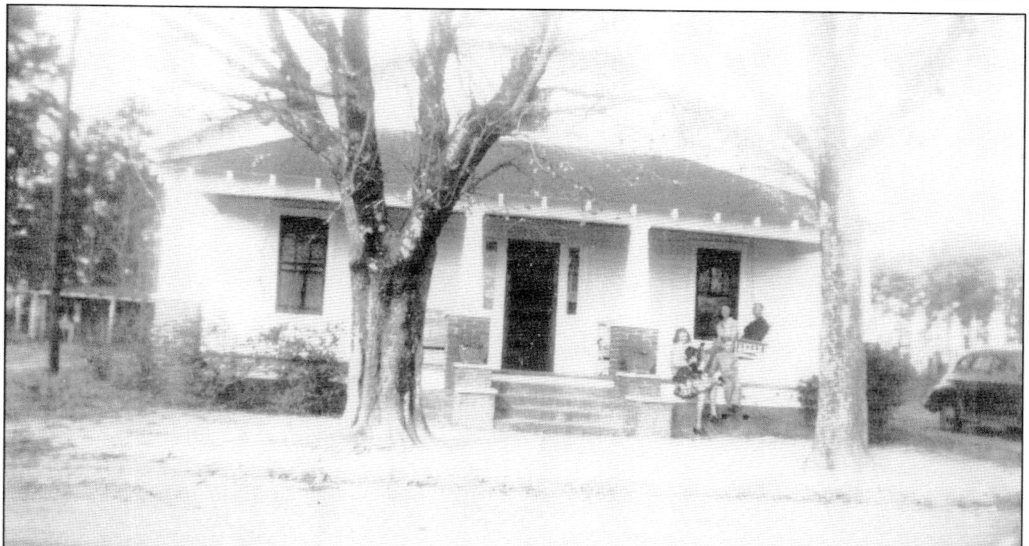

This 1943 photograph taken at the Betts Farm on Cass Holt Road shows the Betts family resting on the front porch. Holding Frank the Irish setter on her lap is Evelyn with her brother Dan sitting next to her. Their parents, Emma (Fuquay) and Hubert, sit on the porch swing. (Bremen and Evelyn Dewar collection.)

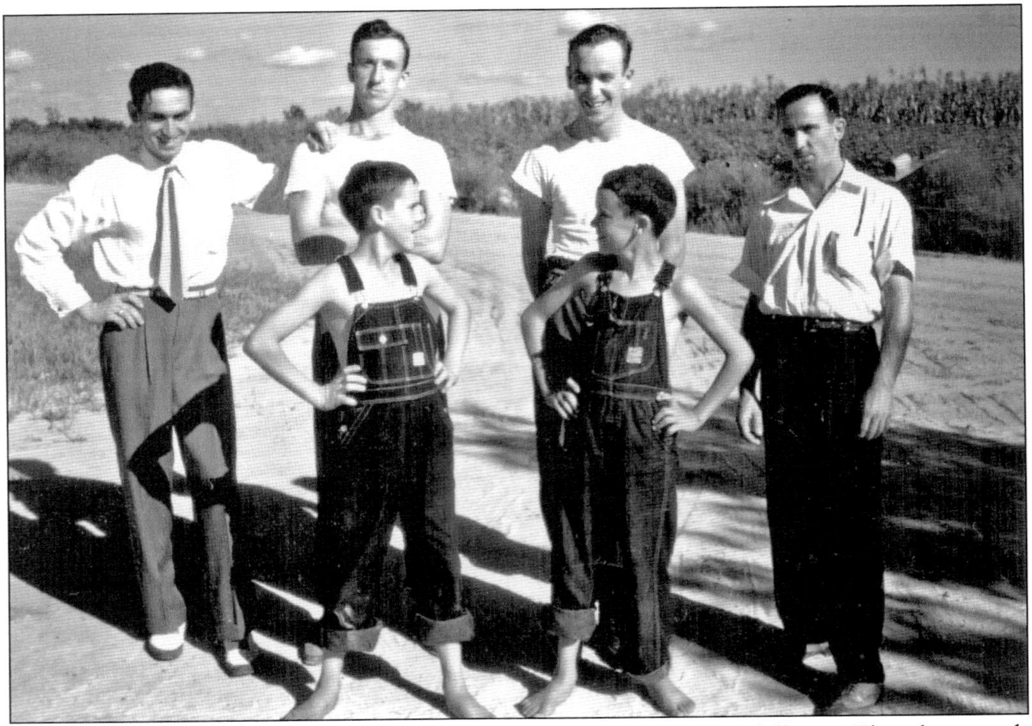

Boys will be boys, and the sons of Cass and Celeste (Tutor) Holt are no different. This photograph taken in 1944 shows the brothers hamming it up for the camera. From left to right are, (first row, wearing overalls) Robert and Billy; (second row) Leon, Calvin, Truby, and Jack. (Billy and Mary Holt collection.)

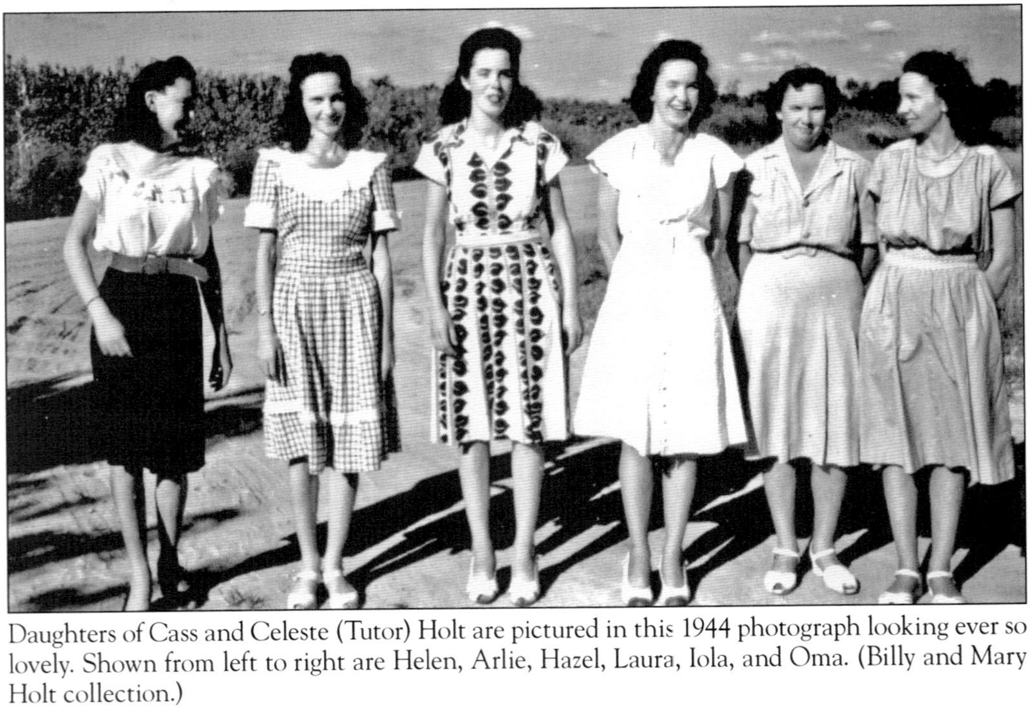

Daughters of Cass and Celeste (Tutor) Holt are pictured in this 1944 photograph looking ever so lovely. Shown from left to right are Helen, Arlie, Hazel, Laura, Iola, and Oma. (Billy and Mary Holt collection.)

This trio of well-dressed folks in the mid-1940s is unidentified, but they are shown standing in front of the Seagraves Hotel at the corner of Ballentine and Main Streets. The Harold Brewer House can be seen in the background on Main Street. This Craftsman-style bungalow was moved to Earp Street in April 1997 to make way for the Village Office Condos. (Doris Jones collection.)

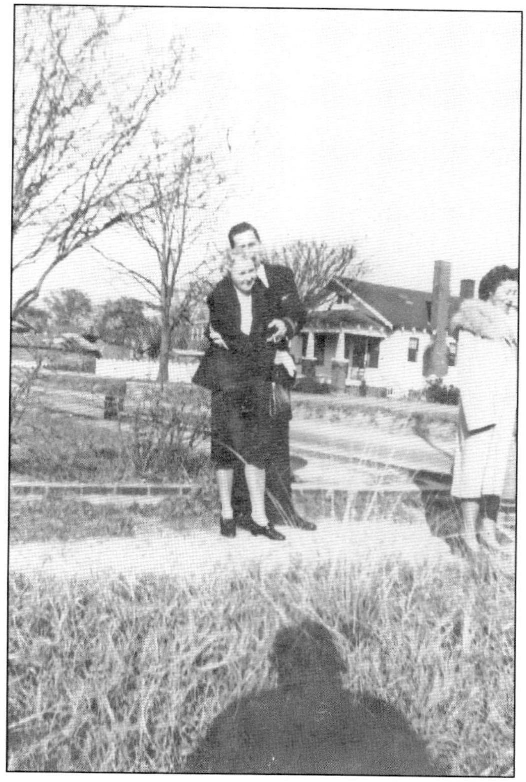

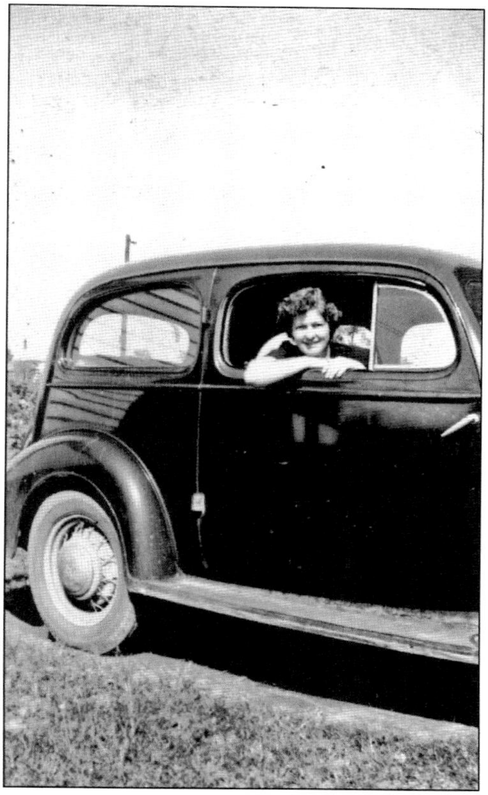

Mary Lee (Utley) Johnson sits awaiting a car ride in this mid- to late-1940s photograph. (Mary Lee Johnson collection, courtesy of Lori Stokes.)

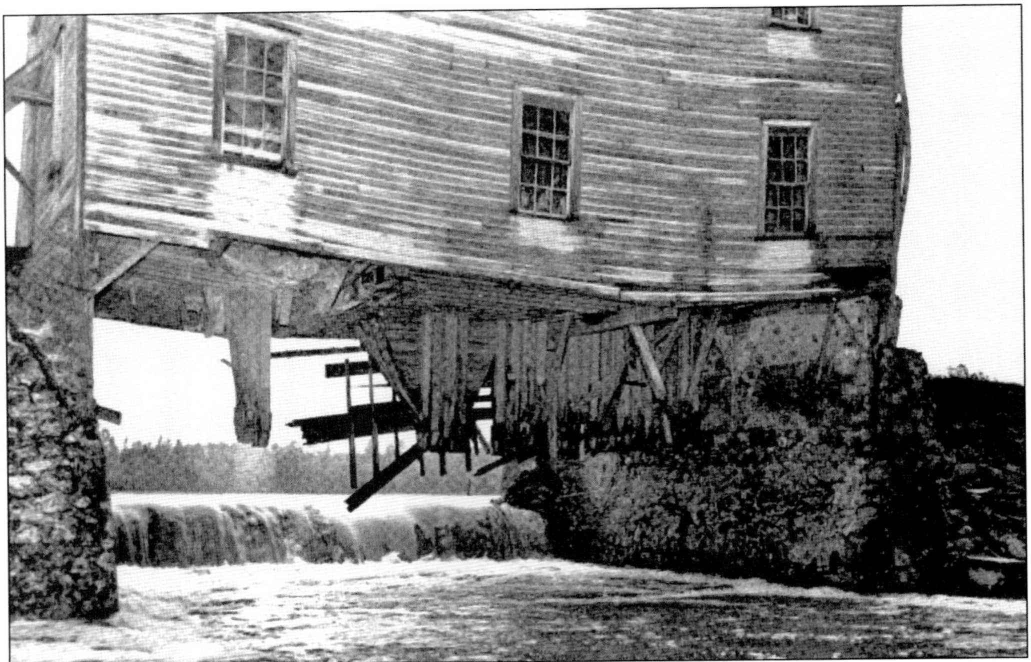

Original owner Needham Norris ran a gristmill on what was known as Norris Mill. Over the years, it changed hands and was referred to by several different names; currently it is called Bass Lake. These 1949 photographs of the three-story mill show the damage to the bottom floor of the structure caused by a hurricane. Over the next couple of days, the mill collapsed and crashed into Bazzel Creek. (Both, courtesy of North Carolina Archives.)

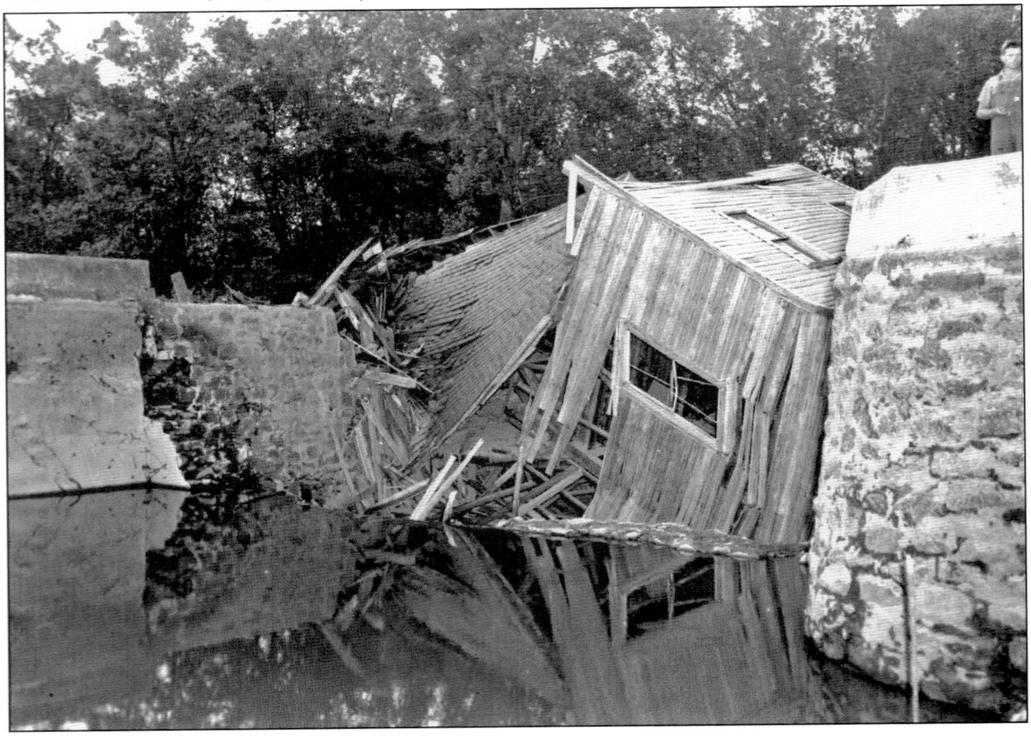

*Two*

# Life in Holly Springs 1950–1976

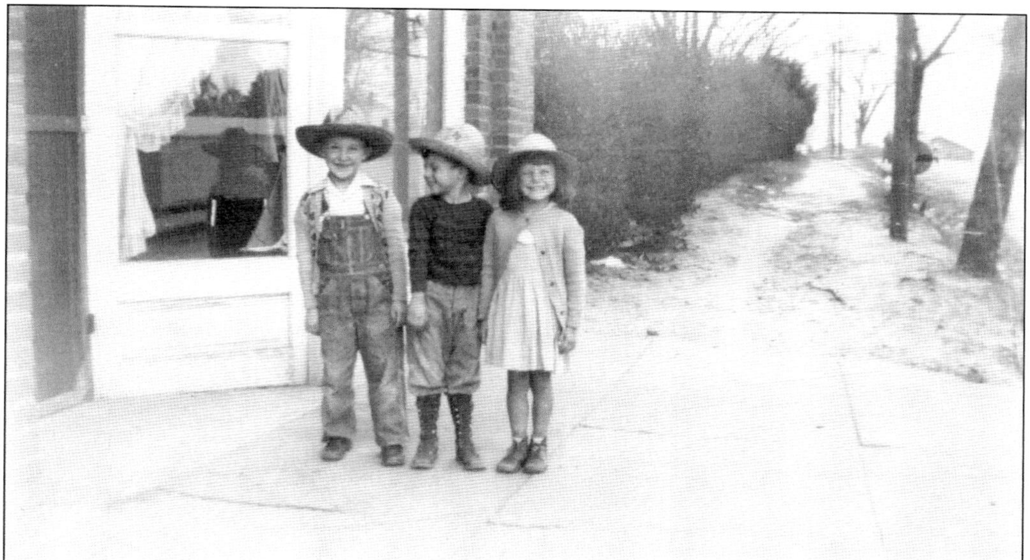

Here is a trio of Holly Springs youngsters. From left to right, Bill Brooks, John Lee Holleman, and Joyce Ann Wilson stopped playing long enough to have their picture taken in front of the store on Ballentine Street that was run by Bill's parents, Claire and Sylvian Brooks. (Sylvian Brooks collection.)

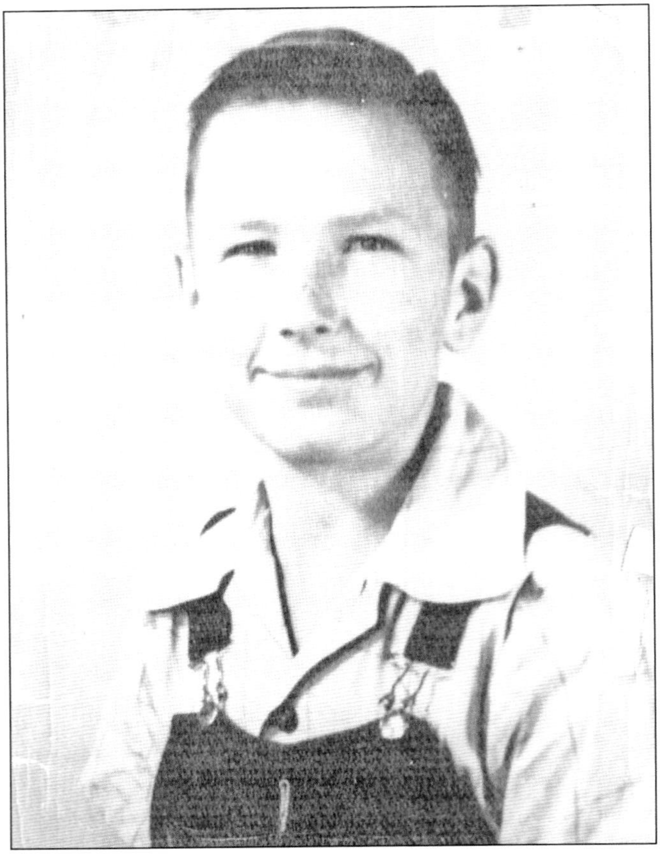

This early-1950s school picture shows a young Gerald W. Holleman, the son of Sherrod "Shake" and Eunice (Cotton) Holleman. Gerald would lead Holly Springs as mayor for 17 years as the town grew both in population and commercial development. In 2000, Holly Springs was recognized as the "Fastest Growing Community in North Carolina." (Courtesy of Gerald W. Holleman.)

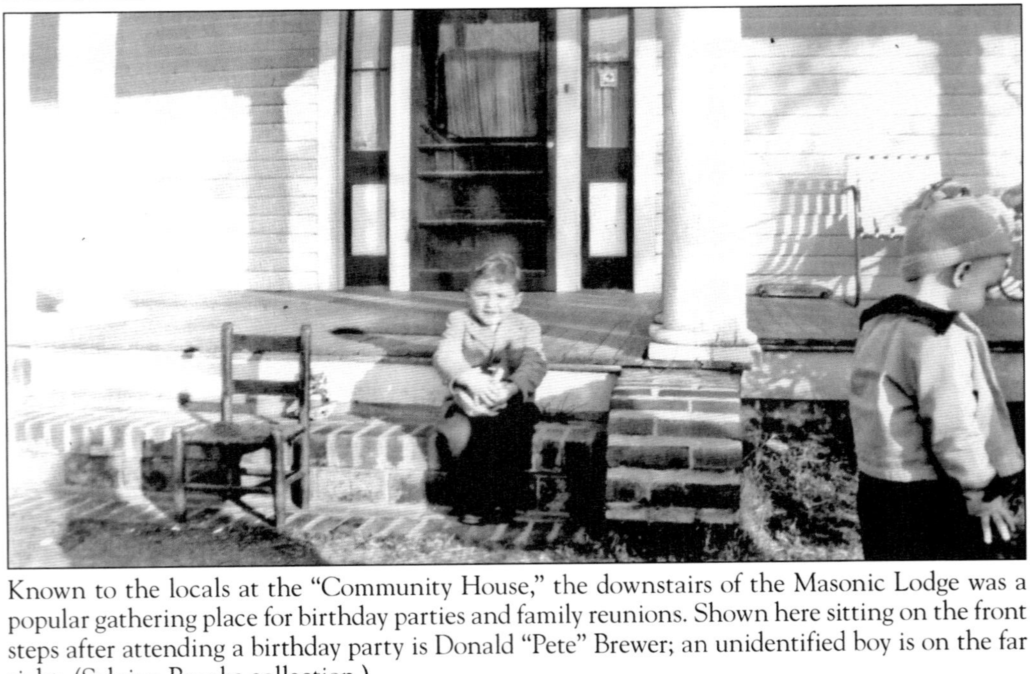

Known to the locals at the "Community House," the downstairs of the Masonic Lodge was a popular gathering place for birthday parties and family reunions. Shown here sitting on the front steps after attending a birthday party is Donald "Pete" Brewer; an unidentified boy is on the far right. (Sylvian Brooks collection.)

Leaning against the front porch of their home, the Leslie-Alford-Mims House, on Easter Sunday of April 1950 and dressed in their Sunday best are, from left to right, Ivan "Ike" and Hubert Edwin "Ed" Mims. (Nathan and Carolyn Williams collection.)

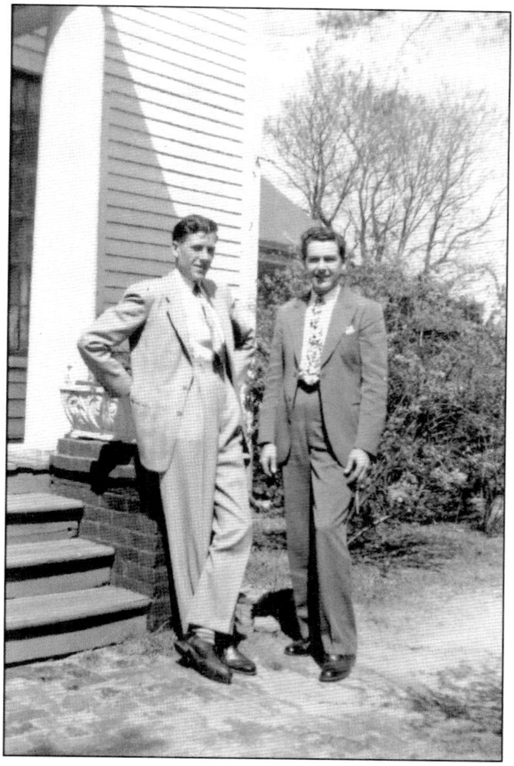

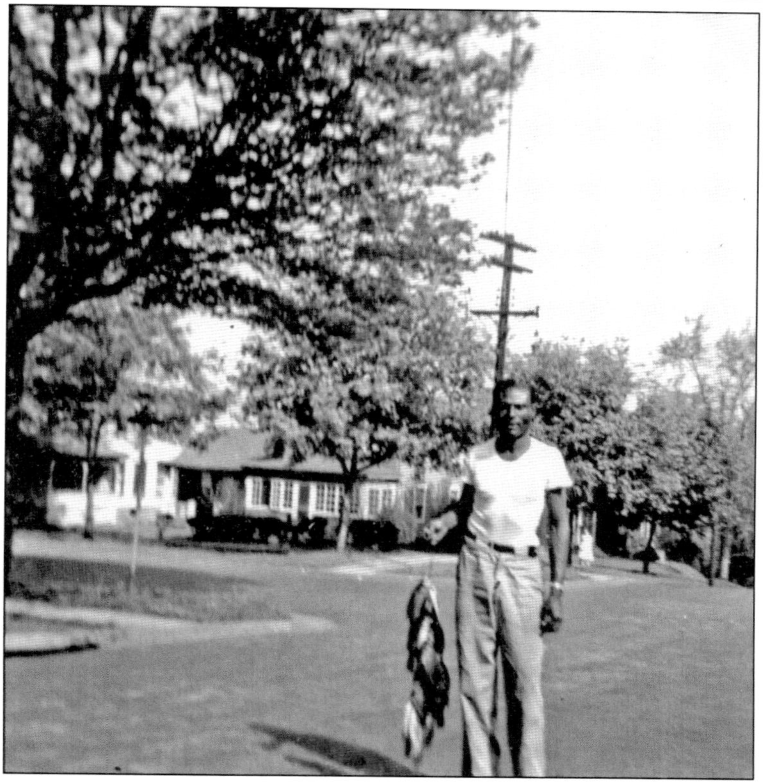

These fish definitely didn't get away from George Adams. This photograph, taken in the late 1950s, features George, son of Lynn and Jennie Belle (Minter) Adams, showing off his prized catch of the day. (Christine Adams-Utley collection.)

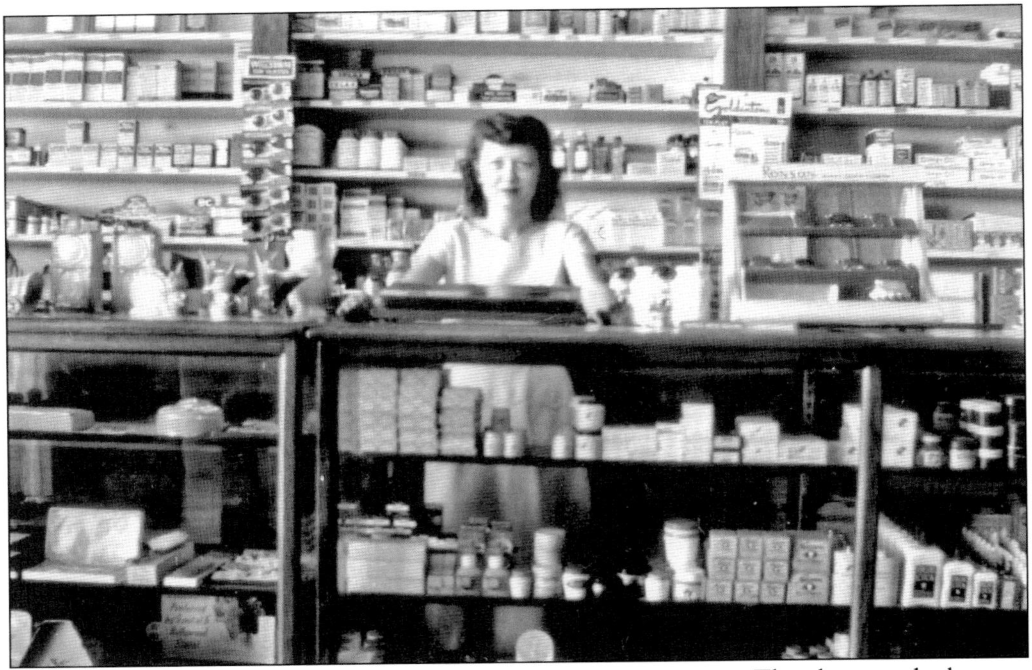

The photograph above was taken of the interior of the Mims Drug Store on West Center Street in the early 1950s. Shown here is Rachel (Hall) Mims, wife of Ivan "Ike" Mims, ready to wait on customers patronizing the store. (Nathan and Carolyn Williams collection.)

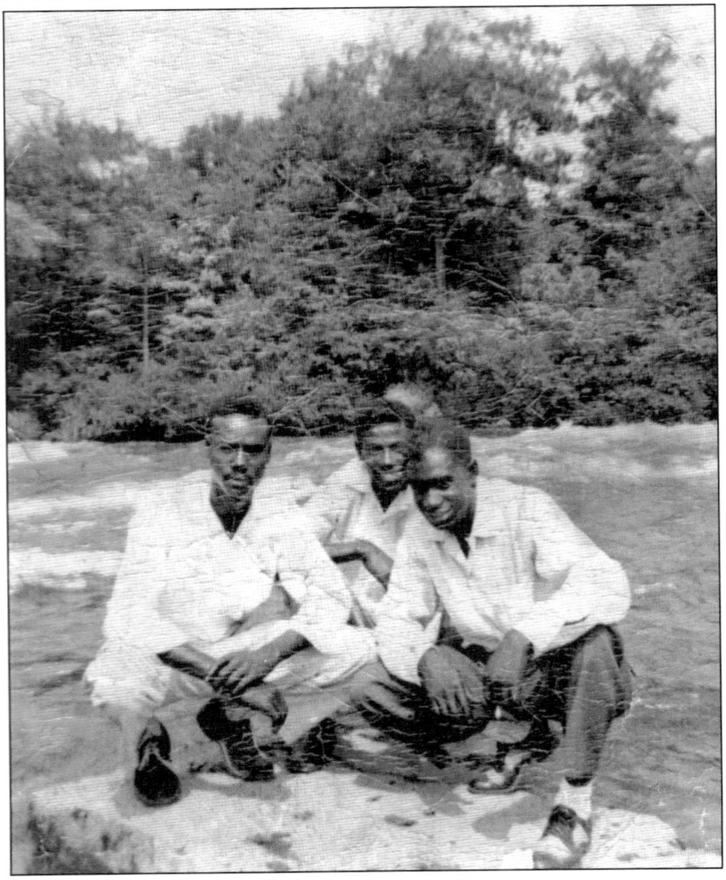

These young Holly Springs men pose for a picture in the mid-1950s. From left to right are Chester Lee Adams, Andrew Adams, and Odell Lockley. (Christine Adams-Utley collection.)

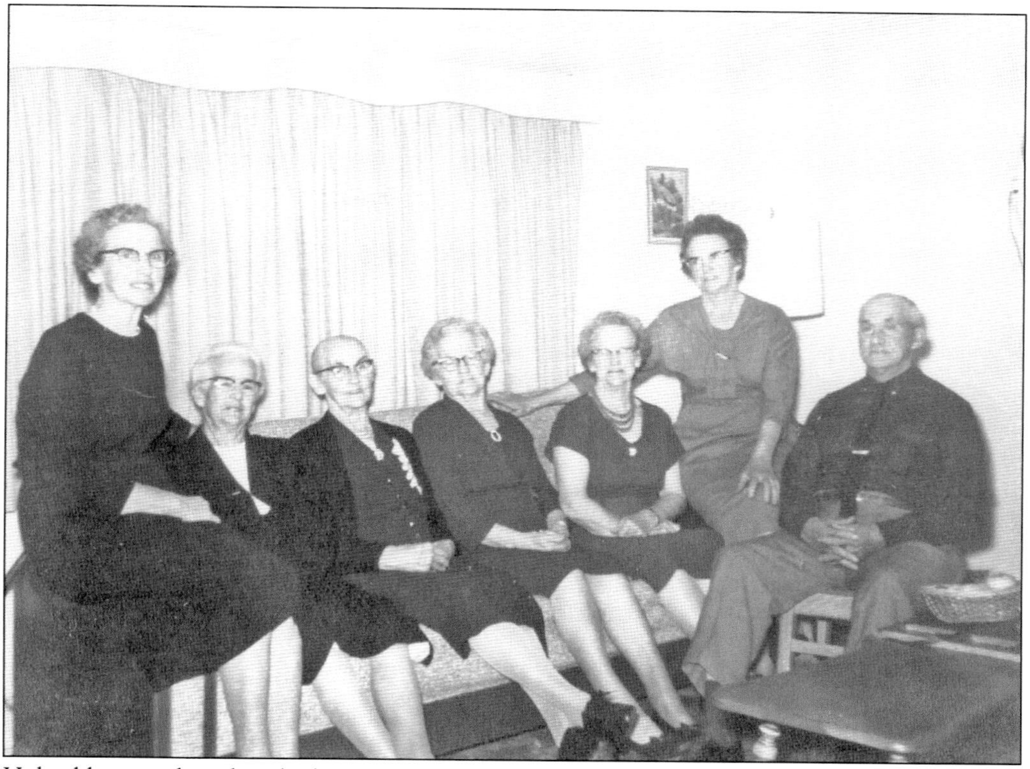

Holt siblings gathered at the home of their sister Ella and her husband, Exum Hare, to celebrate the birthdays of the eldest Holt sister, Ida, and youngest sister, Ella, in this early-1950s photograph. Seated on the couch from left to right are Nula (Holt) Lockamy, Ida (Holt) Seagraves, Missouri (Holt) Powell, Nancy (Holt) Austin, Lessie (Holt) Wilkins, Ella (Holt) Hare, and Cass Holt. (Jimmy H. Hancock collection.)

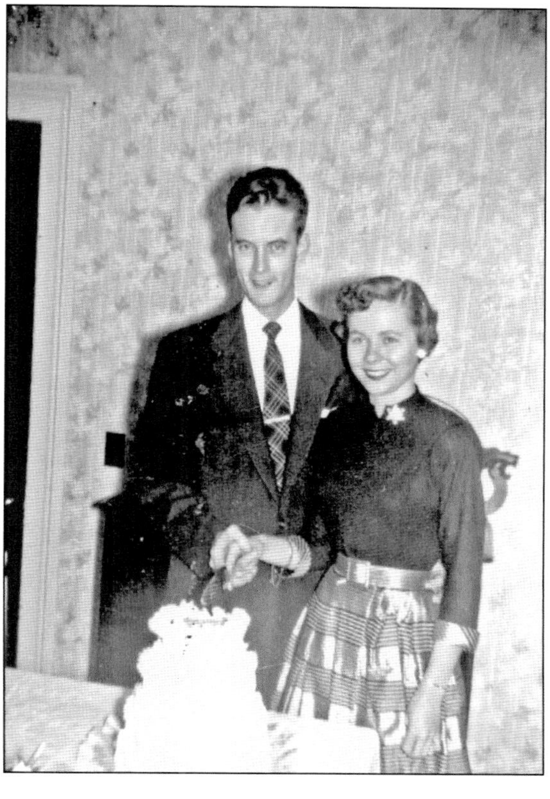

Newlyweds Betsy (Hall) and Tom McCarthy are shown here on December 5, 1953, cutting their wedding cake at the reception held in their honor at the home of Dot and Bob Pearsall on Main Street. (George and Kathy Huegerich collection.)

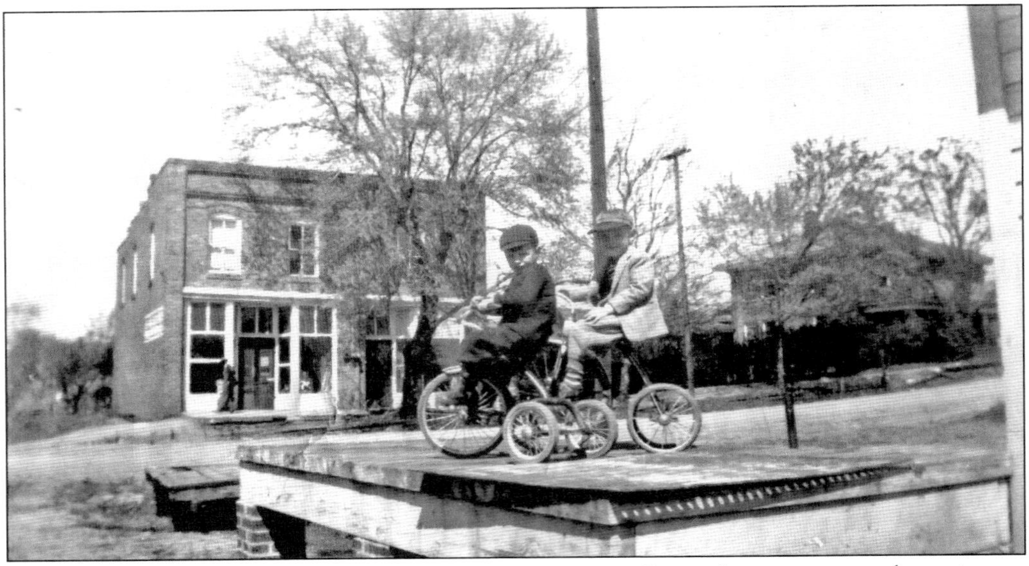

Patiently waiting atop the train platform for the arrival of the mail (above) are John Lee Holleman (left) and Bill Brooks. The railroad tracks started in Harnett County and ran up along the east side of Avent Ferry Road, running behind what are now Dewar's Antiques, Walgreens, and Wendy's. They crossed over Main Street near Quantum Drive to continue along the east side of Main Street all the way to Apex Street. (Sylvian Brooks collection.)

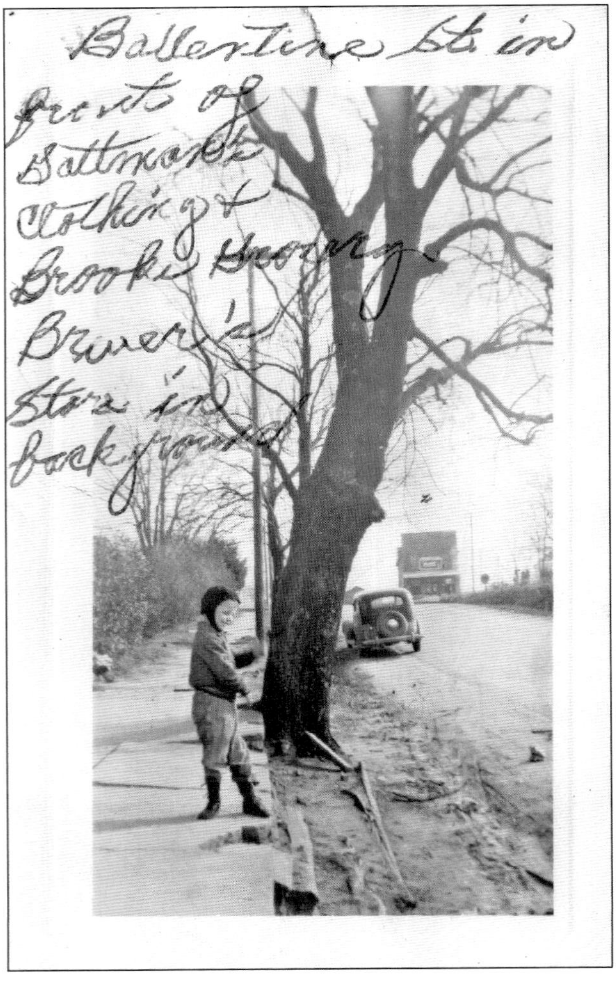


In this c. 1950 photograph, Bill Brooks stands in front of the store his parents ran in the old Seagraves Drug Store building on Ballentine Street, where the town's police station is today. Looking up toward Main Street, Ernie Brewer's Store can be seen in the background. (Sylvian Brooks collection.)

A young Bill Brooks poses near the Durham and Southern train that passed through town. Lifelong residents remember the times when the local children would hear the train approaching and run to greet the conductor, who would throw out candy and wave to them. (Sylvian Brooks collection.)

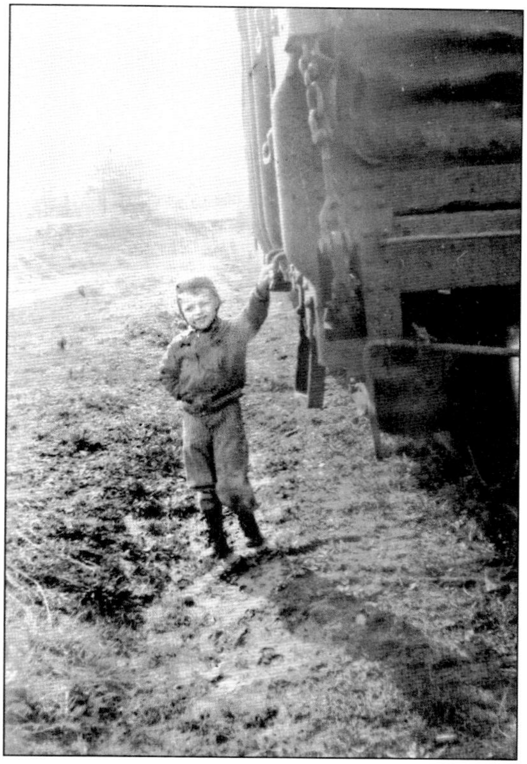

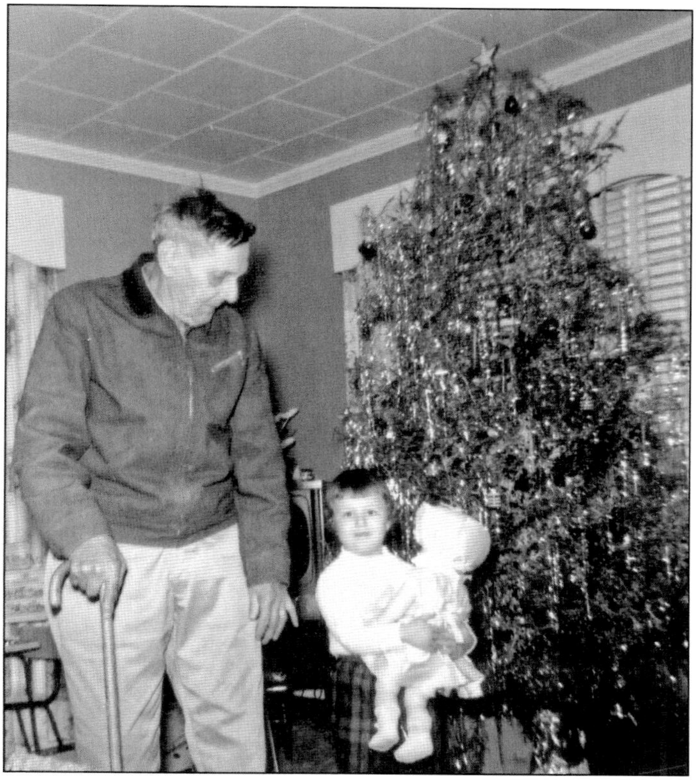

Carl Burch "Burt" Holland and granddaughter Faye (Holland) Congleton, daughter of Burch Wicker "Wick" and Mabel (Olive) Holland, are pictured here at Christmastime in the late 1950s. Faye is holding a brand-new baby doll she had received as a Christmas gift. (Faye and Tim Congleton collection.)

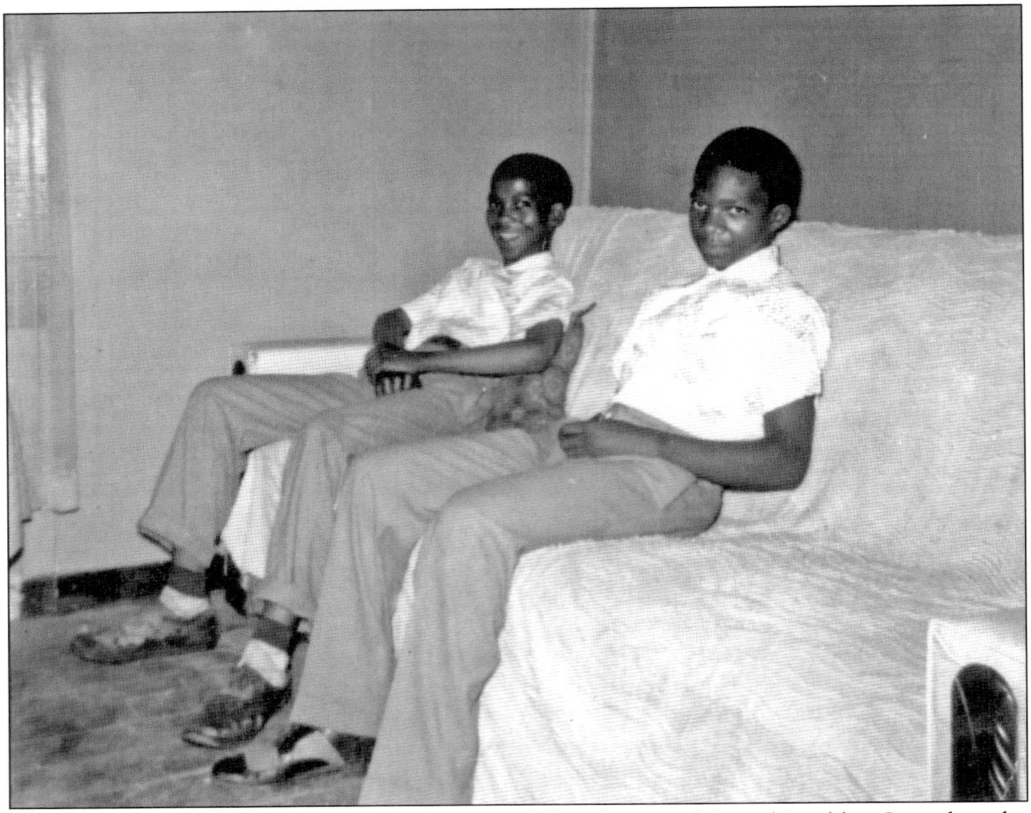

Pictured here are the handsome young sons of Odell and Carrie (Minter) Lockley. Seated on the couch are William Lee (left) and Robert Frank Lockley. (Christine Adams-Utley collection.)

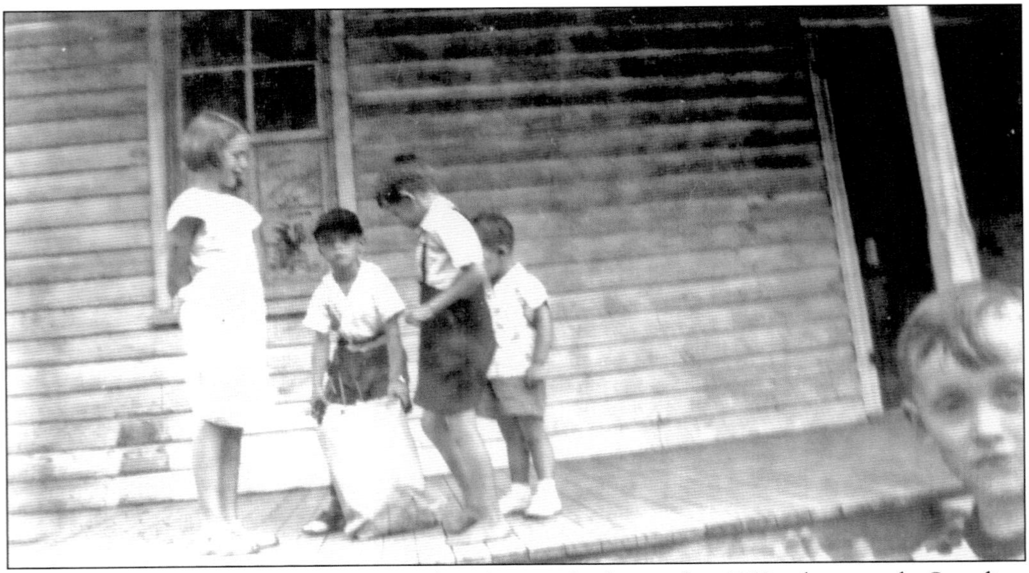

Local youngsters are shown playing at the Masonic Lodge in this 1950s photograph. Standing on the front porch of the lodge are, from left to right, Ilene (Wilson) Bradley, Bill Brooks, Eddie Wilson, Donald "Pete" Brewer, and John Lee Holleman. (Sylvian Brooks collection.)

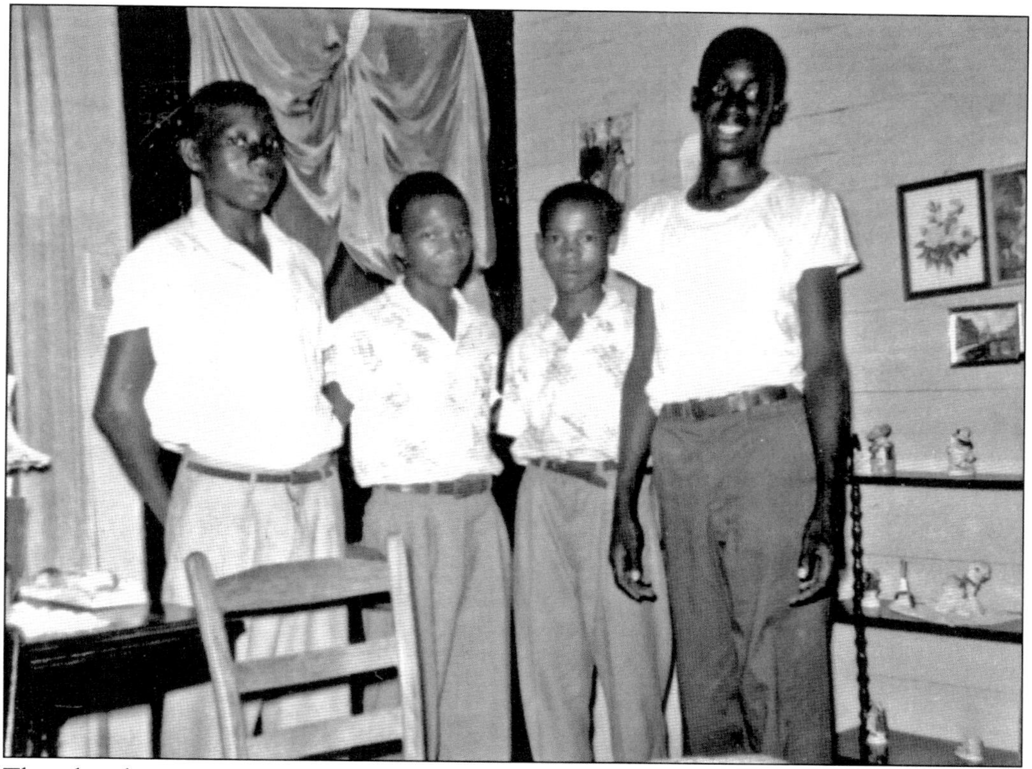

These handsome young men (above) are, from left to right, Benjamin Adams, William Lee Lockley, Robert Frank, and ? Betts in a 1950s photograph. (Christine Adams-Utley collection.)

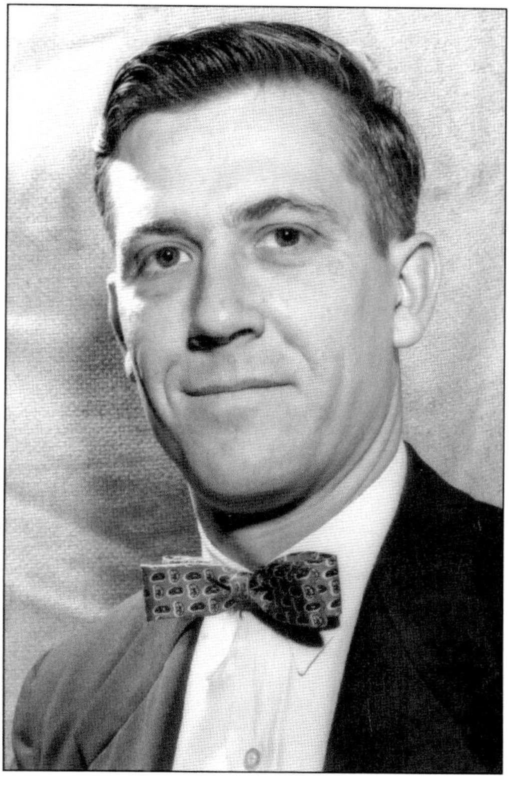

Ivan "Ike" Collins Mims served the community as commissioner from 1947 to 1949 and again from 1961 to 1967. This photograph was taken while Mims was serving as mayor from 1953 to 1955. Mims worked for the *News and Observer* newspaper in Raleigh, North Carolina, for more than 38 years, the last 10 years of which were as the production director. He married the former Rachel Hall on December 25, 1949. (Nathan and Carolyn Williams collection.)

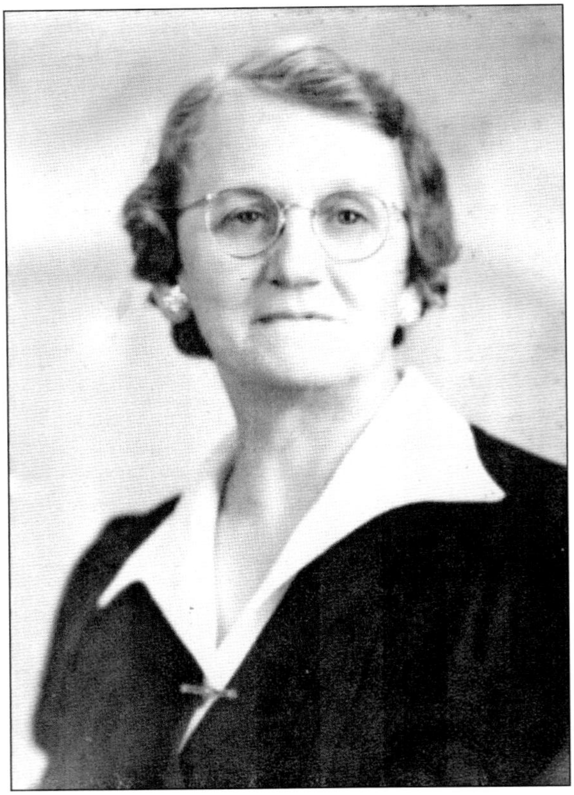

Mamie (Holland) Mann was the daughter of Needham Bennett and Anna Caroline (Partin) Holland and the granddaughter of Simpson Washington and Mary-Ann (Matthews) Holland. Mamie married Lemuel Mann and reared their family on a farm near what is now Harris Lake Park. (Faye and Tim Congleton collection.)

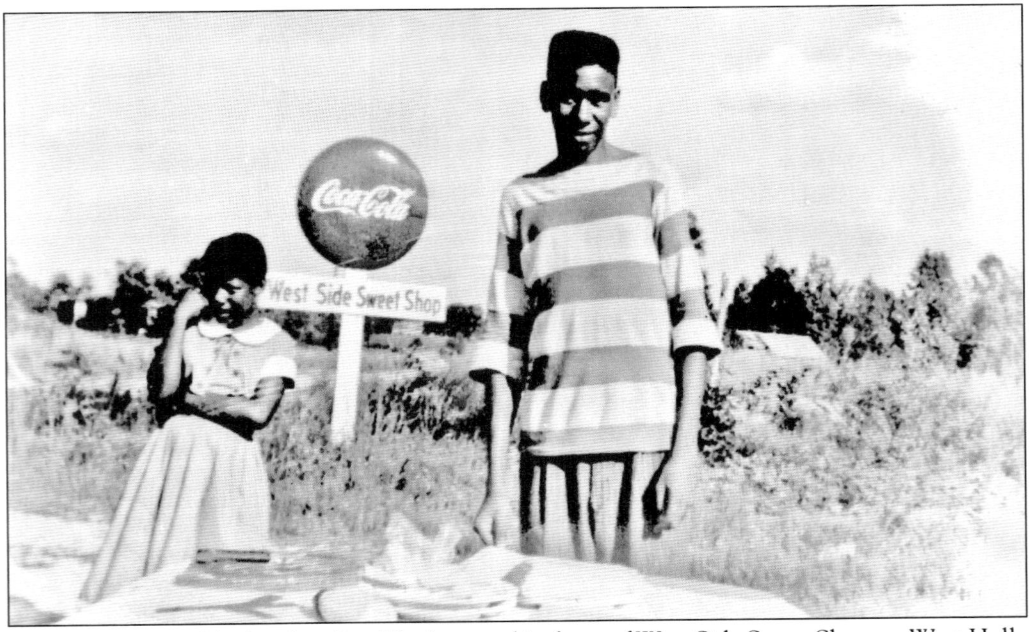


Dorothy and her older brother Cecil Leslie stand in front of West Side Sweet Shop on West Holly Springs Road, or New Hill Road, as it was once called. The Sweet Shop was run by Mr. and Mrs. Essie Baldwin for many years in the area known as West Holly Springs, providing cold soda and candy to the youngsters of Holly Springs. (Dorothy Leslie-Lanier collection.)

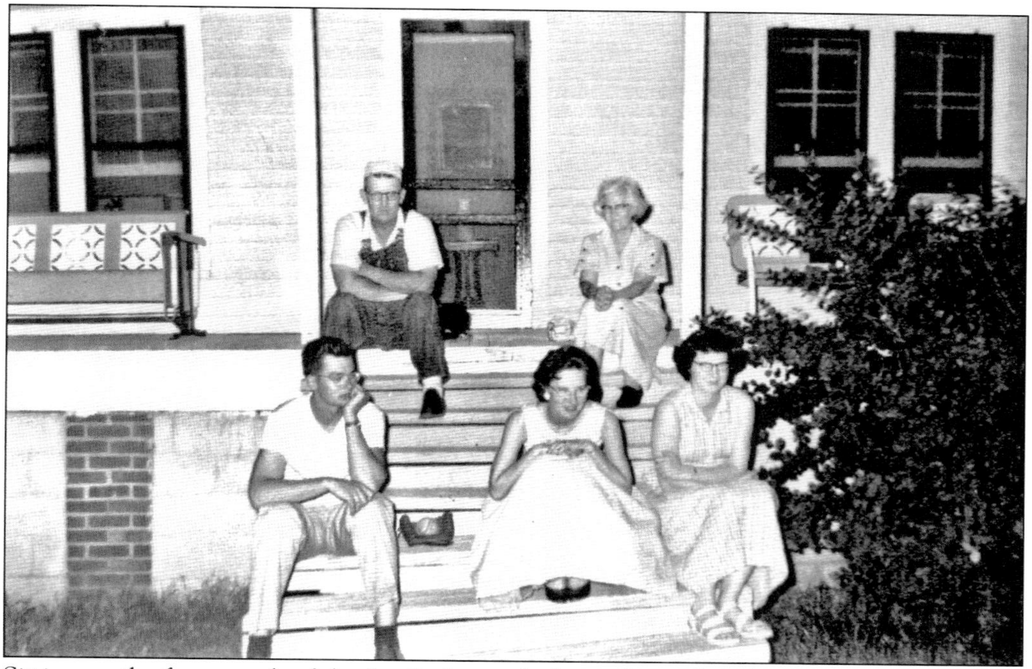

Sitting on the front porch of the family farm, which was located in the vicinity of the current Oak Hall Shopping Center, is the Creech family. In this 1957 photograph are, from left to right, (bottom step) an unidentified friend of the family, Mary, and Georgie Creech; (top step) Arnold and Catherine (Templeton) Creech. (Billy and Mary Holt collection.)

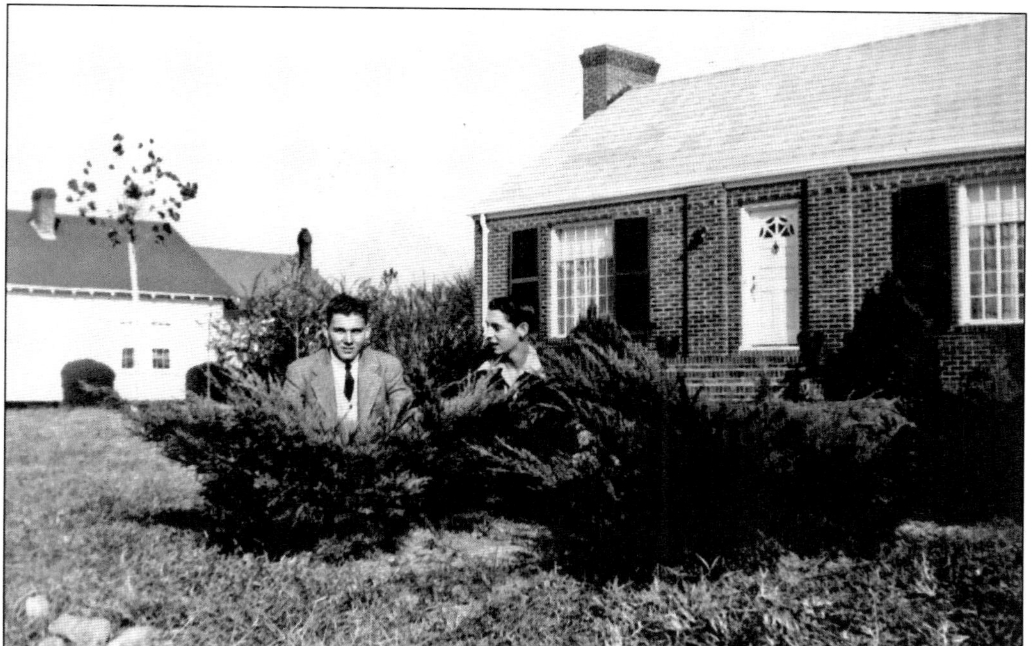

In this 1950s photograph, hiding in the bushes of their buddy Jere Pearsall's front yard at North Main Street, are Willie "Gene" Jones (left) and Jack Beavers. (Doris Jones collection.)

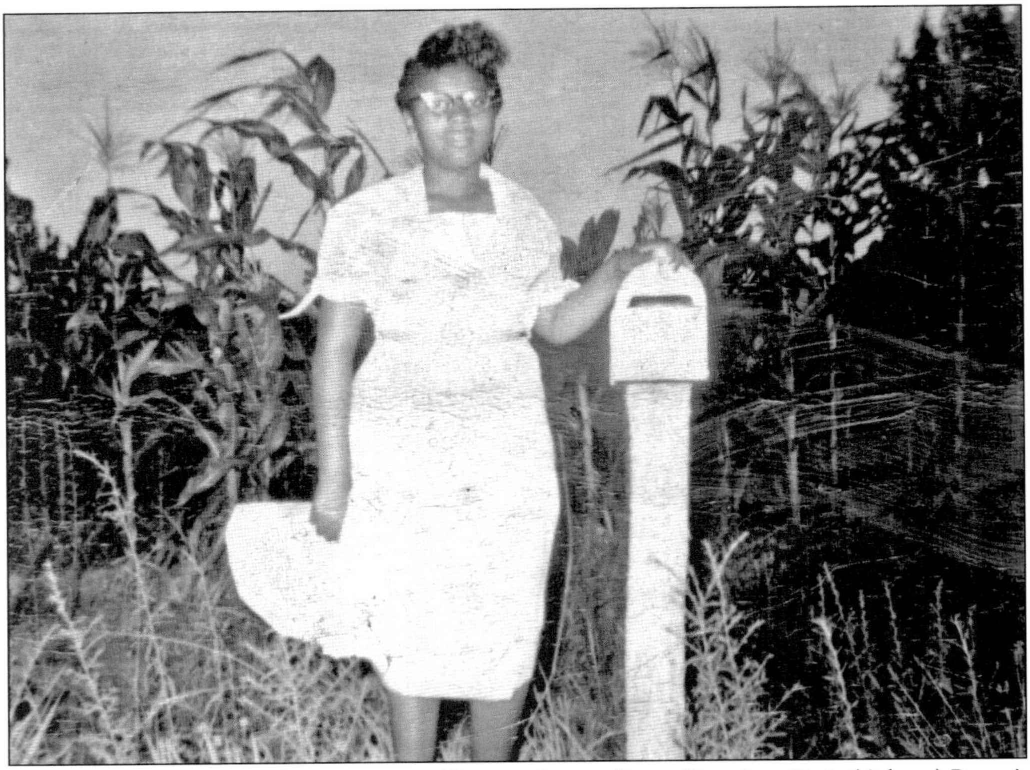

Ten-year-old Christine Adams is pictured here at the mailbox of her sister Essie (Adams) Potter's house on Holly Springs Road in the late 1950s. (Christine Adams-Utley collection.)

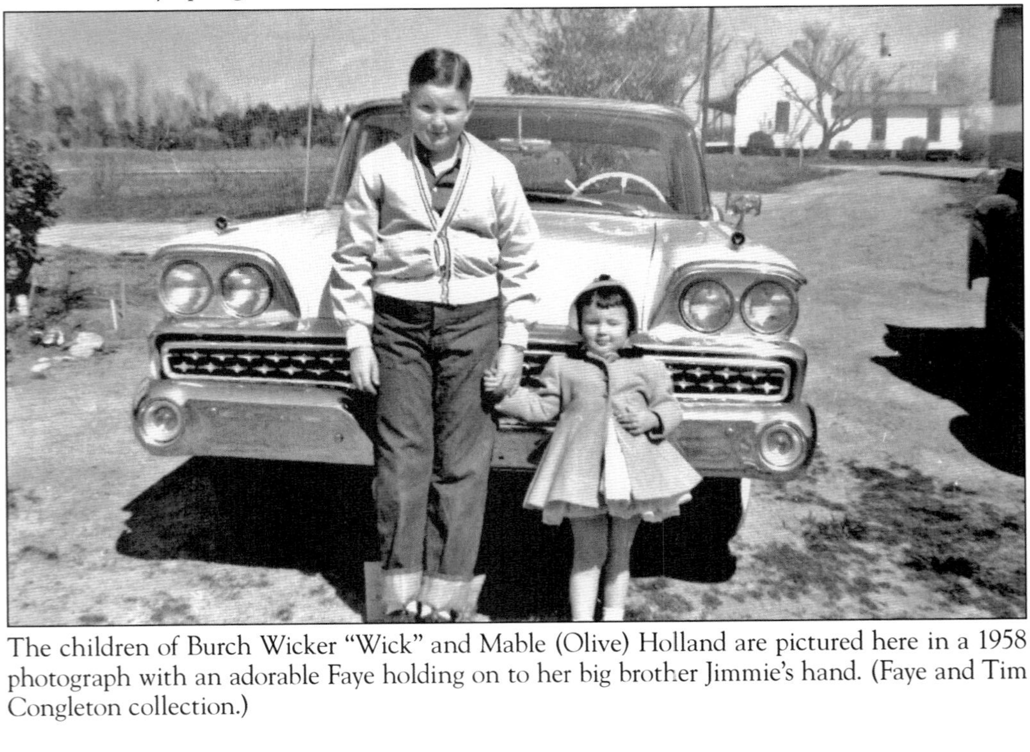

The children of Burch Wicker "Wick" and Mable (Olive) Holland are pictured here in a 1958 photograph with an adorable Faye holding on to her big brother Jimmie's hand. (Faye and Tim Congleton collection.)

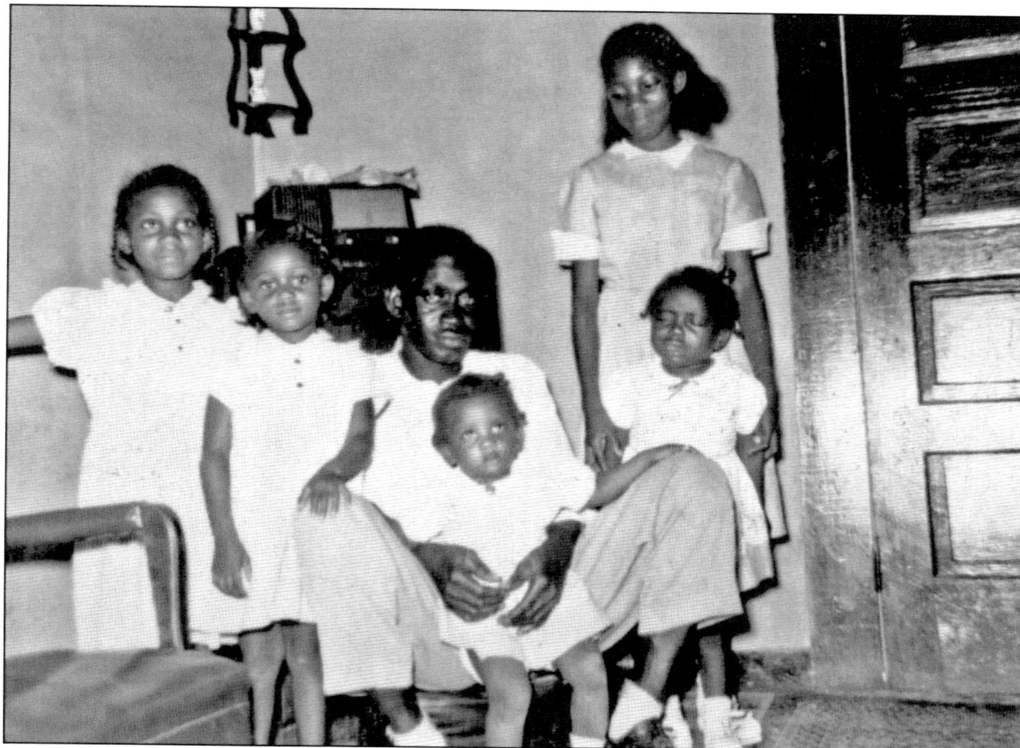

Odell Lockley, son of Willie and Nettie Lockley, is pictured here with his children in the 1950s. From left to right are Reva, Blondell, Odell, Cynthia, Catherine, and Mary Lockley. The children's mother, Carrie (Minter) Lockley, may have taken the photograph. (Christine Adams-Utley collection.)

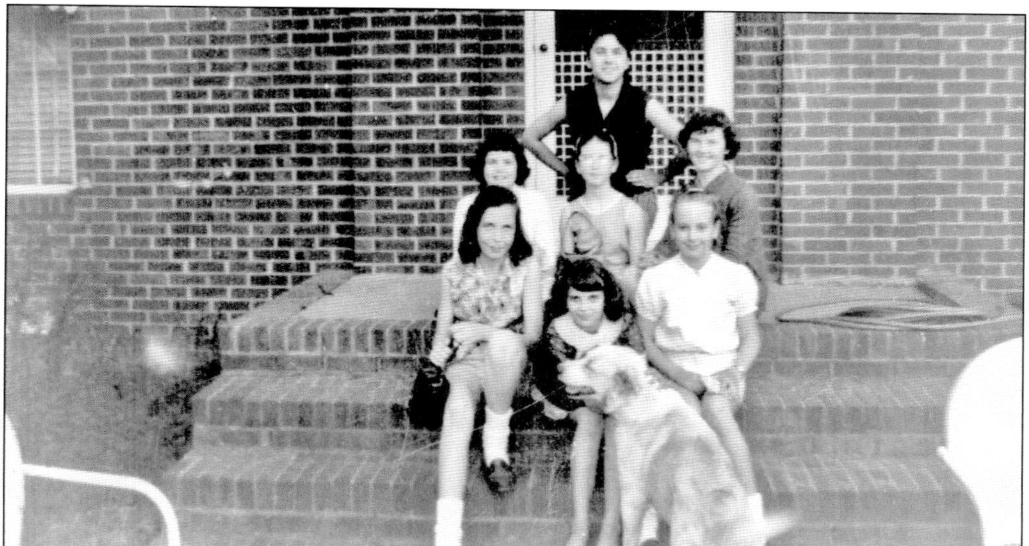

These young ladies are gathered at the birthday party of Kathy Pearsall in May 1959. Seated on the steps are, from left to right, (first row) Lady, the family dog; (second row) Jean Betts, Kathy Pearsall, and Doris Bailey; (third row) Linda Gilliam, Sandra Fuquay, and Diane Morris; (fourth row) Ethel Smith. (George and Kathy Huegerich collection.)

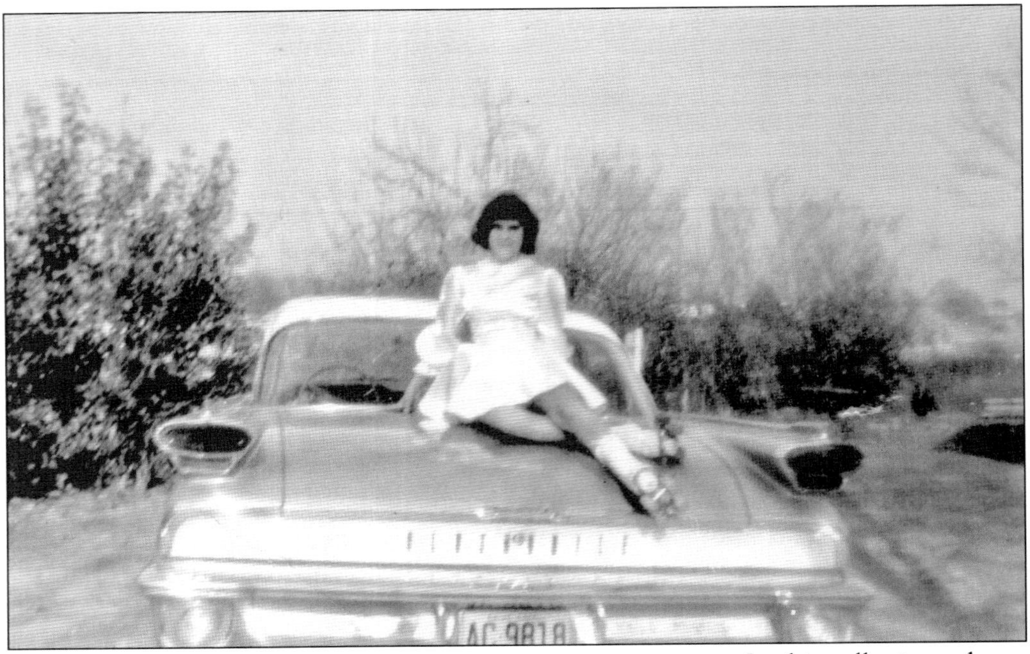

Looking all prim and proper in a fancy dress and her roller skates, perched on the back of an Oldsmobile, is Kathy Pearsall in this 1959 photograph. (George and Kathy Huegerich collection.)

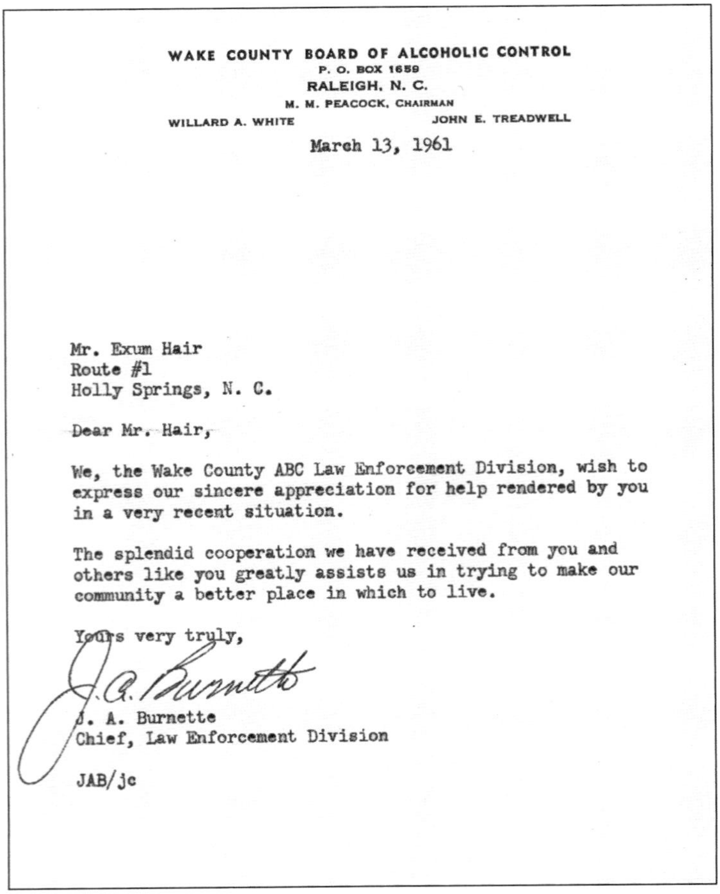

WAKE COUNTY BOARD OF ALCOHOLIC CONTROL
P. O. BOX 1659
RALEIGH, N. C.
M. M. PEACOCK, CHAIRMAN
WILLARD A. WHITE JOHN E. TREADWELL

March 13, 1961

Mr. Exum Hair
Route #1
Holly Springs, N. C.

Dear Mr. Hair,

We, the Wake County ABC Law Enforcement Division, wish to express our sincere appreciation for help rendered by you in a very recent situation.

The splendid cooperation we have received from you and others like you greatly assists us in trying to make our community a better place in which to live.

Yours very truly,

J. A. Burnette

J. A. Burnette
Chief, Law Enforcement Division

JAB/jc

A letter of appreciation from the Wake County Board of Alcoholic Control in Raleigh, North Carolina, acknowledges the assistance of Holly Springs resident Exum Hare for his cooperation in catching local moonshiners in May 1961. (Jean Goodwin collection.)

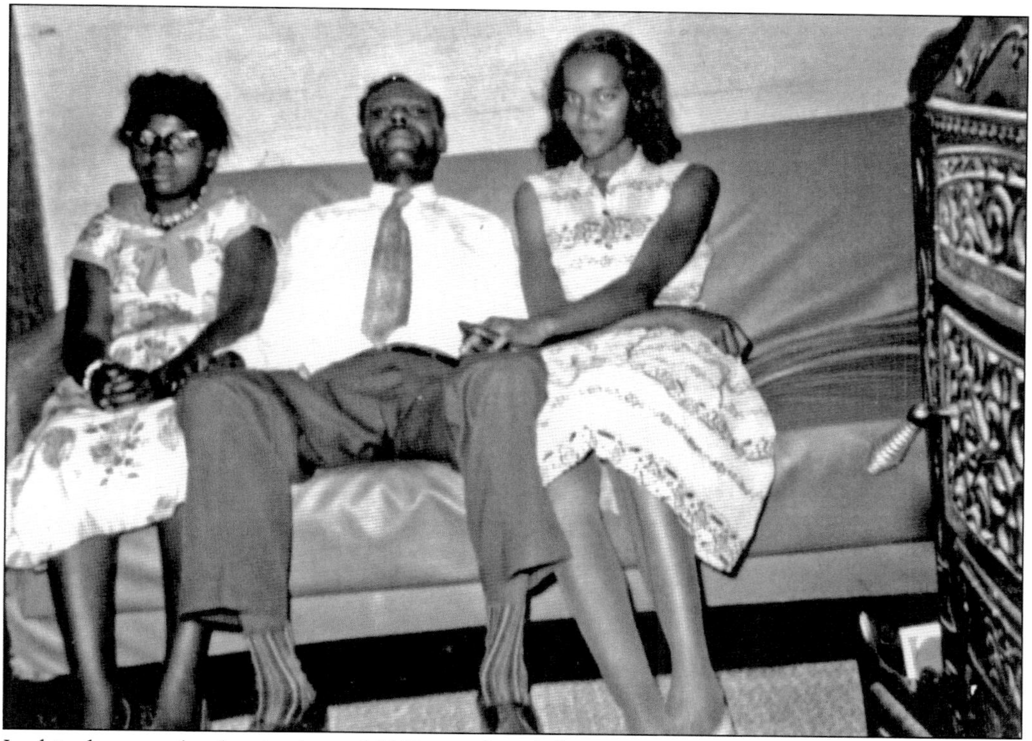

In this photograph taken in the mid-1950s are, from left to right, Christine Adams, her older brother George Adams, and an unidentified young woman. (Christine Adams-Utley collection.)

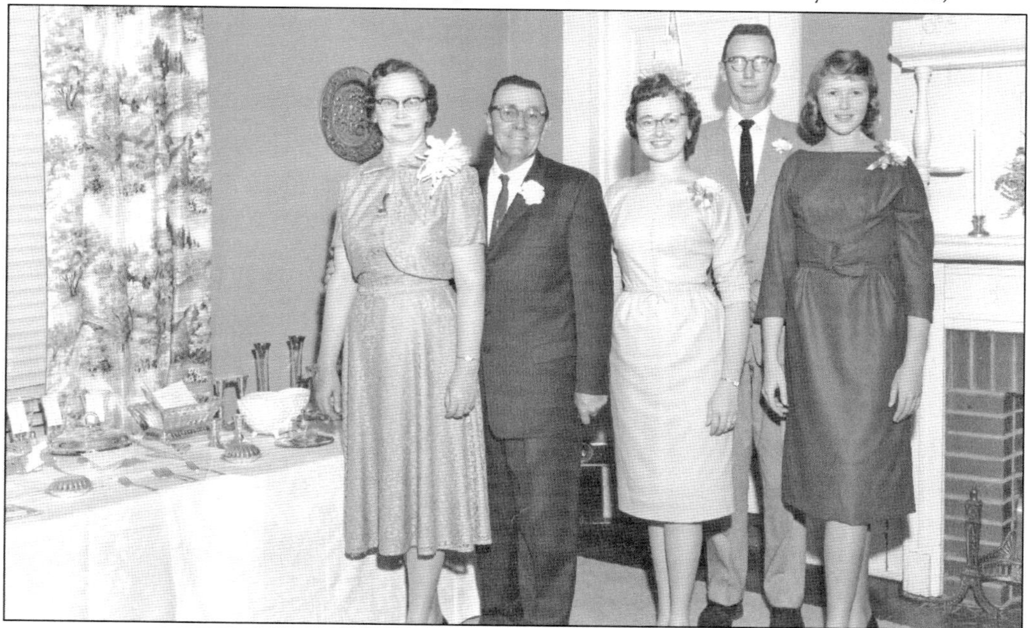

Eunice (Cotton) and Sherrod "Shake" Holleman pose for a family picture with their children, from left to right, Patricia, Gerald, and Rosalyn. This 1960 portrait, taken in the living room of their home on Avent Ferry Road, shows the family gathered to celebrate the 25th wedding anniversary of Eunice and Shake, who were married on December 14, 1935. (Courtesy of Gerald W. Holleman.)

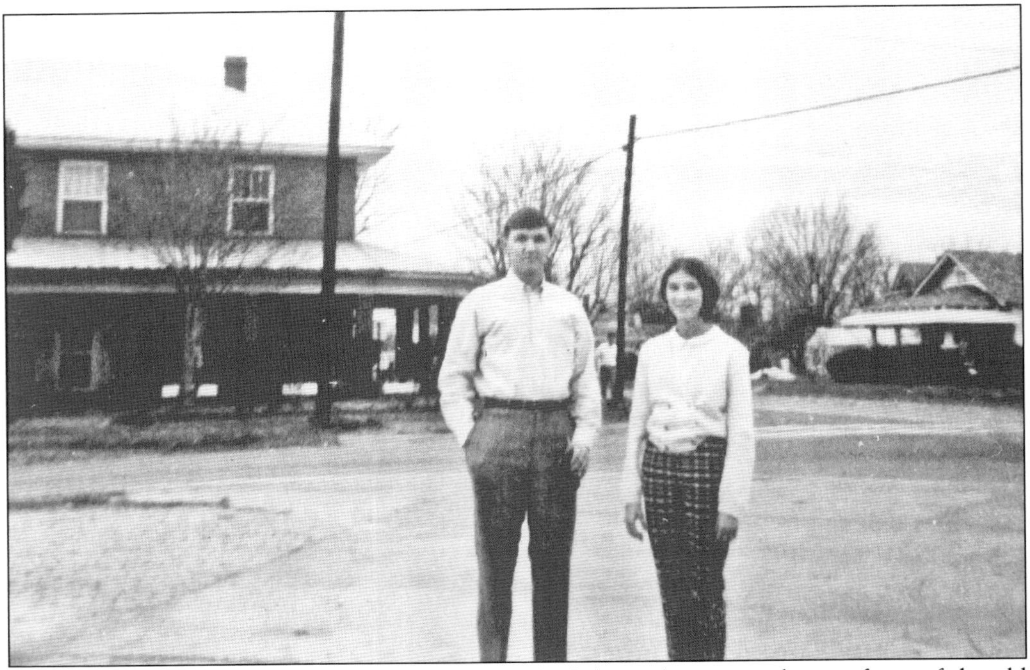

Donald "Pete" Brewer (left) and Patricia Brewer (right) are shown standing in front of the old Seagraves Hotel, now a private home, around 1960. The old hotel building at the corner of Ballentine and Main Streets would see many occupants over the years. It would house a furniture/appliance store, a tire store, and finally the town municipal offices. (Doris Jones collection.)

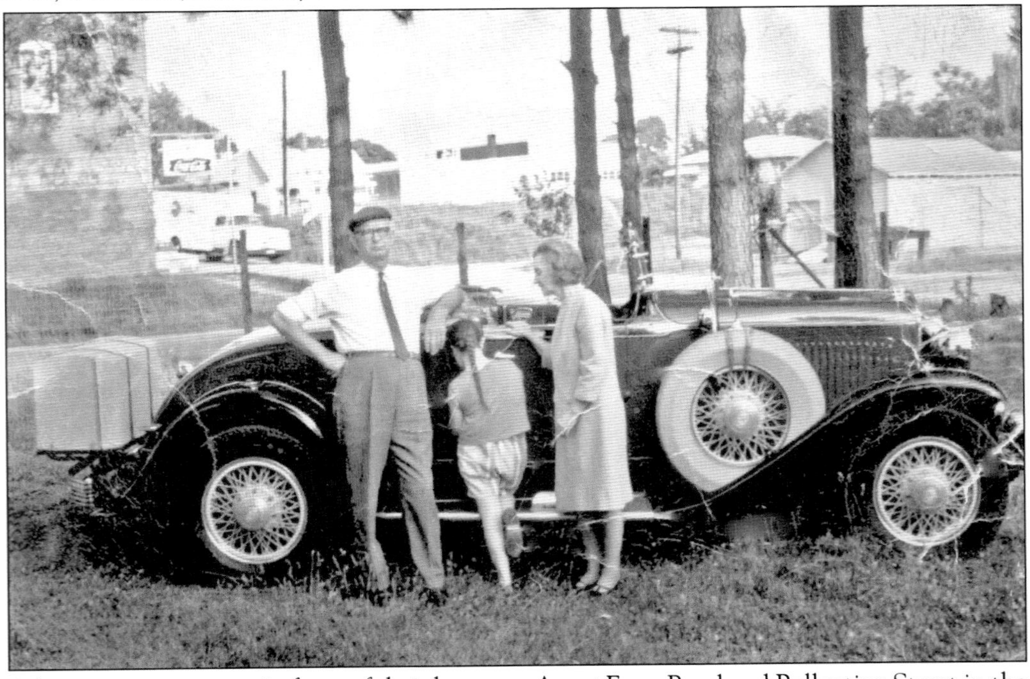

Admiring a vintage car in front of their home on Avent Ferry Road and Ballentine Street in the 1960s are Marvin, Marguerite, and their daughter Bettsye Johnson. (Mary Lee Johnson collection, courtesy of Lori Stokes.)

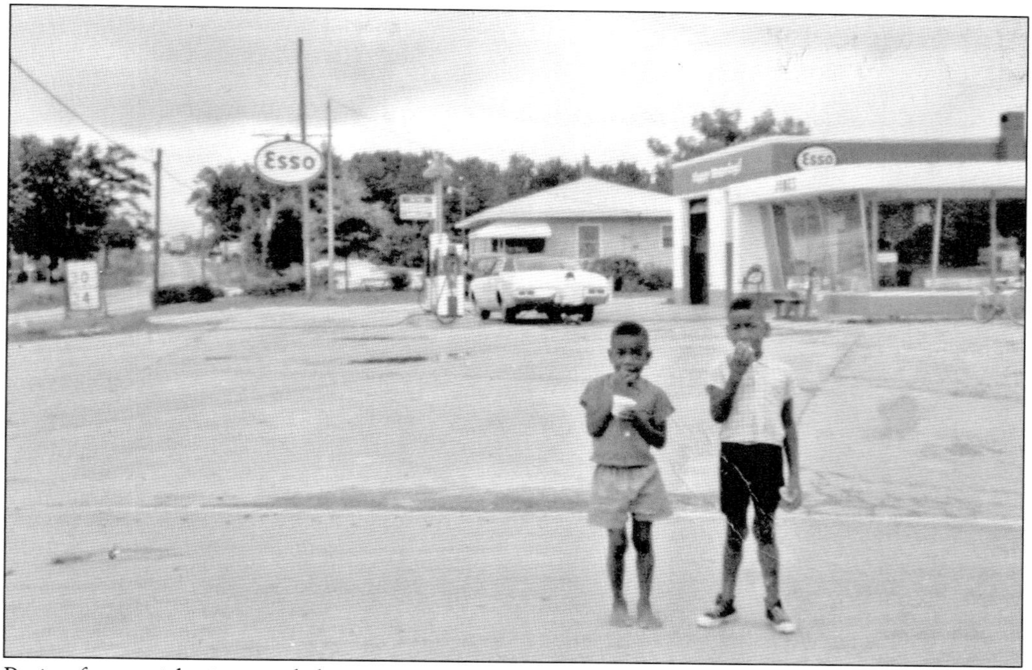

Posing for a quick picture while enjoying ice cream treats on a hot summer day are James Cofield (left) and Tommy Judd. In the background is Jones's Esso Station. Gene Jones, the station owner, is shown here pumping gas at a whopping 30¢ per gallon. The station was located at the corner of Ballentine and Main Streets across from the current town hall. (Courtesy of LaVerne Cofield.)

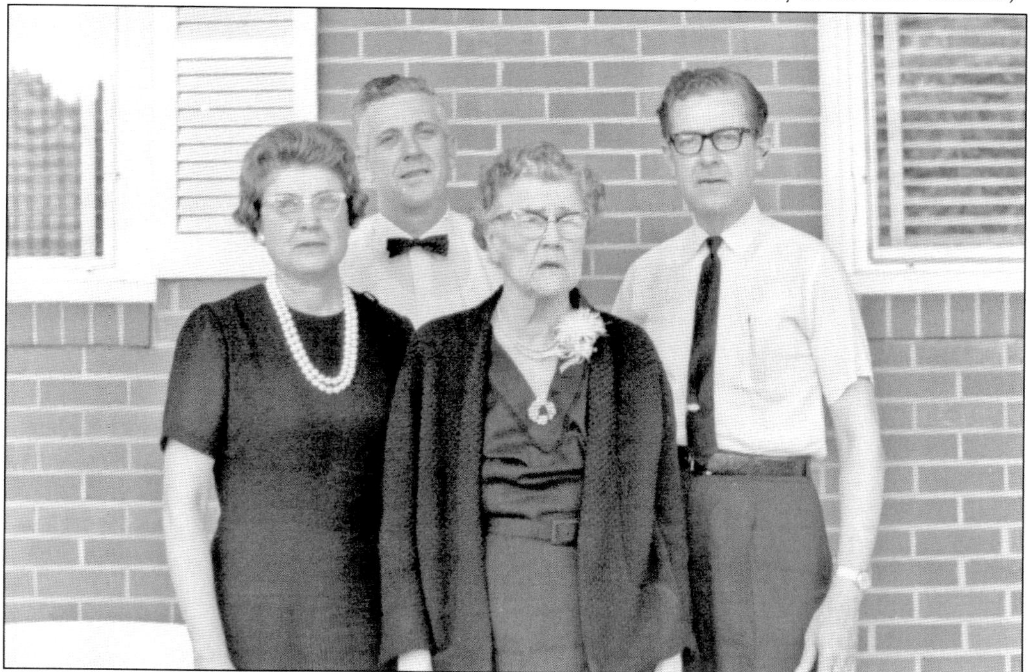
Taking a moment to capture a lasting memory on Mother's Day in 1968 are, from left to right, Margaret (Mims) Wright, Ivan "Ike" Mims, Delcie (Collins) Mims, and Hubert Edwin "Ed" Mims. (Nathan and Carolyn Williams collection.)

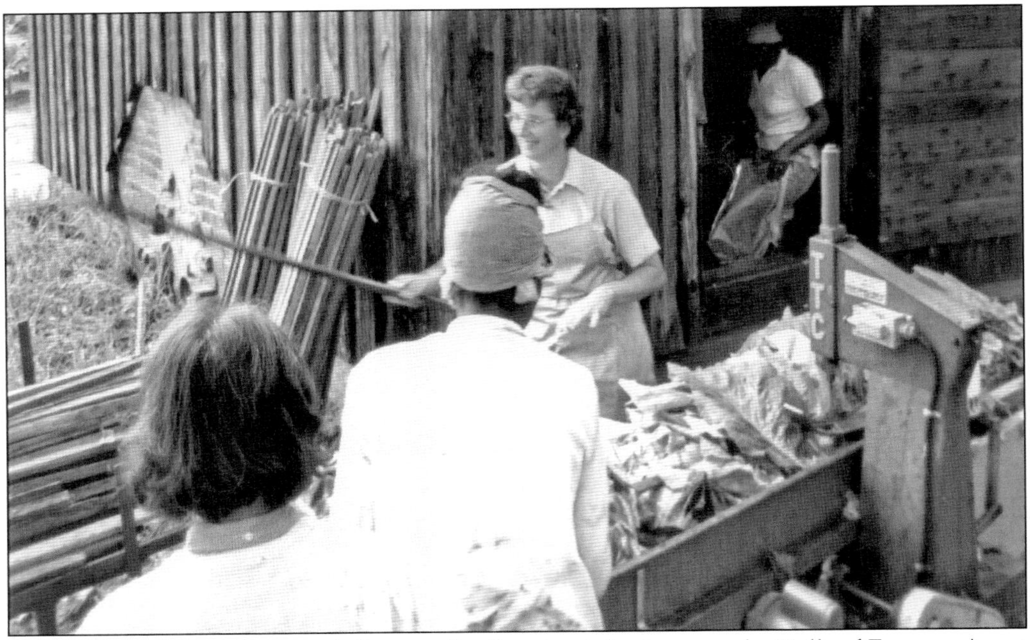

Shown in this 1960s photograph "barning" or "putting in" tobacco at the Holland Farm on Avent Ferry Road is Mable Holland, who had a reputation for being the fastest "looper" in the family. Looping is the term used for binding tobacco leaves with twine, attaching the bundle to a stick, which is then hung to dry on tiered poles inside the barn. (Faye and Tim Congleton collection.)

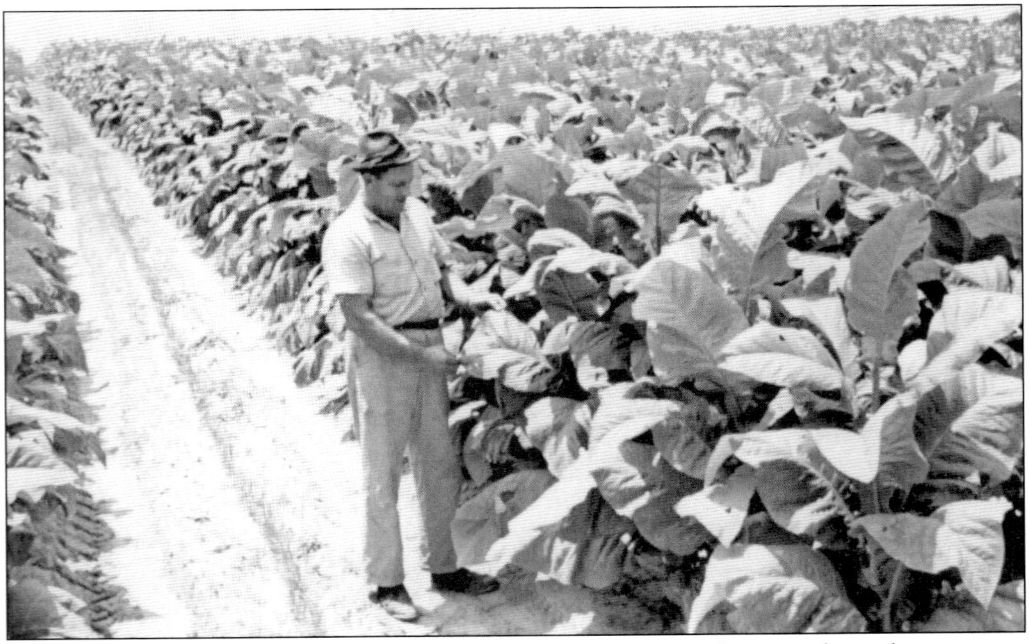

The Burch Wicker "Wick" Holland farm on Avent Ferry Road, across from the entrance to Holly Glen subdivision, was one of many farms in the area that produced a bountiful harvest. This mid-1960s photograph shows Wick admiring a sturdy row of tobacco. (Faye and Tim Congleton collection.)

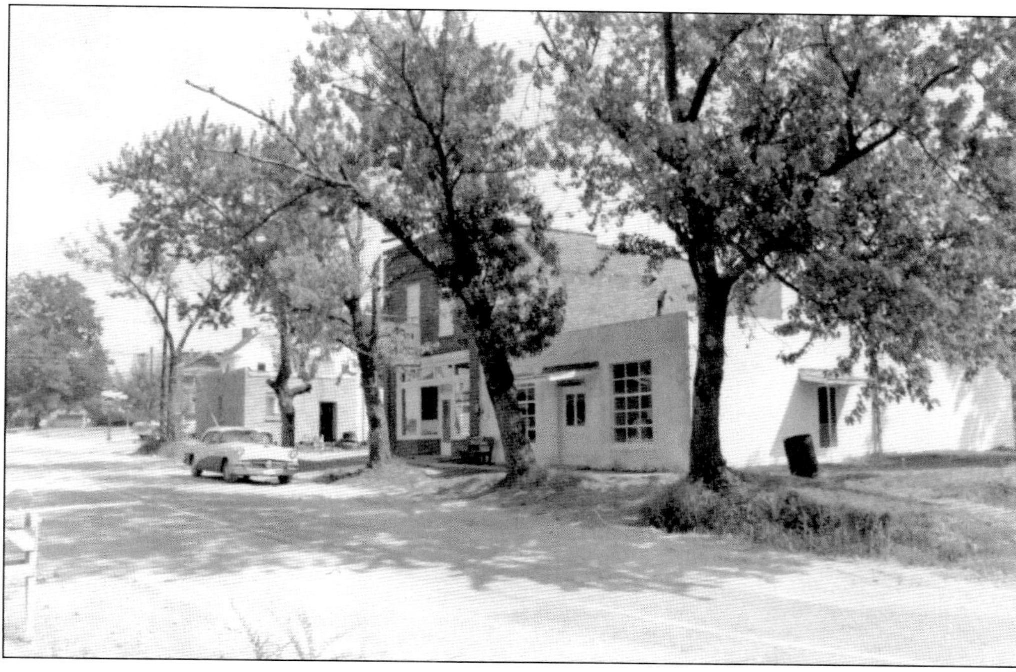

These before and after photographs of the Mims Drug Store taken in September 1968 show the difference curbs, gutters, and a new paved street can make on the curb appeal of a business. (Both, Nathan and Carolyn Williams collection.)

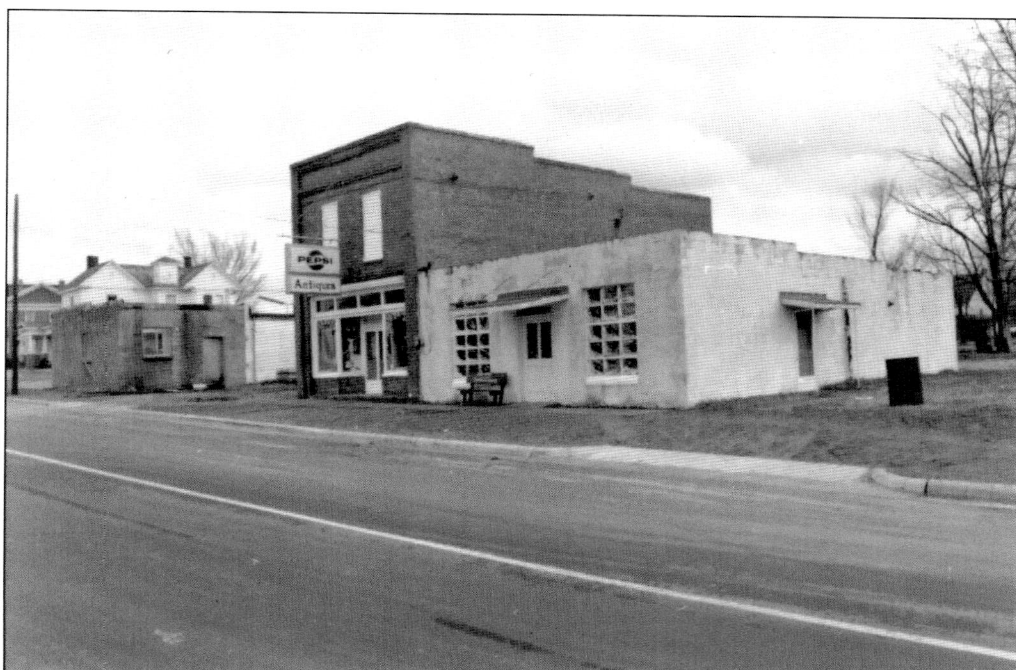

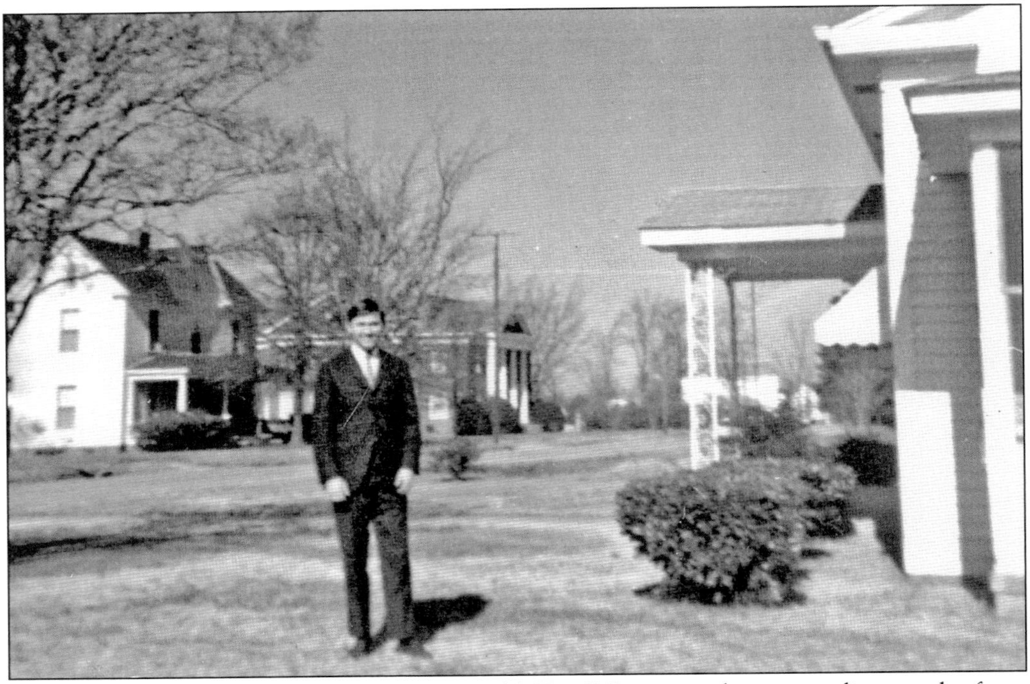

Around the 1960s, a handsome, young Donald "Pete" Brewer is shown standing on the front lawn of his parents Ernie and Cleo Brewer's house on Raleigh Street. In the background are the Holly Springs Baptist Church and the Utley-Wright House, which was moved from Raleigh Street to its new location behind the Leslie-Alford-Mims House and now houses 919 Marketing. (Doris Jones collection.)

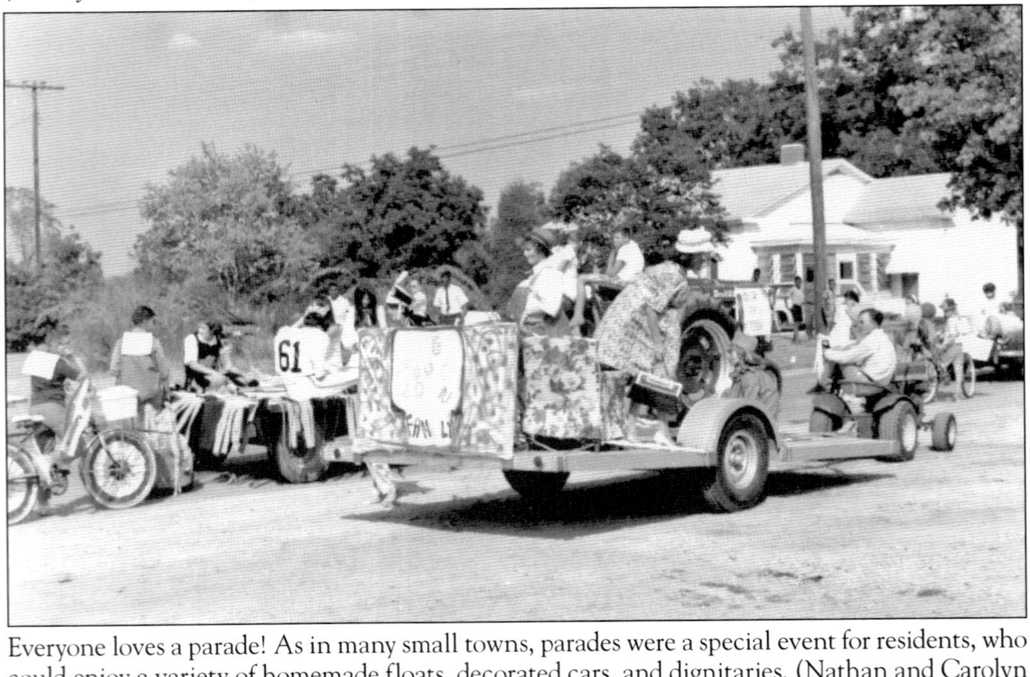


Everyone loves a parade! As in many small towns, parades were a special event for residents, who could enjoy a variety of homemade floats, decorated cars, and dignitaries. (Nathan and Carolyn Williams collection.)

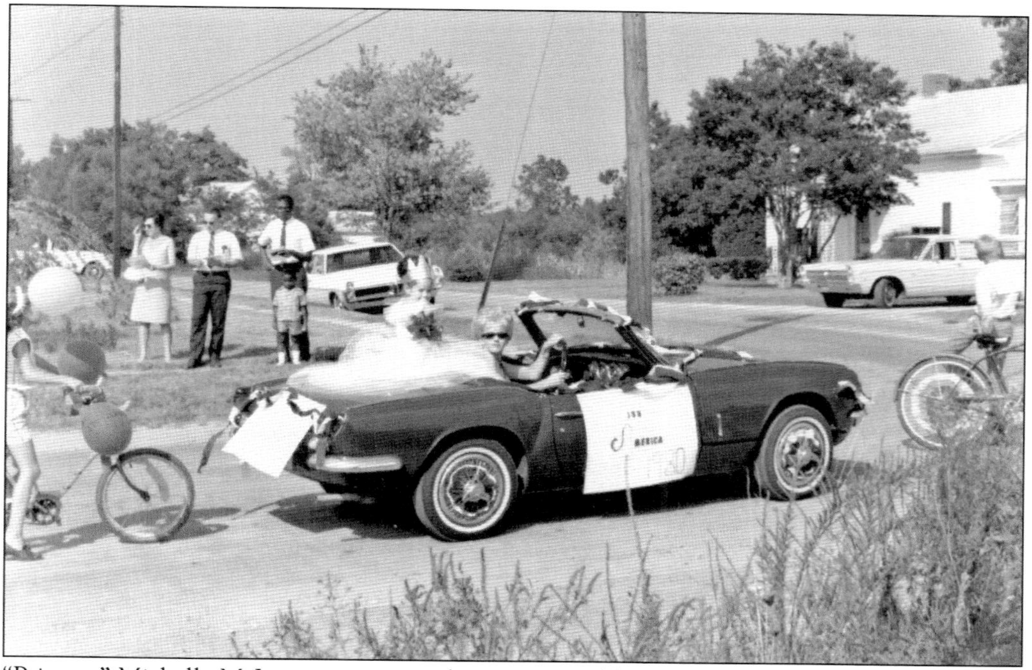

"Princess" Michelle McLean was escorted in a convertible for the Holly Springs Parade in the summer of 1968. Proud parents can be seen in the background with cameras loaded with film to capture their child's picture as they paraded by. (Nathan and Carolyn Williams collection.)

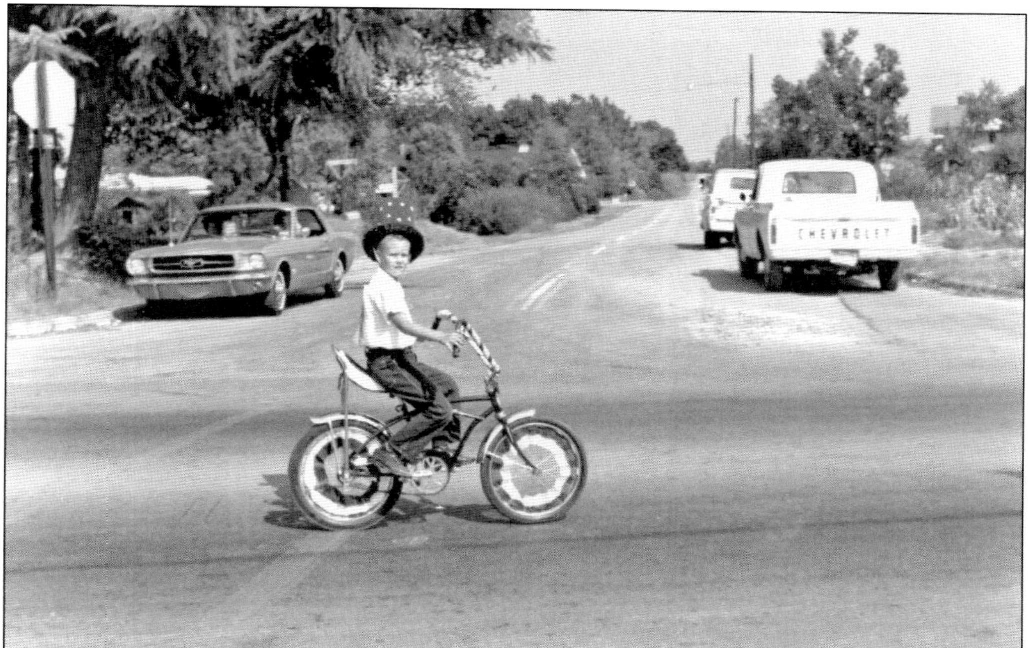


Kevin Williams, son of Nathan and Carolyn Williams, proudly shows off his patriotically decorated bicycle in the parade in the summer of 1968. Traffic stopped along Main Street for this wonderful hometown event. (Nathan and Carolyn Williams collection.)

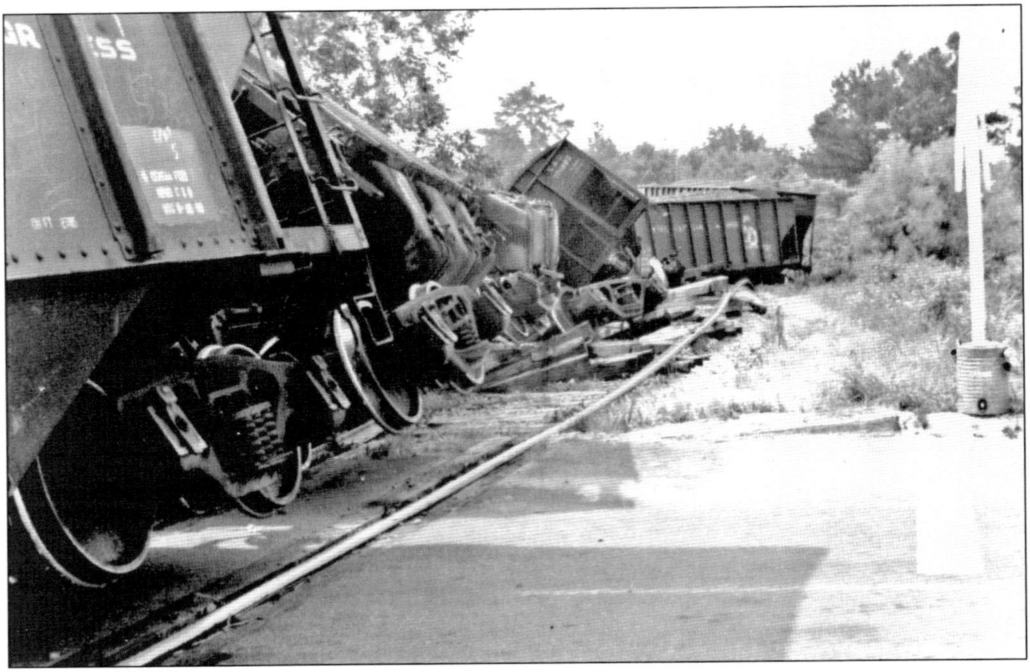

A broken rail near the Center Street track crossing was given as the cause for a freight train car derailment on Sunday, June 29, 1969. Ernie Brewer, who owned a store next to the track, said the derailed train came to rest about 100 feet from the back door of his store. (Both, Nathan and Carolyn Williams collection.)

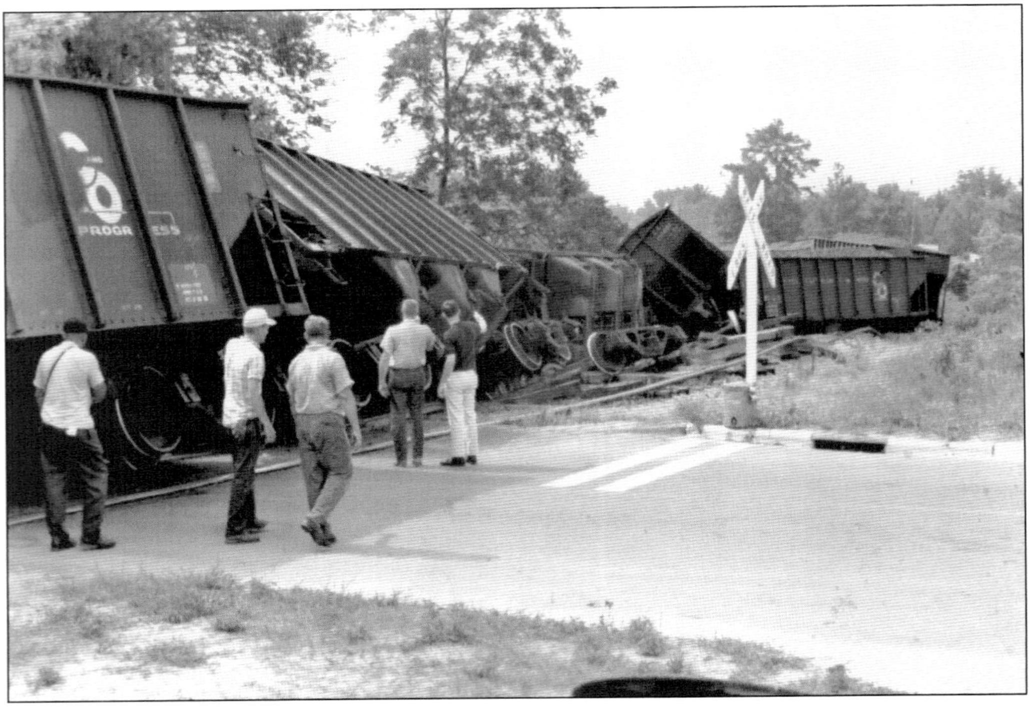

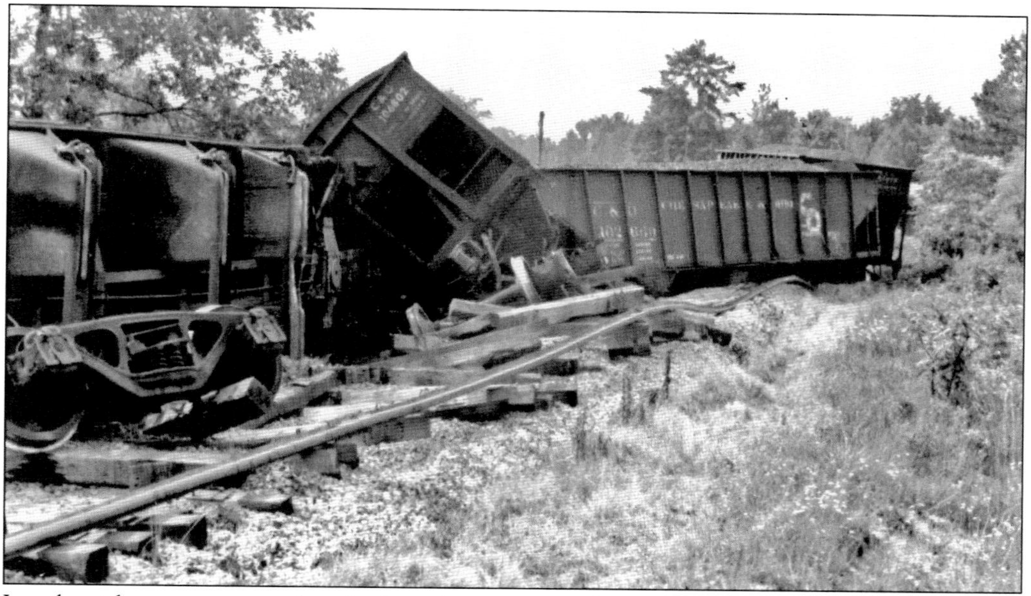

Local residents get an up-close look at the train derailment in 1969. Brakeman Frank Leach, who was in the main engine's cab when the accident occurred, explained that with daytime temperatures in the 90s, the heat may have expanded the steel tracks, causing the cars to derail. The derailed cars, loaded with coal, were near the rear of the 50-car train. (Nathan and Carolyn Williams collection.)

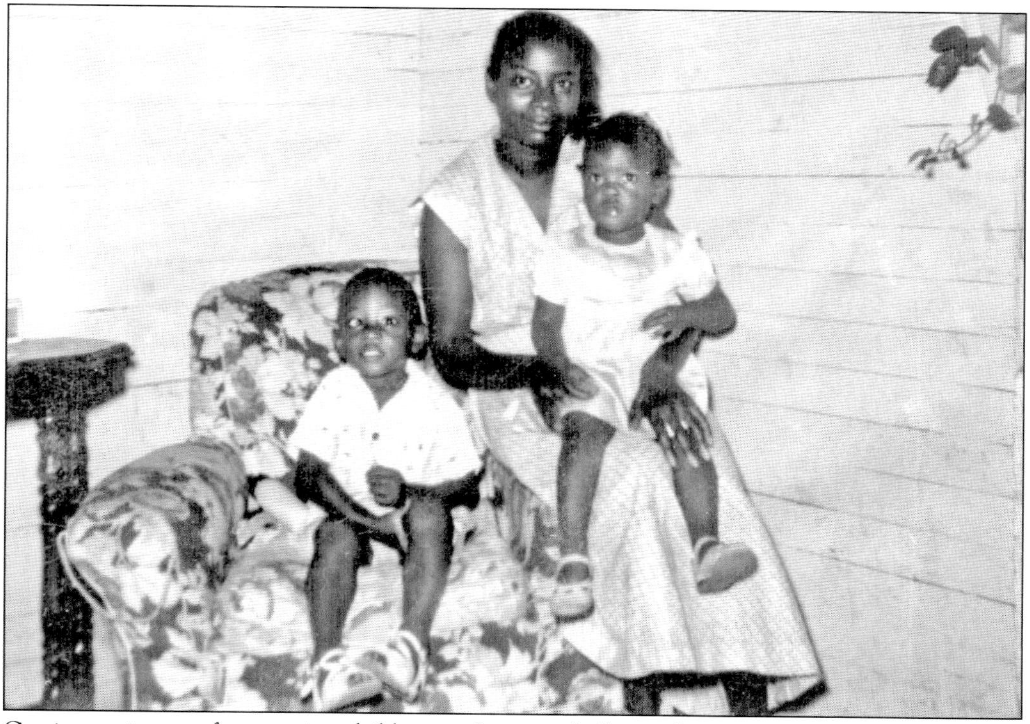

Getting a picture of two active children is always a challenge for any parent. Shown sitting on the chair are, from left to right, James Adams, Elnora Adams, and Phyllis Adams. (Christine Adams-Utley collection.)

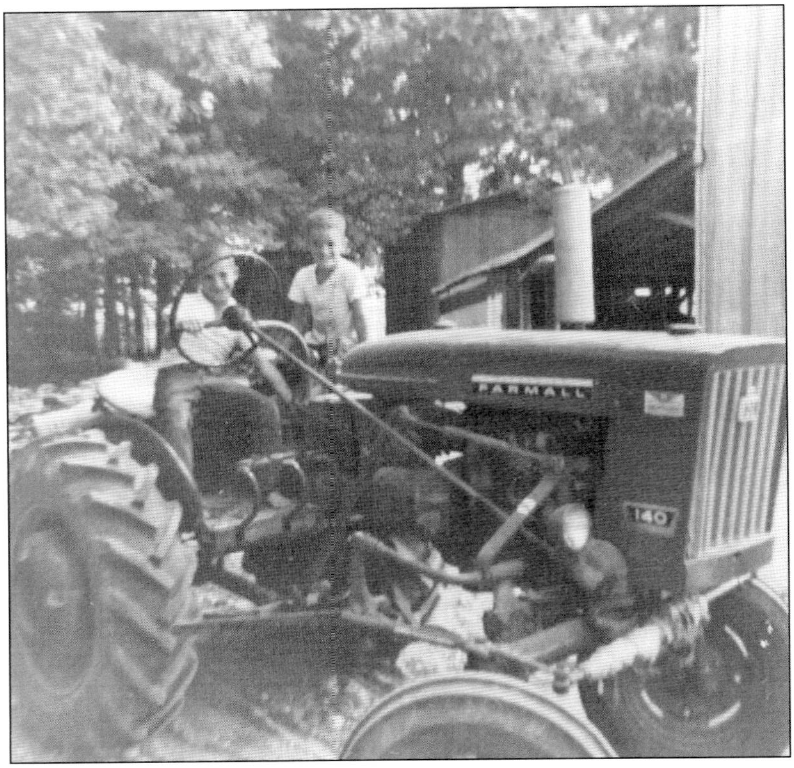


This summer of 1966 photograph shows the sons of Billy and Mary (Creech) Holt, Joel (left) and Wayne, trying out the seat of Grandpa Cass Holt's tractor. (Billy and Mary Holt collection.)

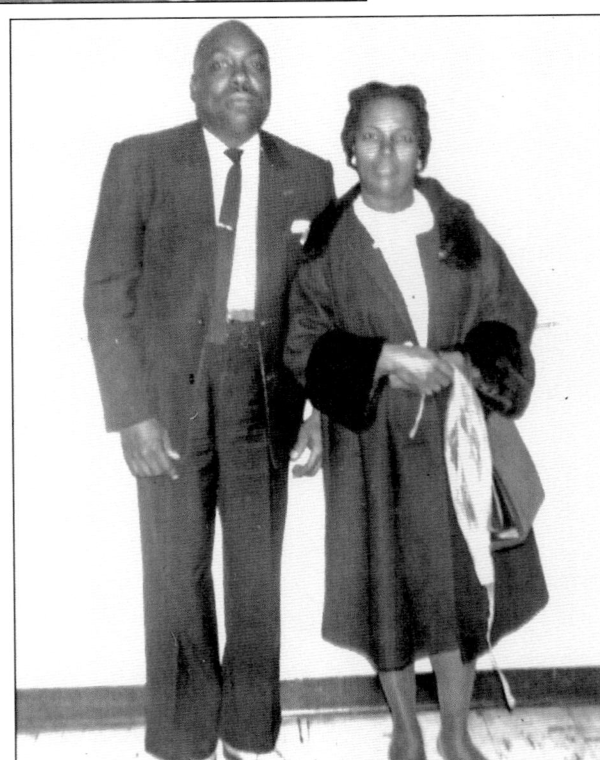

William Bernice and Cora Mae (Norris) Lassiter are pictured here in a c. 1960 photograph. Bernice shares the honor with James Norris of being elected in 1973 as the first black men to serve on the Holly Springs Board of Commissioners. Cora was appointed to the town council in 1981 to fill a vacated seat. She is the official historian of the Holly Springs United Church of Christ. (Courtesy of Cora Lassiter.)

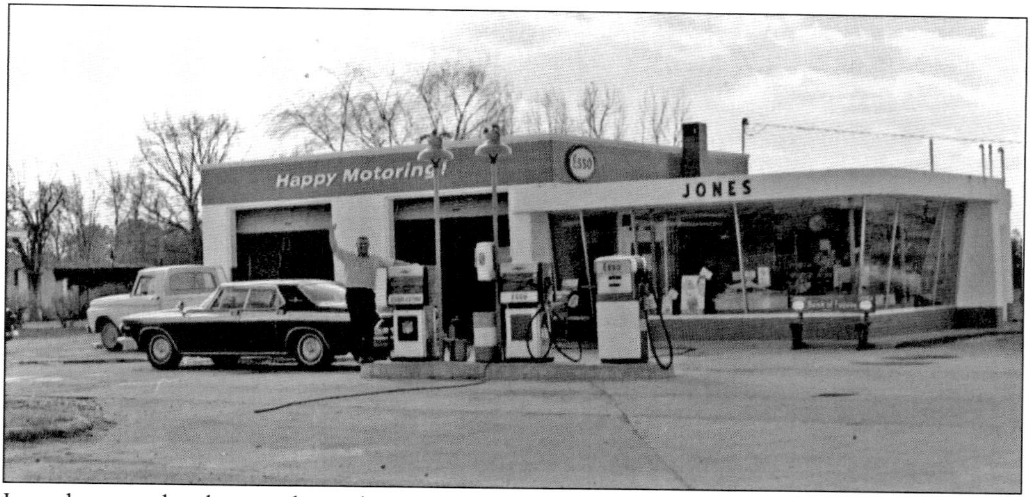


In a photograph taken in the early 1970s, Willie Eugene "Gene" Jones waves from the front of his Esso station, located at the corner of Main and Ballentine Streets. Gene ran a full-service gas station, which meant that he checked the engine oil level and tire air pressure, washed the windshield, and pumped gas. Jones' Esso Station served the community from 1954 to 1978. (Doris Jones collection.)

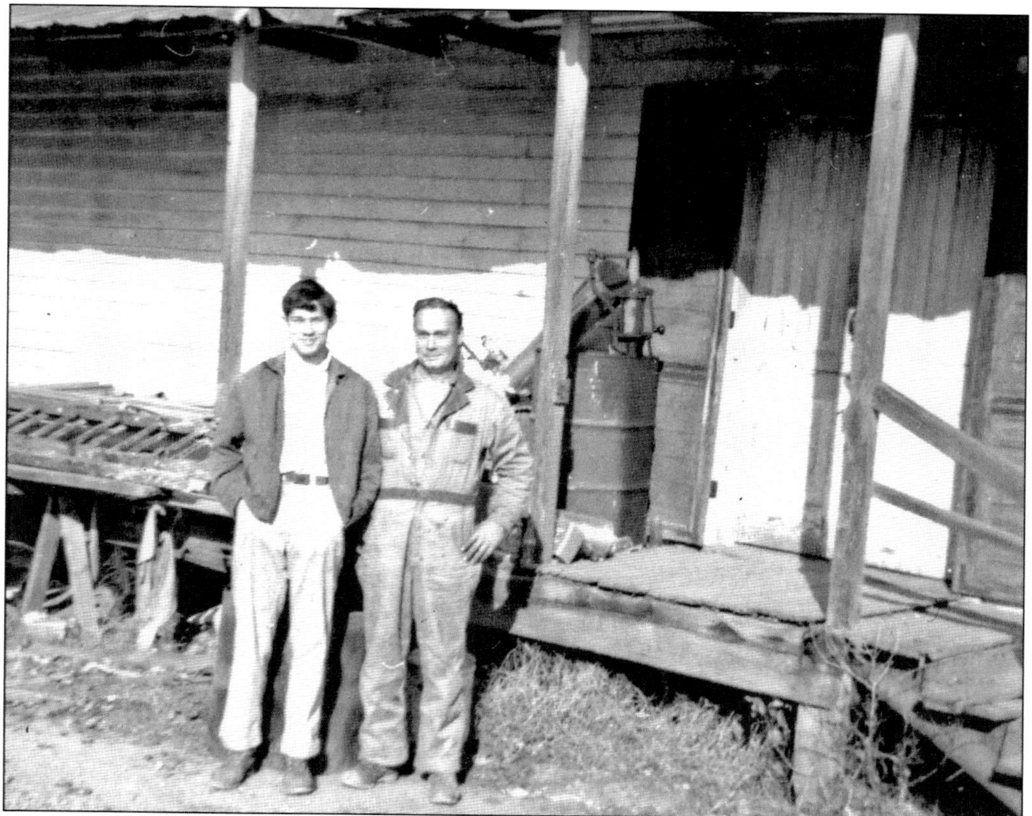

Rufus Bell, the owner of Bell's Heating and Air, who ran his sheet metal shop out of the Alford-Lashley Store, is pictured here on the right. Also pictured is Rufus's son Tim (left) in this 1960s photograph. (Doris Jones collection.)

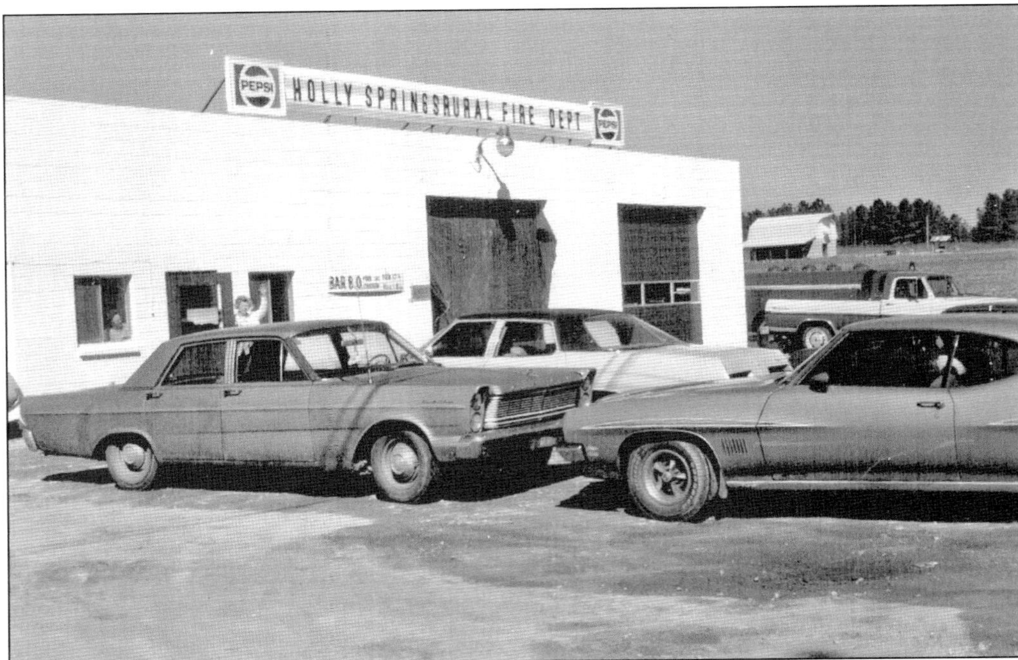


In July 1971, the Holly Springs Rural Volunteer Fire Department was founded, led by Jimmie Holland, the first chief. The station sits on land donated by Jack Stephens. Volunteer firemen have always been important to Holly Springs. It was not uncommon for a farmer to leave a field half plowed or the store-owner to close his shop when the sound of sirens pealed through town. (George and Kathy Huegerich collection.)

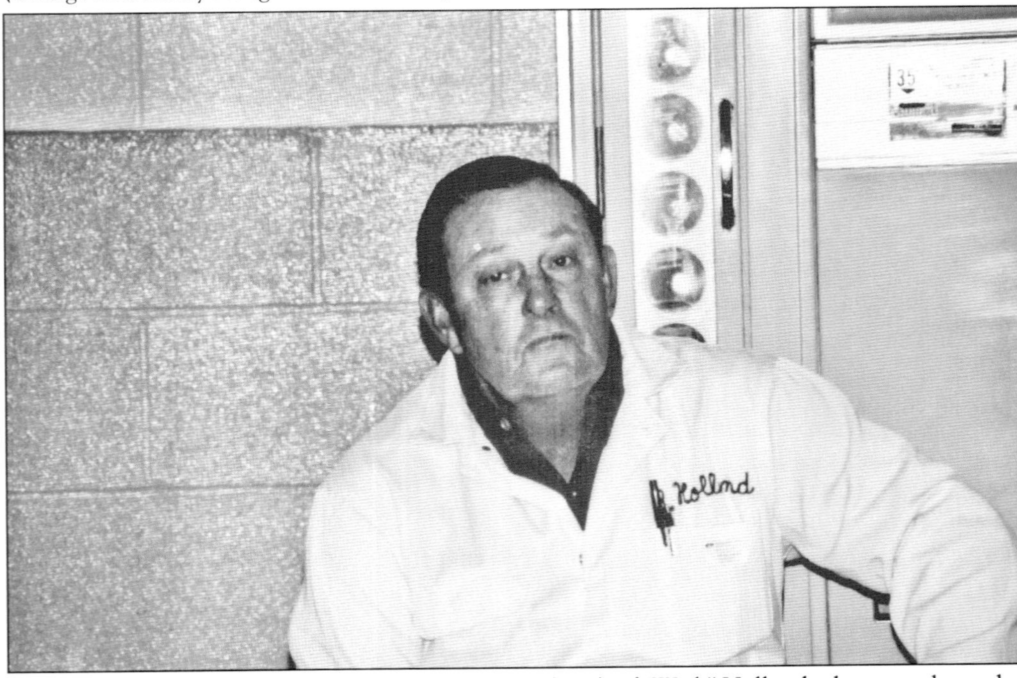

Holly Springs Rural Volunteer Department assistant fire chief "Wick" Holland takes a much-needed break at a barbecue fund-raiser at the firehouse. (George and Kathy Huegerich collection.)

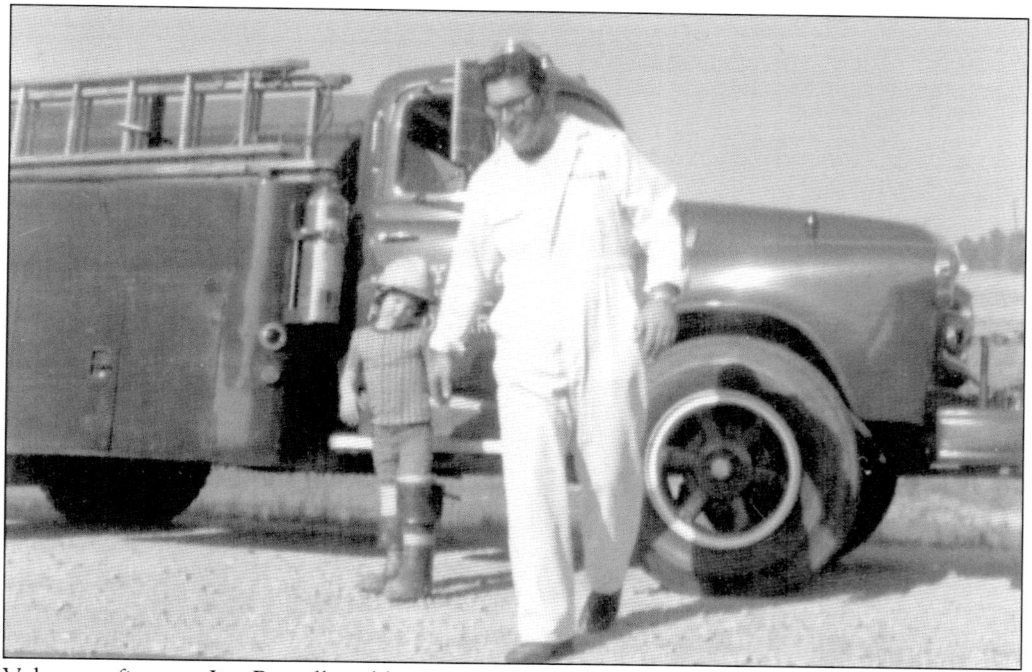

Volunteer fireman Jim Russell and his "junior firefighter" daughter Jennifer Russell are shown in this early-1970s photograph with a 1951 International tanker fire truck. This fire truck was graciously donated to Holly Springs by the Fairview Fire Department. (George and Kathy Huegerich collection.)

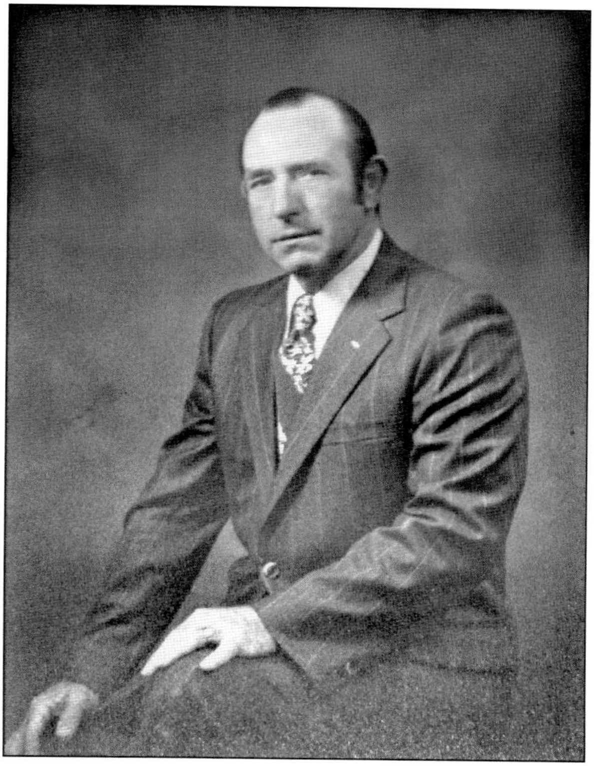

Mallie "Jack" Stephens Jr. left in January 1942 to serve in World War II, in which he was awarded five Bronze Stars and a Good Conduct Medal. After the war, he married hometown girl Dorothy "Dot" Shaw. Jack served as the lodge master in 1955 and held the office of mayor from 1969 until 1975, a total of three terms. (Courtesy of Holly Springs Masonic Lodge No. 115 AF&AM.)

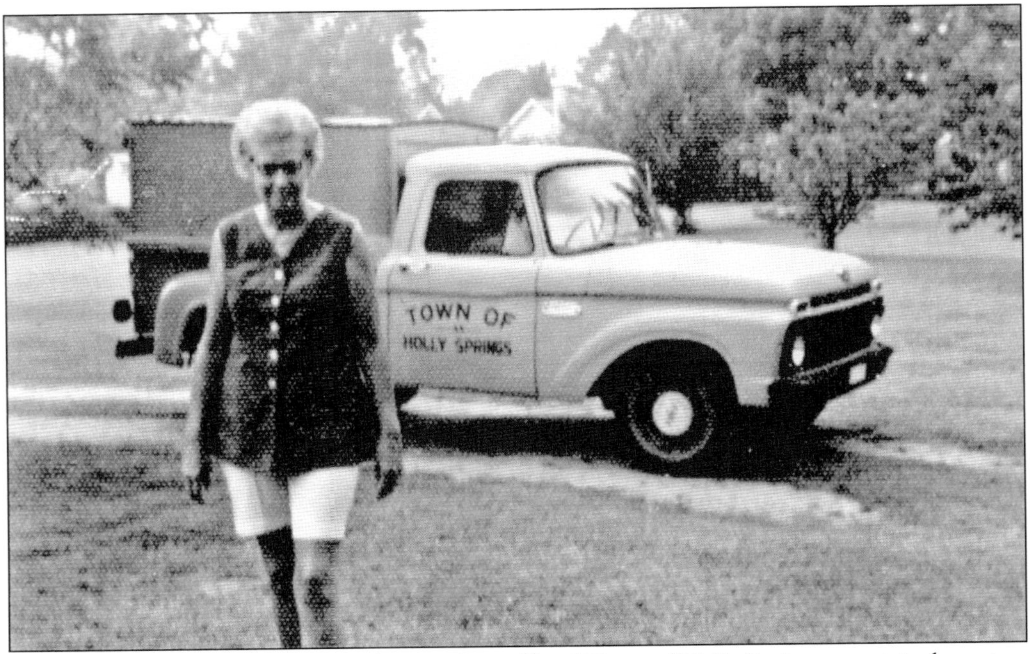


Sylvian Brooks stands in front of the very first official Town of Holly Springs municipal services truck, acquired from Fort Bragg army surplus at no charge. The town invested $783 for a tune-up, paint job, new seat covers, and tires. Sylvian's husband, Claire A. Brooks, was the water superintendent at the time. (Sylvian Brooks collection.)

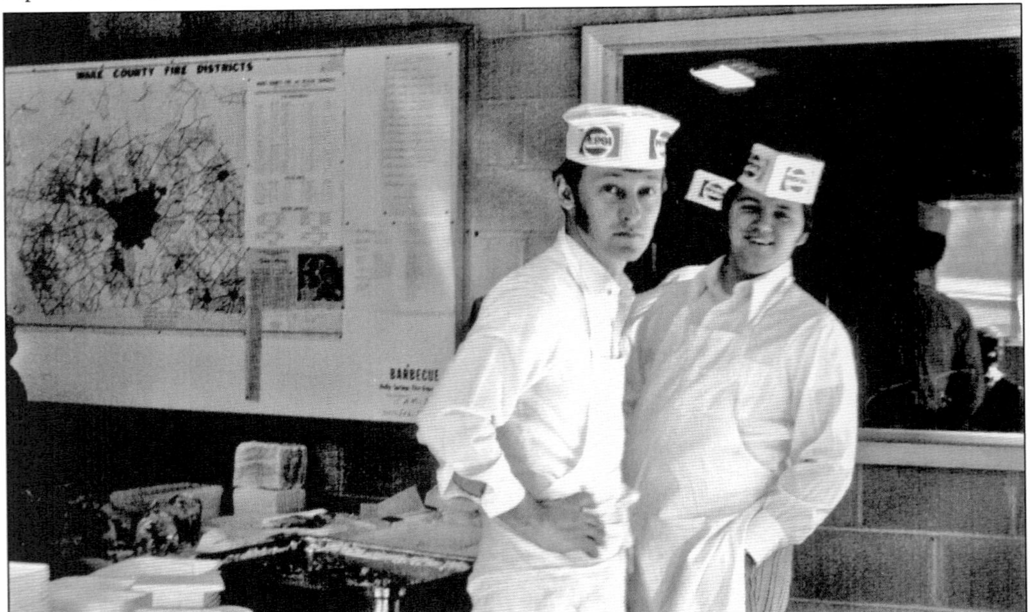


The annual fire department barbecue fund-raisers, held in February and September, were anticipated events in the community for many years. The wives would make the coleslaw, potato salad, and baked goods. Shown here ready to serve up a plate of pork or chicken barbecue are volunteer firemen John Lee Holleman (left) and "Pete" Brewer. The money raised help acquire new equipment. (George and Kathy Huegerich collection.)

Willie Archie "Monk" Jones is shown at right in a mid-1970s photograph. Retired from the Wake County Public Schools after 20-plus years, he started a second career as the owner of Jones's Backhoe Service. He served as a Holly Springs commissioner from 1977 to 1979 and was a member of the Masonic Elijah Lodge No. 821. He was married to Dora (Beckwith), and they had one daughter, Jean. (Courtesy of Jean Jones.)

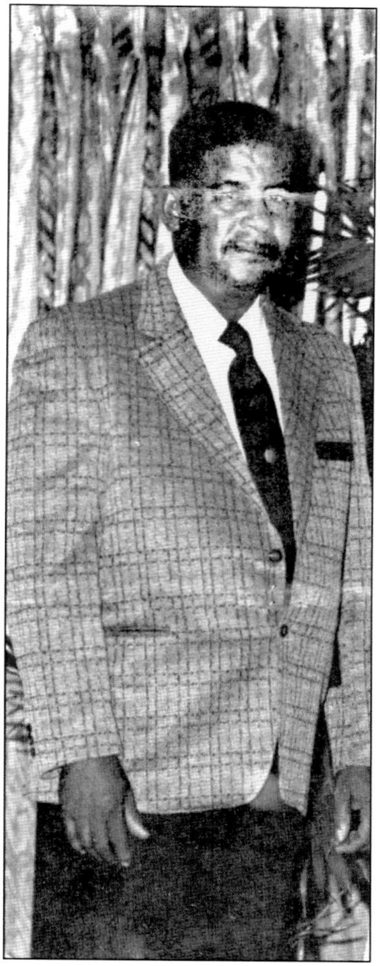

Meetings and training seminars were always a vital part of the duties of the firemen. Chatting during a break in a meeting are, from left to right, Jim Russell, Howard Weatherspoon, and Bobby Ragland. (George and Kathy Huegerich collection.)

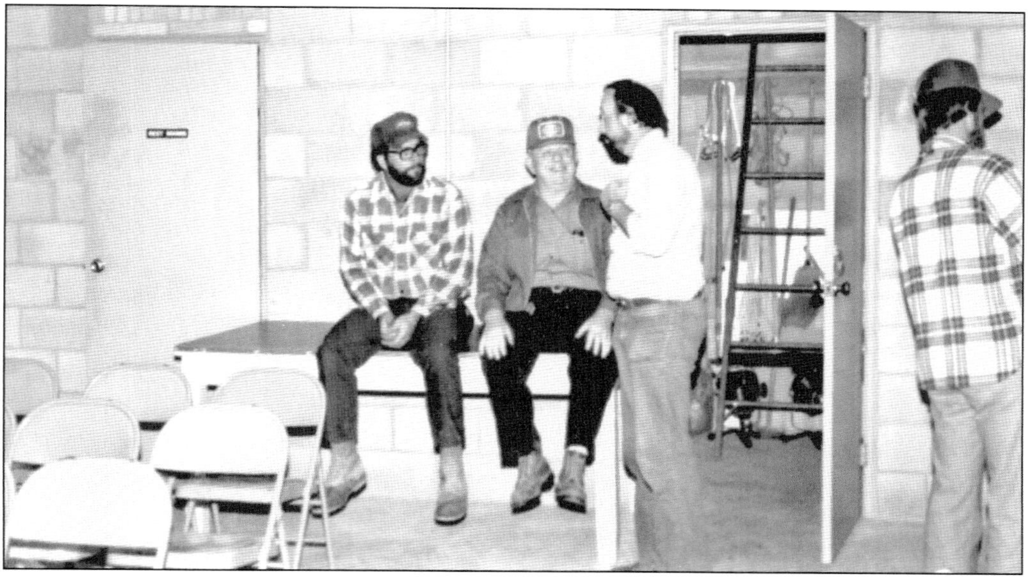

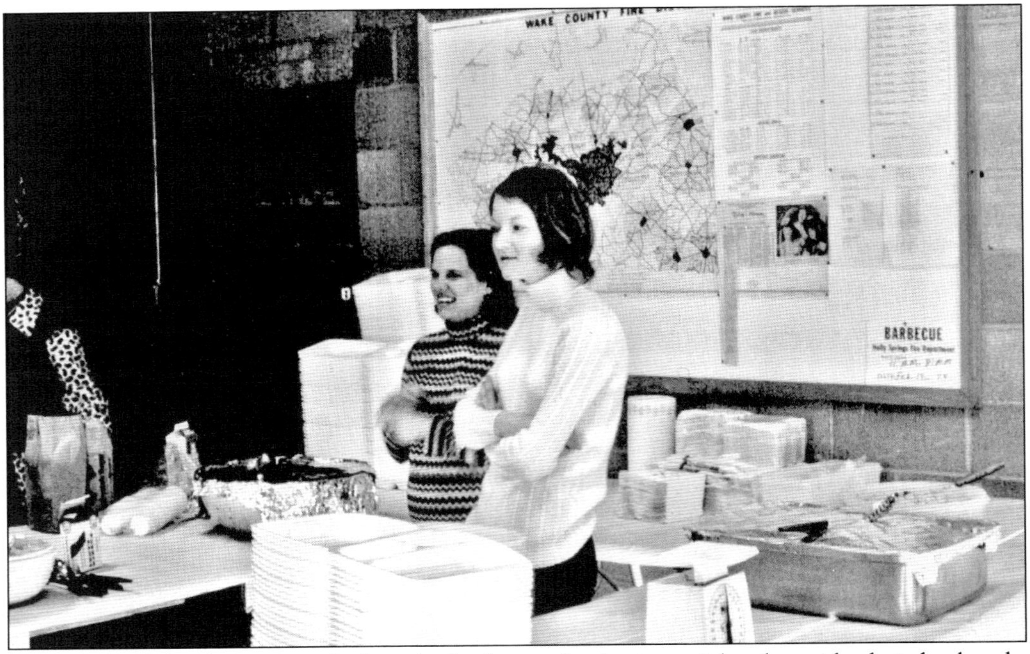


The wives of the firemen worked at the barbecue fund-raisers right alongside their husbands. Pictured from left to right are Kathy Huegerich and Joann Holland. The residents of the community took an active role in preparation for the barbecue, as the ladies were given bags of raw potatoes to peel, dice, and cook. Firemen would then pick them up to be made into potato salad by their wives. (George and Kathy Huegerich collection.)

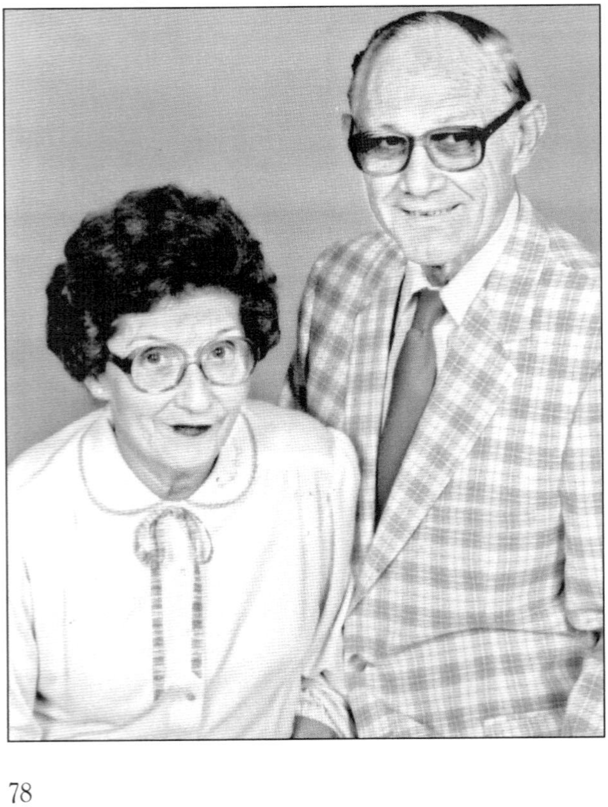

In this mid-1970s photograph used in the Holly Springs Baptist Church directory are Elmer Brewer and his wife, Cleo (Jones) Brewer. Cleo ran Brewer's Grocery after her brother-in-law, Ernie Brewer, became sick. In 1971, he sold the store to Elmer and Cleo. Elmer was a rural letter carrier for the U.S. Postal Service for 32 years. (Nathan and Carolyn Williams collection.)

Sweet as she can be, little two-year-old Deanna (Cofield) Hamilton, daughter of LaVerne (Prince) and Wiley Cofield, is pictured standing on Utley Street in 1975. On the left is Elm Street, which intersects with Main Street. (Courtesy of LaVerne Cofield.)

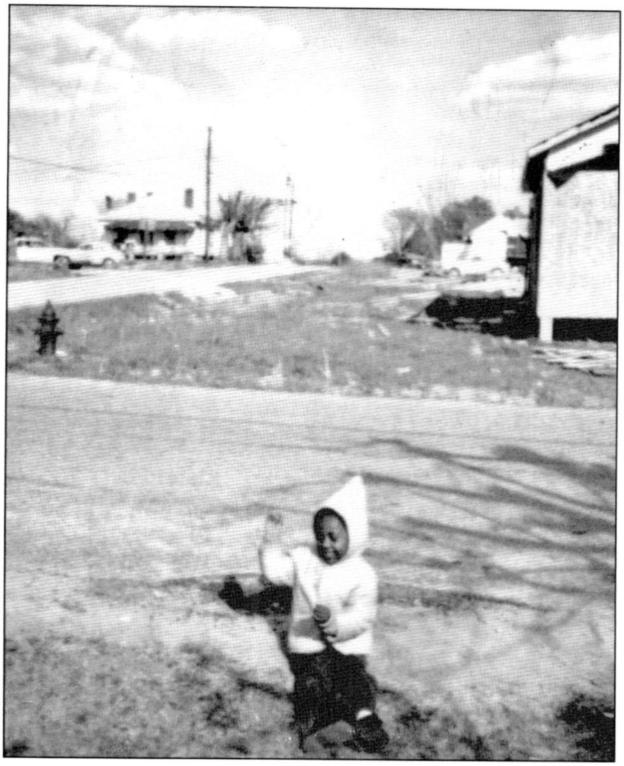

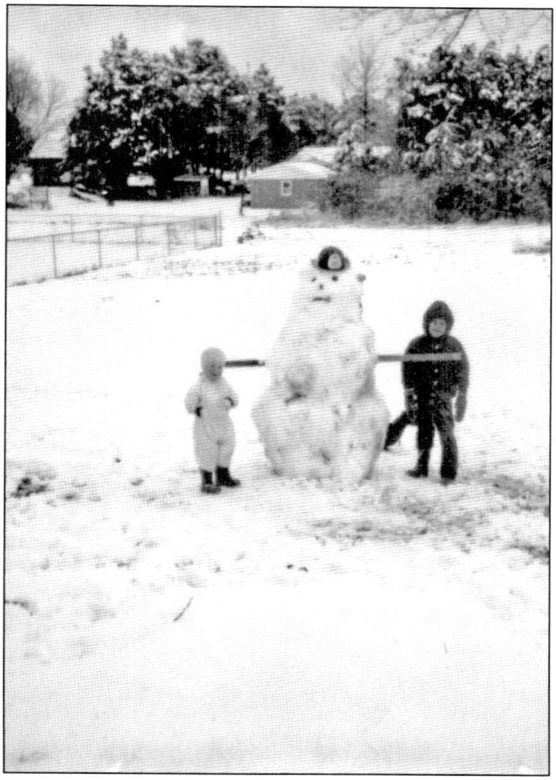

It does snow in the South! The Huegerich boys, Paul (left) and Karl, stand beside an excellent example of a snowman, complete with a fireman's hat, more than likely made with the assistance of their father, George. (George and Kathy Huegerich collection.)

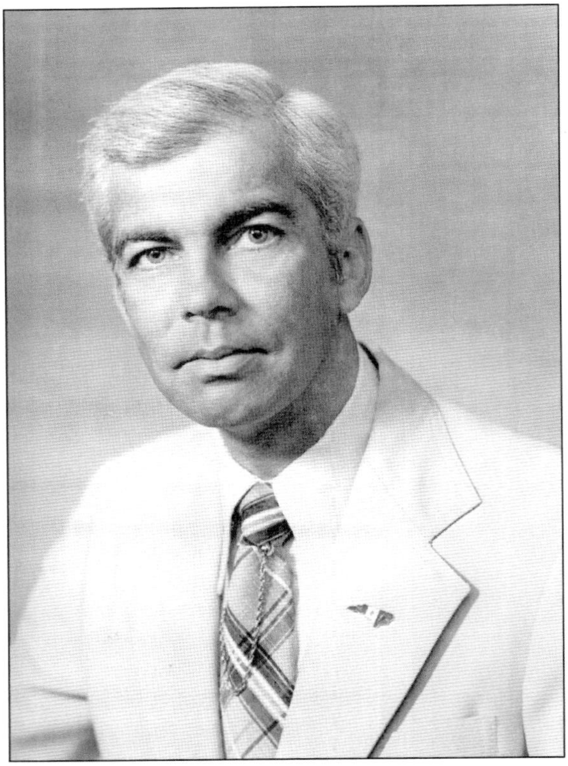

Jimmy H. Hancock served the community of Holly Springs by being elected as a commissioner in 1971–1973 and reelected to serve an additional two-year term in 1973–1975. In 1975, Hancock was elected as mayor, an office he held until 1980. (Jimmy H. Hancock collection.)

Shown below in a mid-1970s photograph is Holly Springs' one-man police department, Richard "Lee" Carroll (left), receiving the keys to the town's first police vehicle from Mayor Jimmy H. Hancock (right). Two auxiliary policemen were available to support Carroll in the event that any one of the 960 residents needed assistance. (Jimmy H. Hancock collection.)

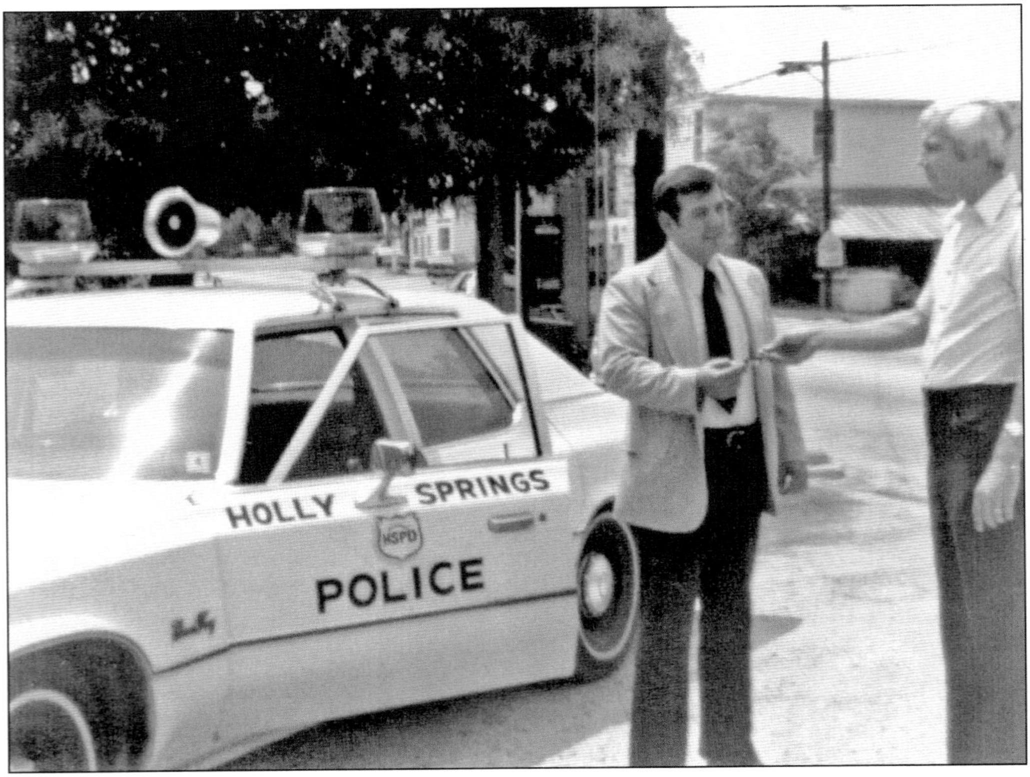

Marie (Adams) Yates, daughter of Lynn and Jennie Belle (Minter) Adams and wife of Lennis Yates, is shown here in a stylish scarf that was ever so popular in the 1970s. (Christine Adams-Utley collection.)

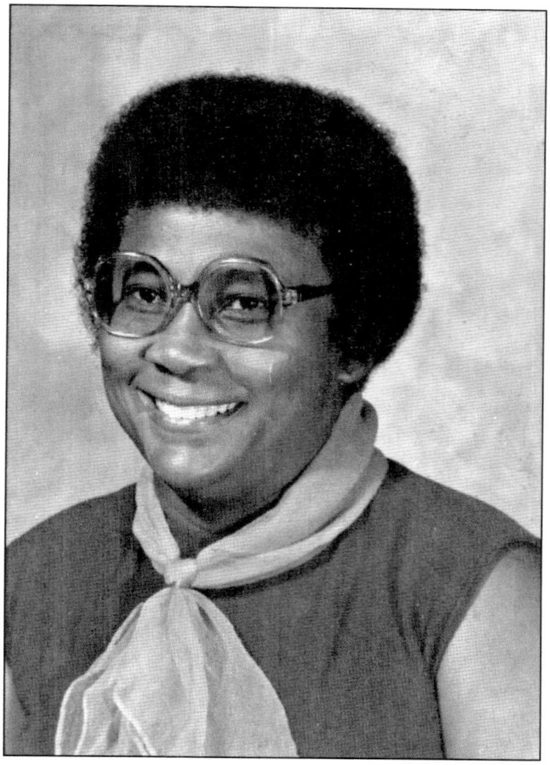

Holly Springs residents were given the opportunity to meet the candidates running for office in the 1976 upcoming general election. At the reception are, from left to right, Elizabeth Cofield, Bernice Lassiter, Nancy Womble, and Vasser Sherrill. (Jimmy H. Hancock collection.)

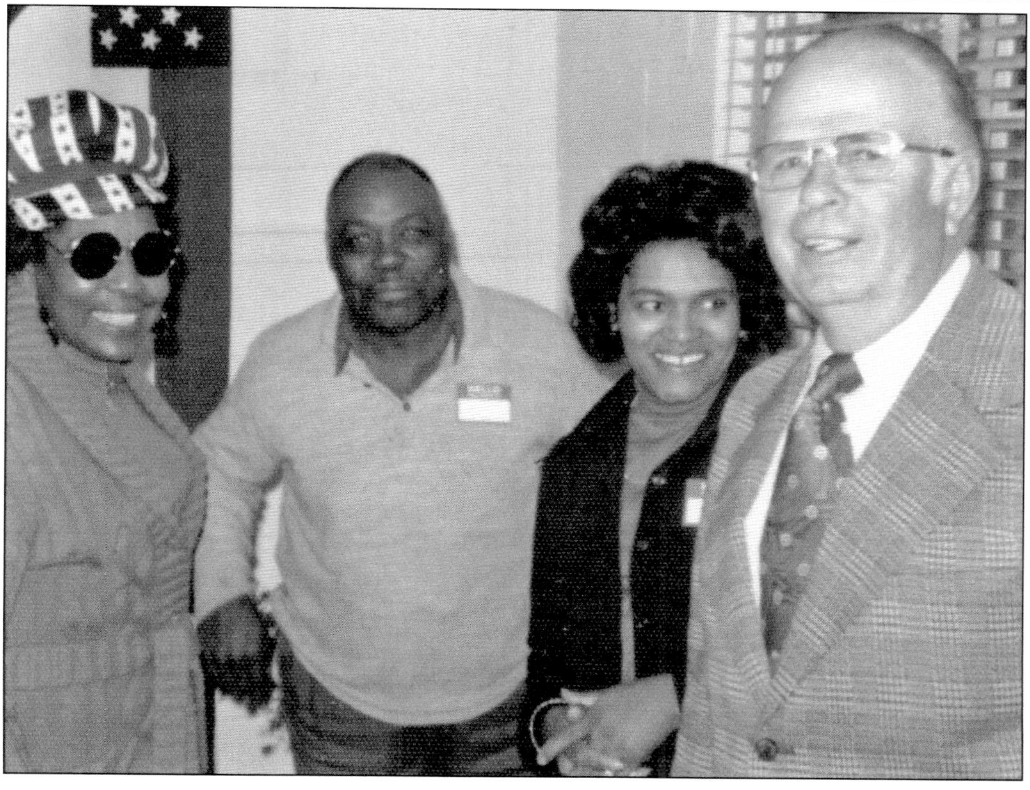

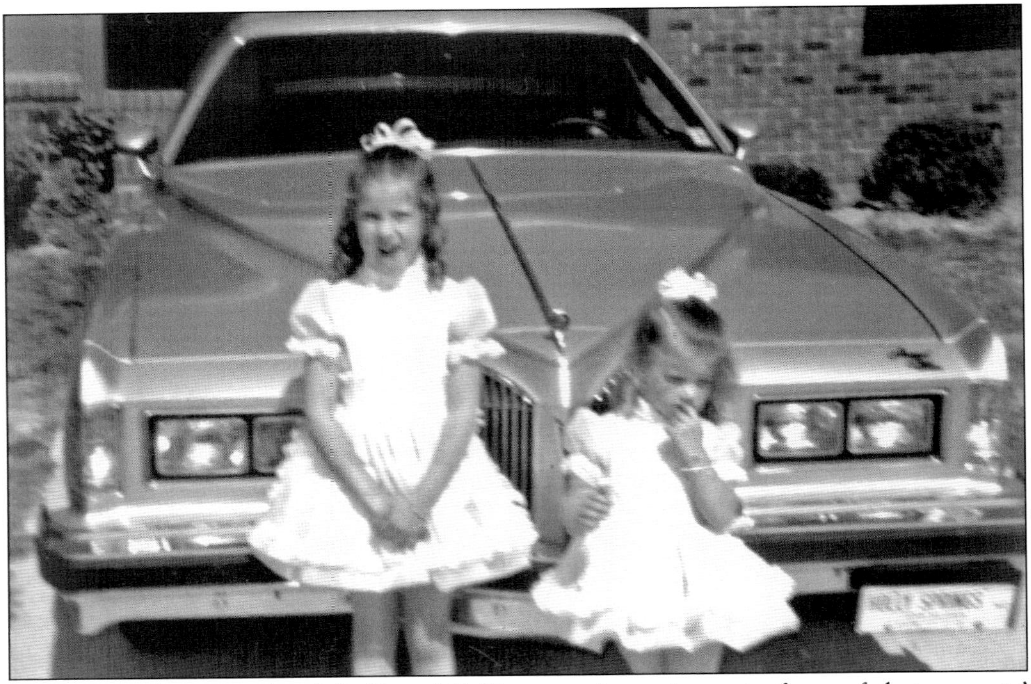

The Hancock sisters, April (left) and Kellie, pose for a picture in front of their parents' car. Notice the front license plate, which was created to honor the town's centennial. (Jimmy H. Hancock collection.)

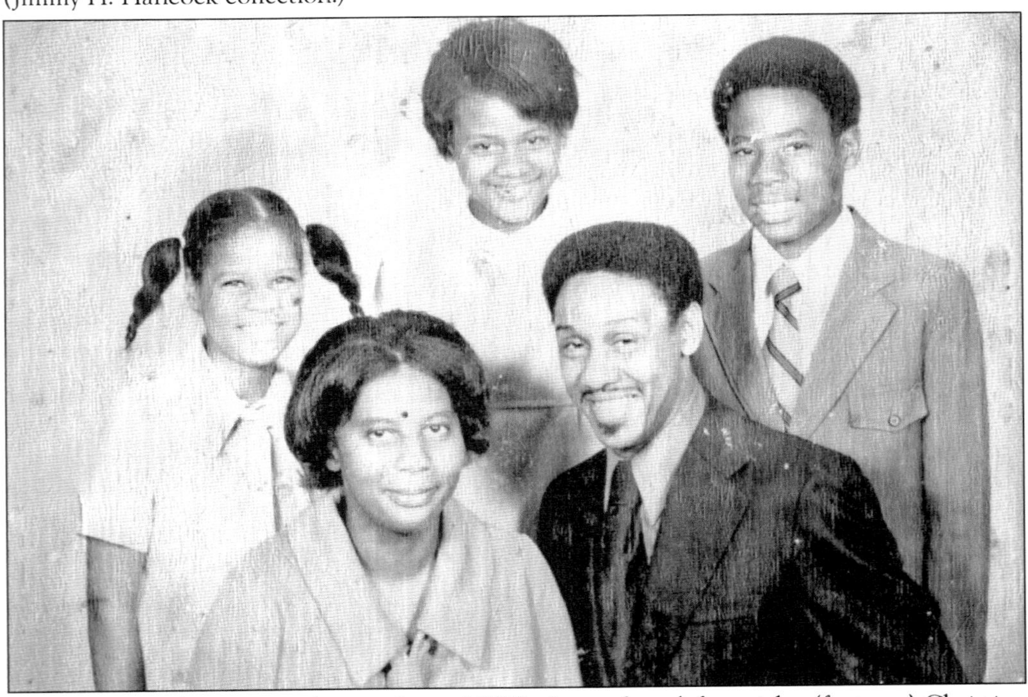

This Utley family portrait taken in the mid-1970s shows, from left to right, (first row) Christine (Adams) and Joe Utley; (second row) Vickie, Marjorie Gail, and Derek Utley. (Christine Adams-Utley collection.)

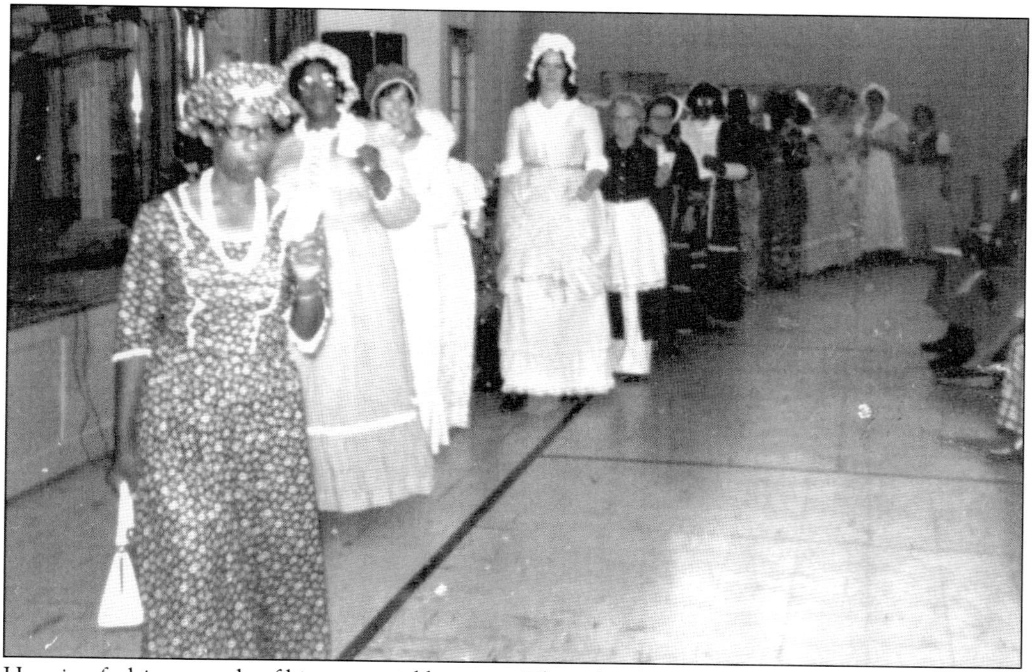

Here is a fashion parade of bicentennial beauties. These lovely Holly Springs ladies show off their period costumes in front of an admiring crowd. They spent months designing and hand-sewing their costumes in preparation for the big event. (Both, Jimmy H. Hancock collection.)

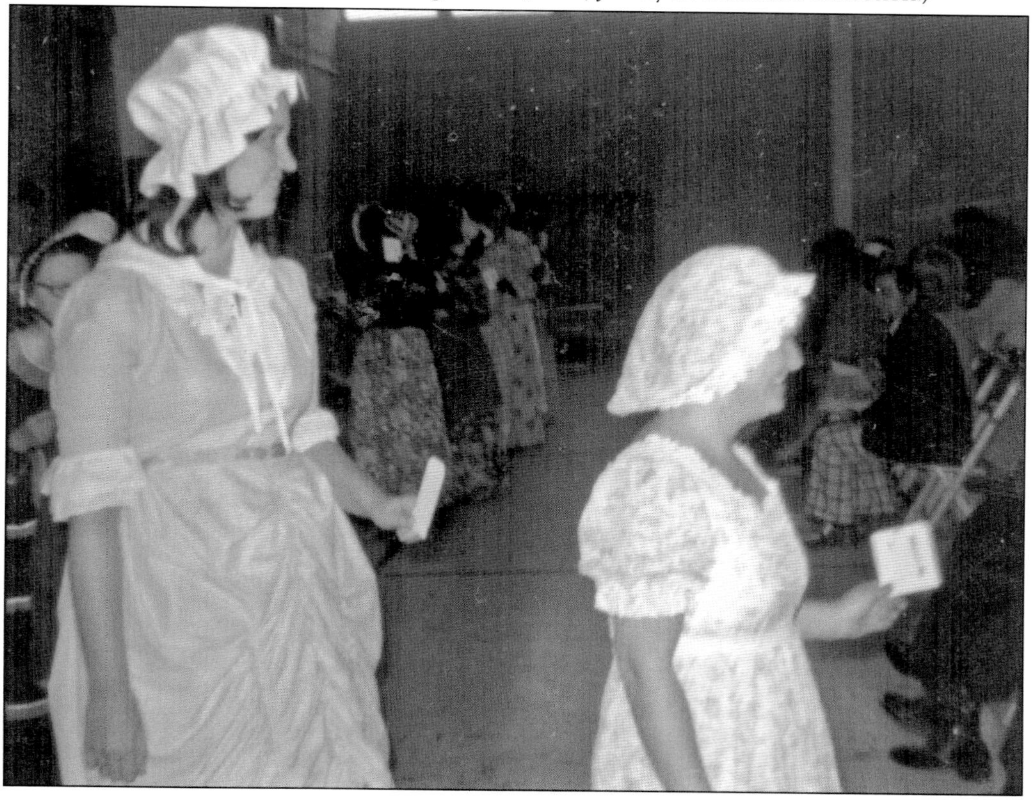

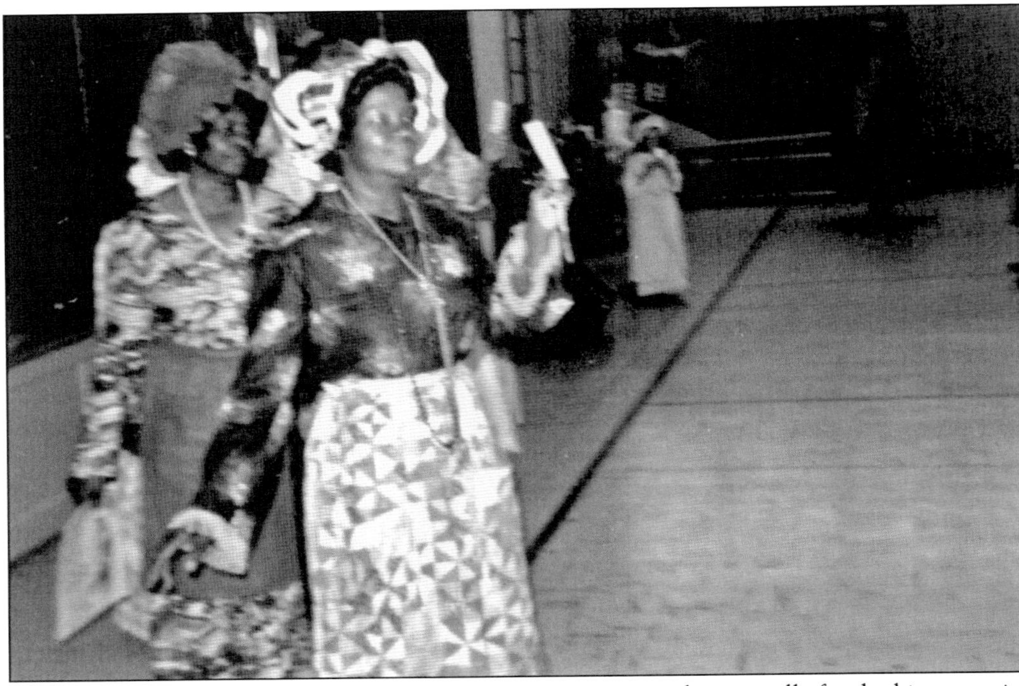

Here are more lovely ladies modeling their period costumes made especially for the bicentennial celebration. (Jimmy H. Hancock collection.)

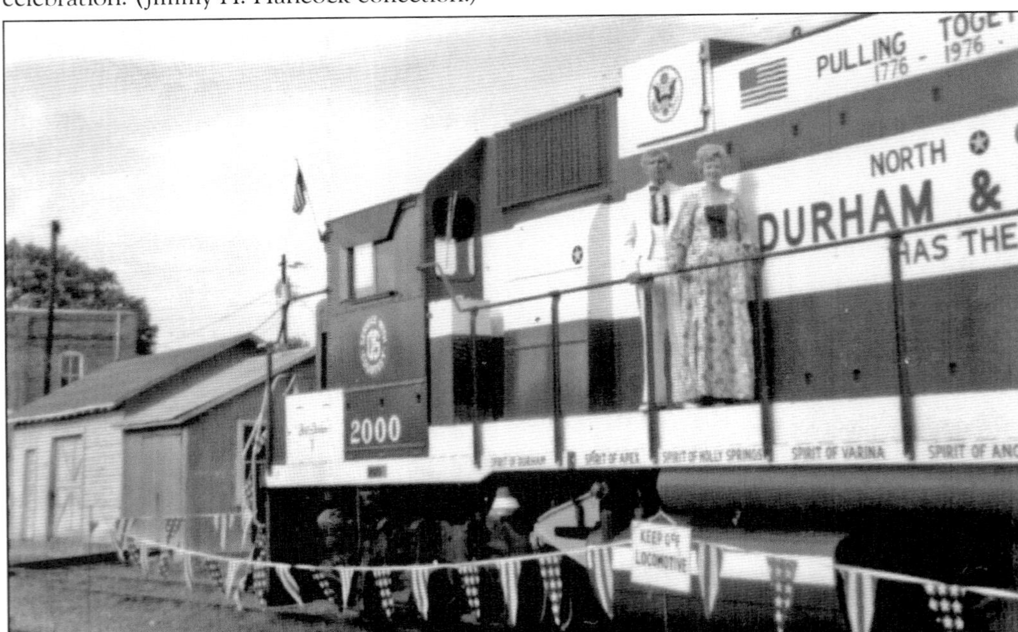


The Durham and Southern Railroad designed a special engine commemorating our nation's bicentennial. Parked in Holly Springs for a period of one month for the residents to enjoy, the engine was an exciting addition to the many festivities planned by the town. Attired in their period costumes in this 1976 photograph are Mayor Jimmy H. and his wife, Rosalyn (Holleman) Hancock. (Jimmy H. Hancock collection.)

# *Three*

# PLACES OF WORSHIP

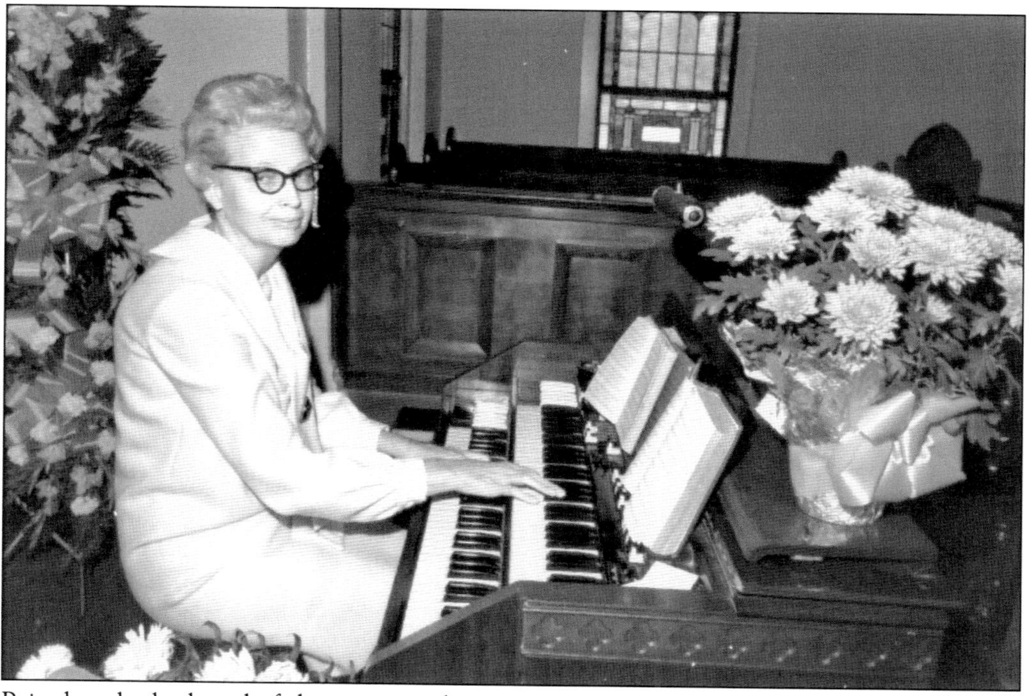

Poised at the keyboard of the organ in the sanctuary of the Holly Springs United Methodist Church on Avent Ferry Road is Sylvian (Knowles) Brooks, shown here in a 1970 photograph. Parishioners have enjoyed the heavenly music provided by Brooks for many years. (Nathan and Carolyn Williams collection.)

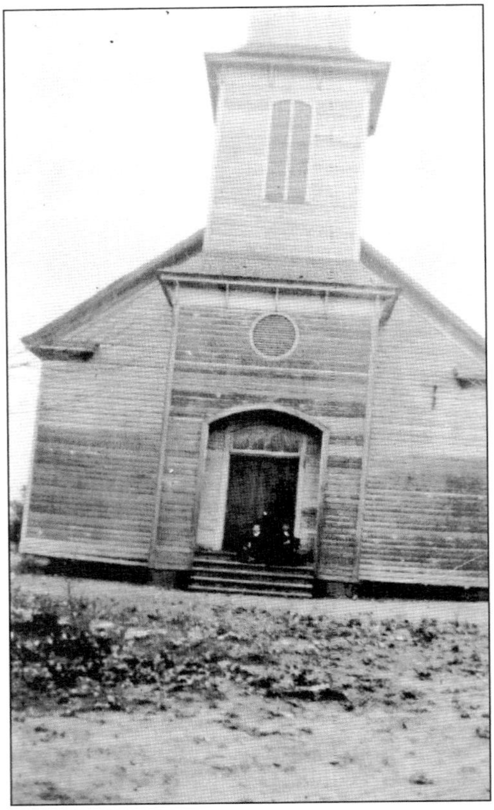

The Holly Springs Baptist Church was formed in 1822. The site of the original building was on the west side of the Leslie-Alford-Mims property, which was used until 1928, when the building was sold and moved to Durham. The current church sits at the corner of Raleigh and Center Streets on land donated by W. A. Seagraves. The modern, brick education building was added in 1971. (Both, Town Historical collection.)

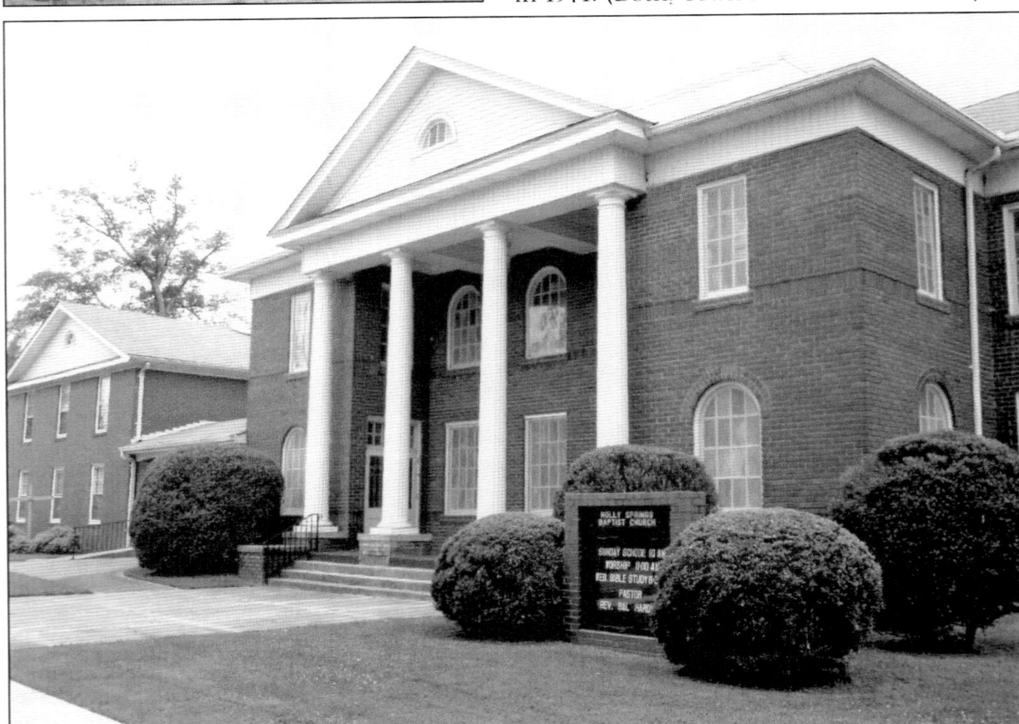

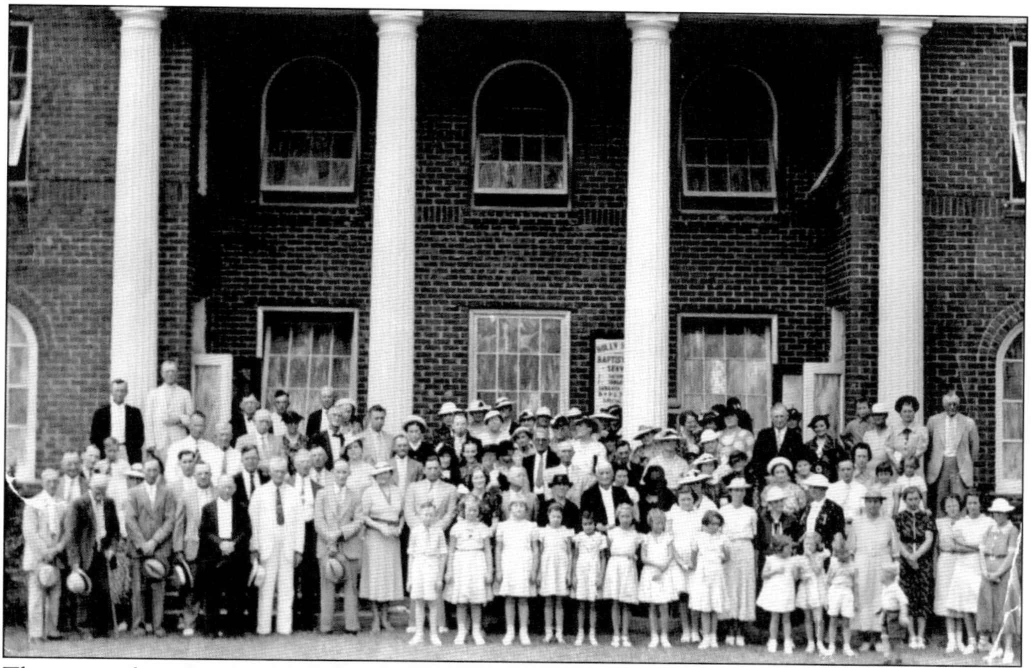

The group of parishioners poses for a 1950s photograph outside of the Holly Springs Baptist Church, which is located on the corner of Center and Raleigh Streets. David A. Baker, grandfather of Vada (Cummings) Fiegler, is standing at the far right on the top row. (Vada Fiegler collection.)

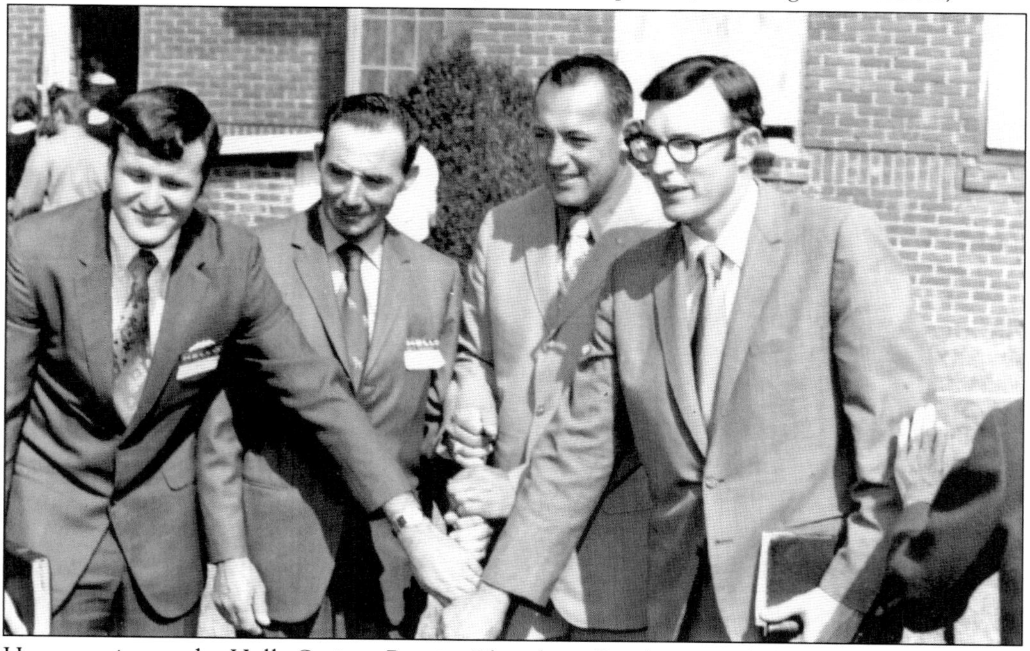

Homecoming at the Holly Springs Baptist Church in October 1970 held more than the usual speeches and ceremonies. On this occasion, the ground-breaking for the educational building was the highlight of the day. Standing here with shovels in hand are, from left to right, Pastor R. D. Ramey, James Yarborough, Harvey Montague, and Gene Williams. (Nathan and Carolyn Williams collection.)

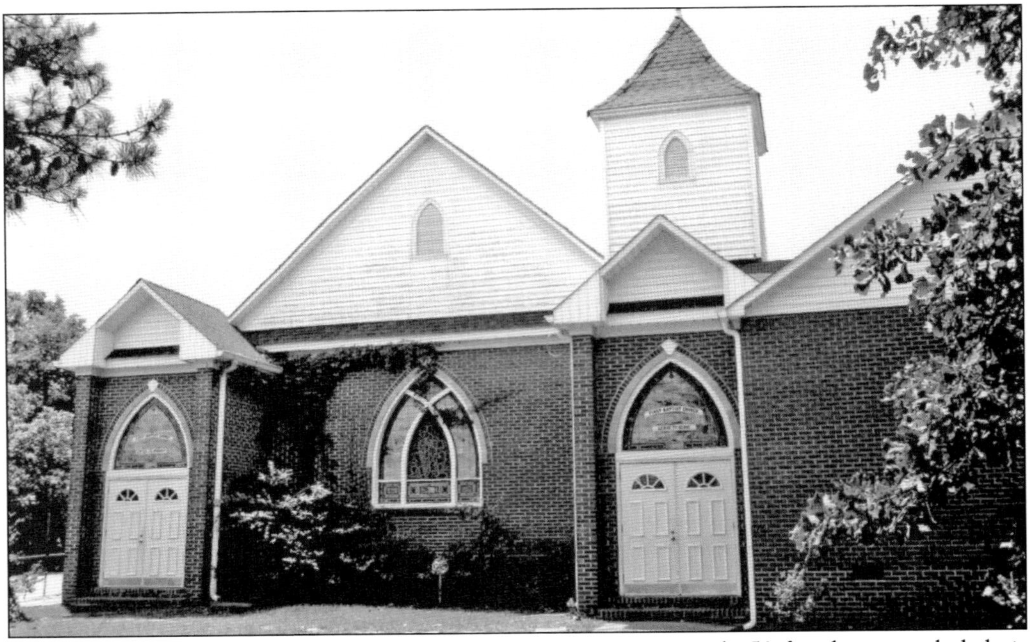

In 1866, the First Baptist Church was formed when approximately 50 freedmen pooled their resources and bought a half-acre plot of land that held a log cabin. Two years later, a new church was built, but it was destroyed by fire. A new frame building was erected soon after the fire, and it was renovated in 1935 and again in 1952 with added brick veneer and modern amenities. (Town Historical collection.)

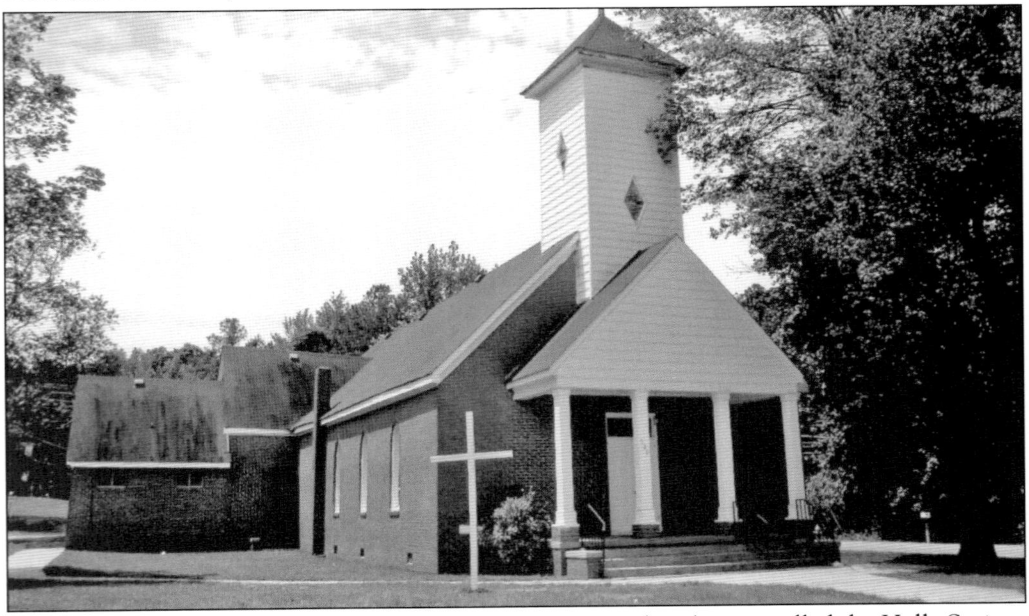

Formed in 1871 by freedmen, the Holly Springs Christian Church, now called the Holly Springs United Church of Christ, was led by Rev. Jackson Jefferson with a membership of three: Price Page, Ned Ballentine, and Edie Page. Originally a wood-frame building, the building was enlarged and improved as the membership grew. In 2004, a larger facility on Third Street was to become its new home. (Town Historical collection.)

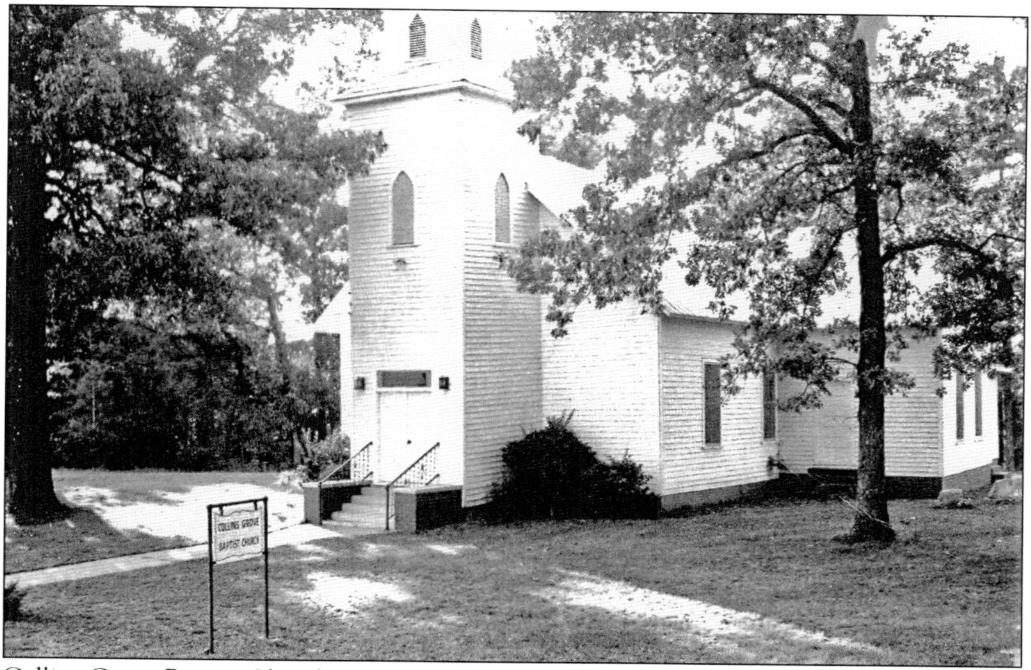

Collins Grove Baptist Church was organized in 1870 in the community known as Holleman's Crossroads and met in the homes of its parishioners. It was not until 1877 that Jessie A. Norris, the grandson of John Norris Jr., gave the church one acre of land upon which to construct the building. The church cemetery holds most of the older, original, deceased families of the area. (Courtesy of North Carolina Archives.)

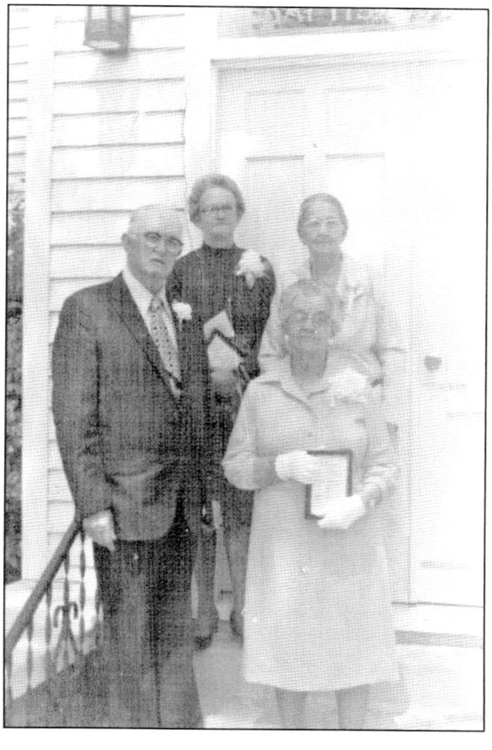

This 1970 photograph shows members of the Collins Grove Baptist Church being honored for their commitment to the church. Standing from left to right are (first row) Exum Hare and Estelle Womble; (second row) Ella (Holt) Hare and Mary Holleman. (Mary Macon collection.)

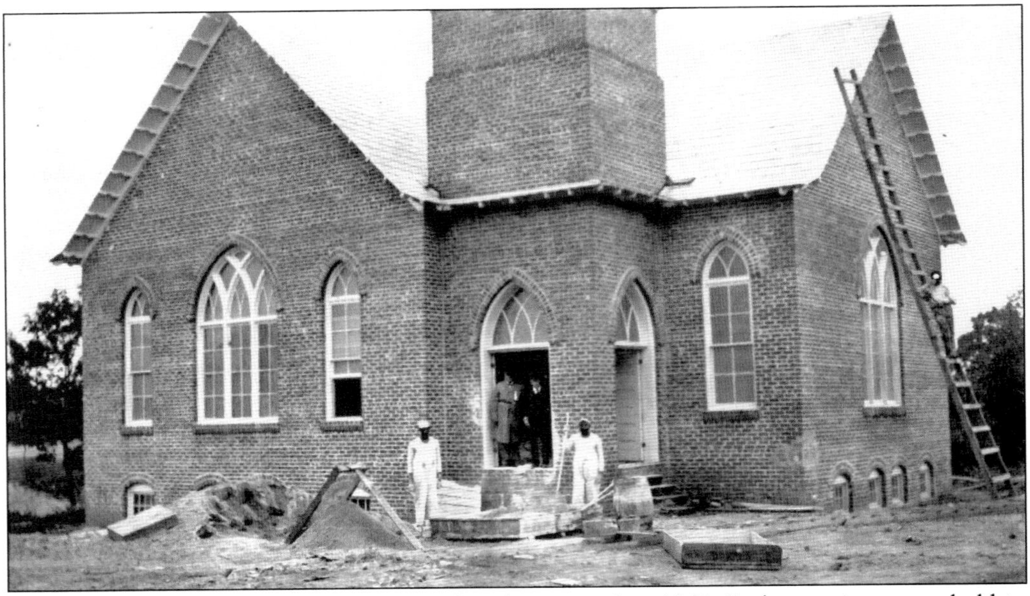

The inception to establish a Methodist church occurred in 1860. Early meetings were held in homes until the congregation purchased the old Holly Springs Academy, which was located on the hill bordering the present cemetery. In 1917, land for the current church and the bricks were donated by George Benton Alford. Alford can be seen in the doorway in his trademark uniform during the construction stage. (Wright collection.)

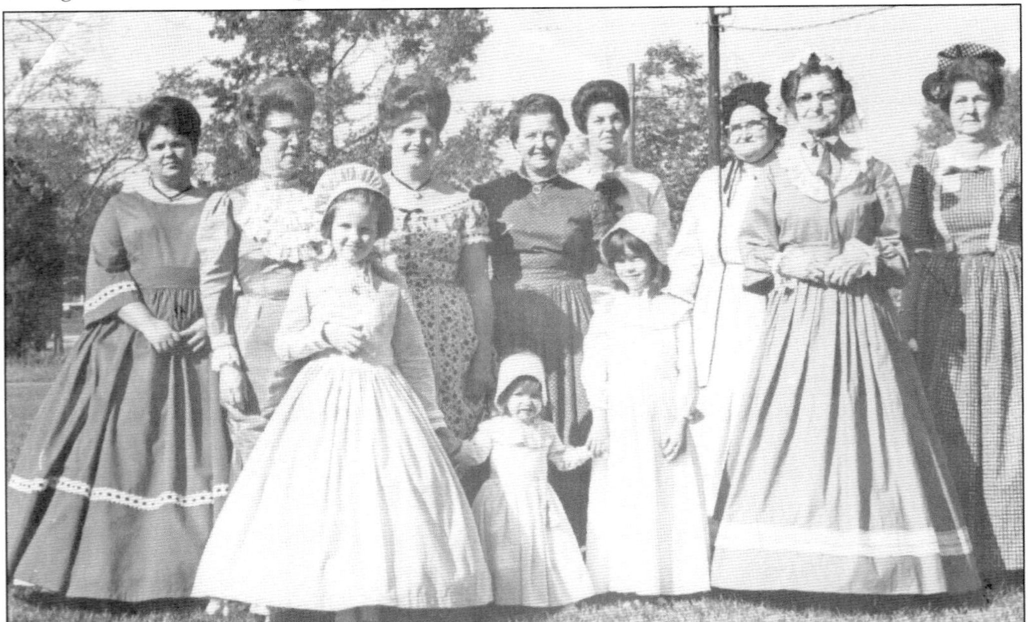

Dressed in period costumes to celebrate the Holly Springs United Methodist Church Centennial on November 8, 1970, are the ladies of the church. The lovely ladies are, from left to right, (first row) Lugene Bradley and the two unidentified children of Charles Pollock; (second row) Mildred Wilson, Kathryn Cummings, Ilene Bradley, Louise Turner, Doris Jones, Jessie Wilson, Blanche Holt, and Mary Lee Johnson. (Mary Lee Johnson collection, courtesy of Lori Stokes.)

As in so many small towns, churches in Holly Springs were gathering spots for the community. On Sundays, residents would come into town to worship and socialize. The group shown here from the Holly Springs United Methodist Church is, from left to right, Keith Glover (pastor), Ed Belton, Irma Gattman, unidentified, Bethel Wright, Emma Betts, unidentified, and Evelyn Belton. (Mary Lee Johnson collection, courtesy of Lori Stokes.)

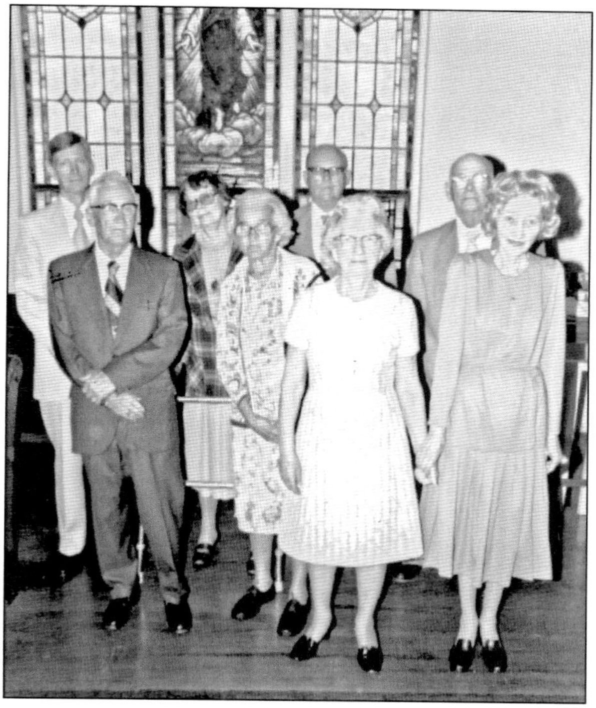

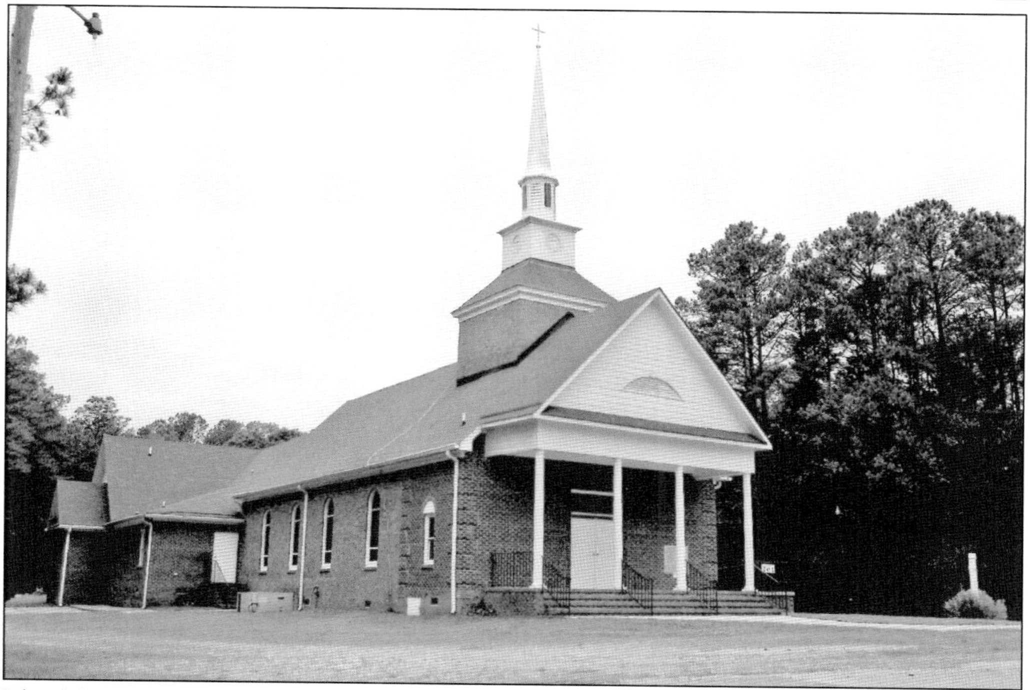

The African Methodist Episcopal Zion Church was organized early in the 1900s and met in the old Champion School west of Holly Springs. In 1925, the local Methodist congregation sold their church building to what is now known as Douglas Chapel AMEZ, named in honor of the late Frank Douglas. With logs used to roll the building down the street, the church was relocated to its present location on Douglas Street. (Town Historical collection.)

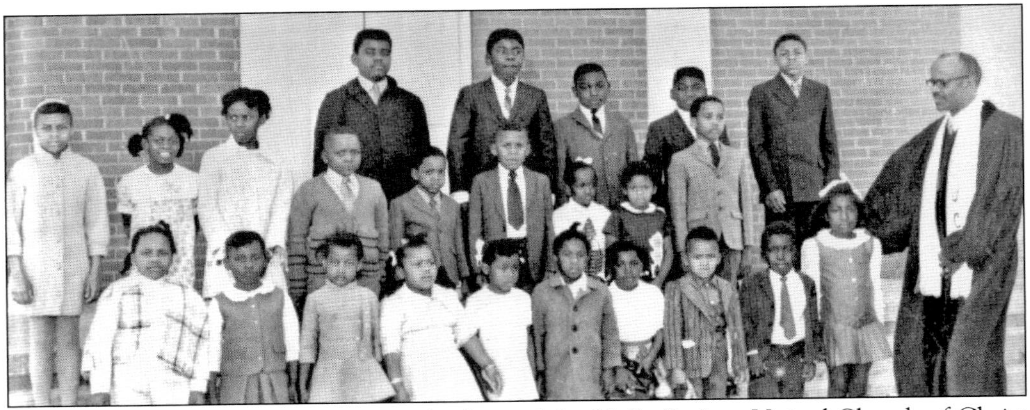

This 1970 photograph shows the angelic faces of the Holly Springs United Church of Christ "Beginners." From left to right are (first row) Sandra Judd, Debbie Whitaker, Vanessa Snellings, Sherry Judd, Myra Harris, Jackie Harris, Kate (Richardson) Macon, Patrick McNeil, Reggie Mann, Toni (Richardson) Gass, and Rev. John Henry Jones; (second row) Doris Jean Prince, Molly (Lockley) Laws, Denise (Harrington) Coates, Dwight Judd, Eric Corbin, Anthony Harris, Yvette Richardson, Terrie (Harris) Shaw, and Matthew Corbin; (third row) Carlton Mann, James Mann Jr., Darryl Kimble, Jerome Mann, and Wade Prince Jr. (Courtesy of John McNeil.)

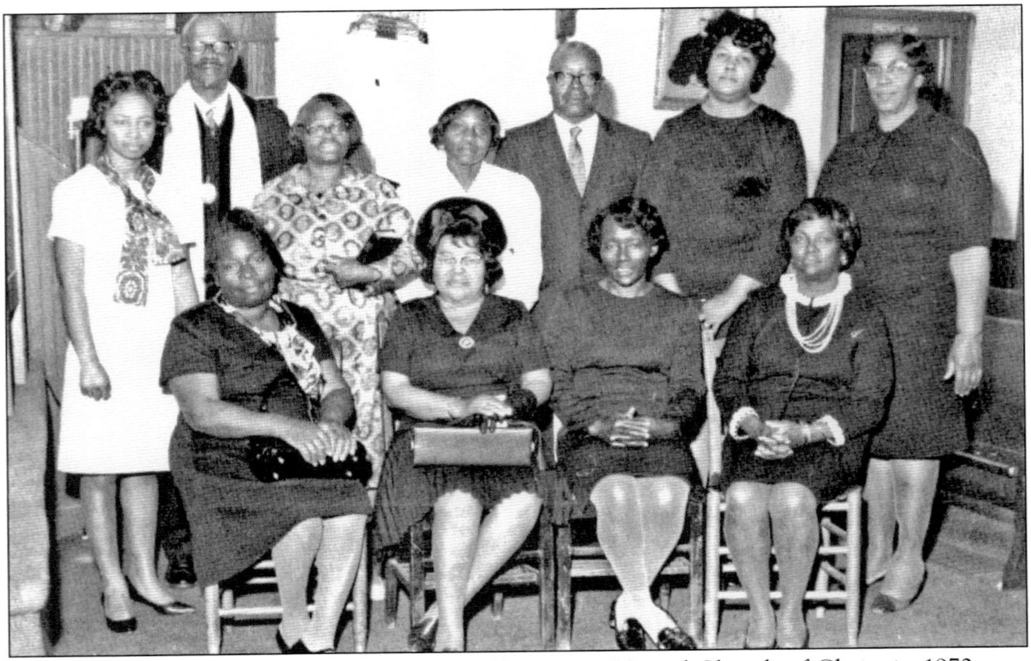

Members of the Missionary Circle of the Holly Springs United Church of Christ in 1970 pose for a photograph to be included in the church's centennial book 1871–1971. From left to right are (first row) Alice Kimble, Dala Rogers, Martha Utley, and Cora Mae Lassiter; (second row) Delois (Johnson) Whitaker, Rev. John Henry Jones, Coretta Merritt, Bertha Turner, Rev. Robert Johnson, Sue Carroll (Leslie) Barbee, and Alechia Betts. (Courtesy of John McNeil.)

# *Four*

# THE SCHOOL HOUSE

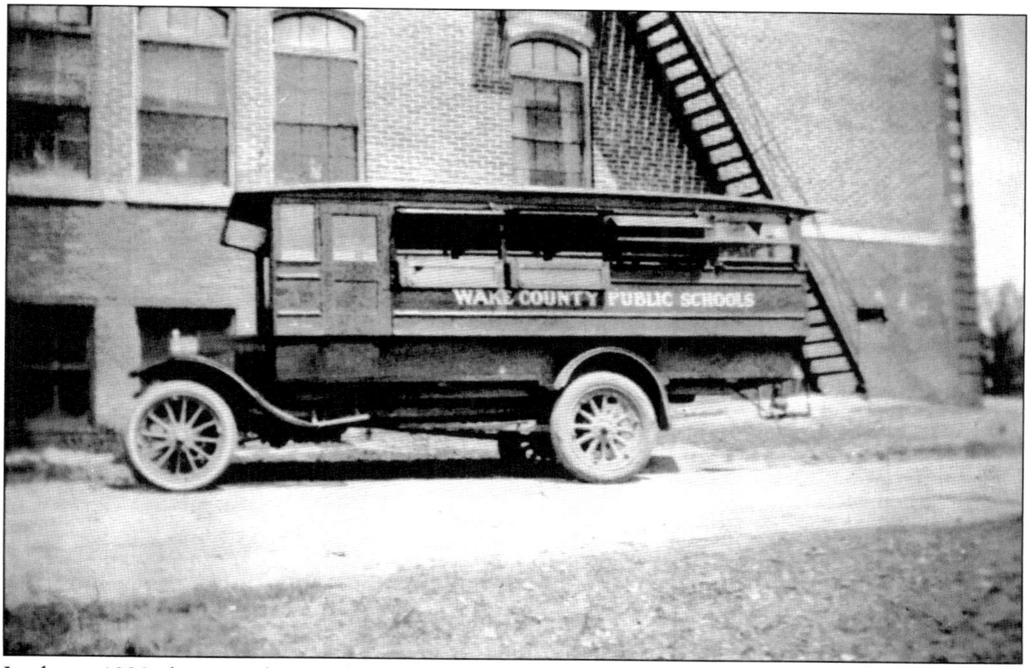


In this c. 1920 photograph, a Wake County Public School bus parked outside of the Holly Springs High School stands ready to deliver another load of students safely to their destination. (Mary Lee Johnson collection, courtesy of Lori Stokes.)

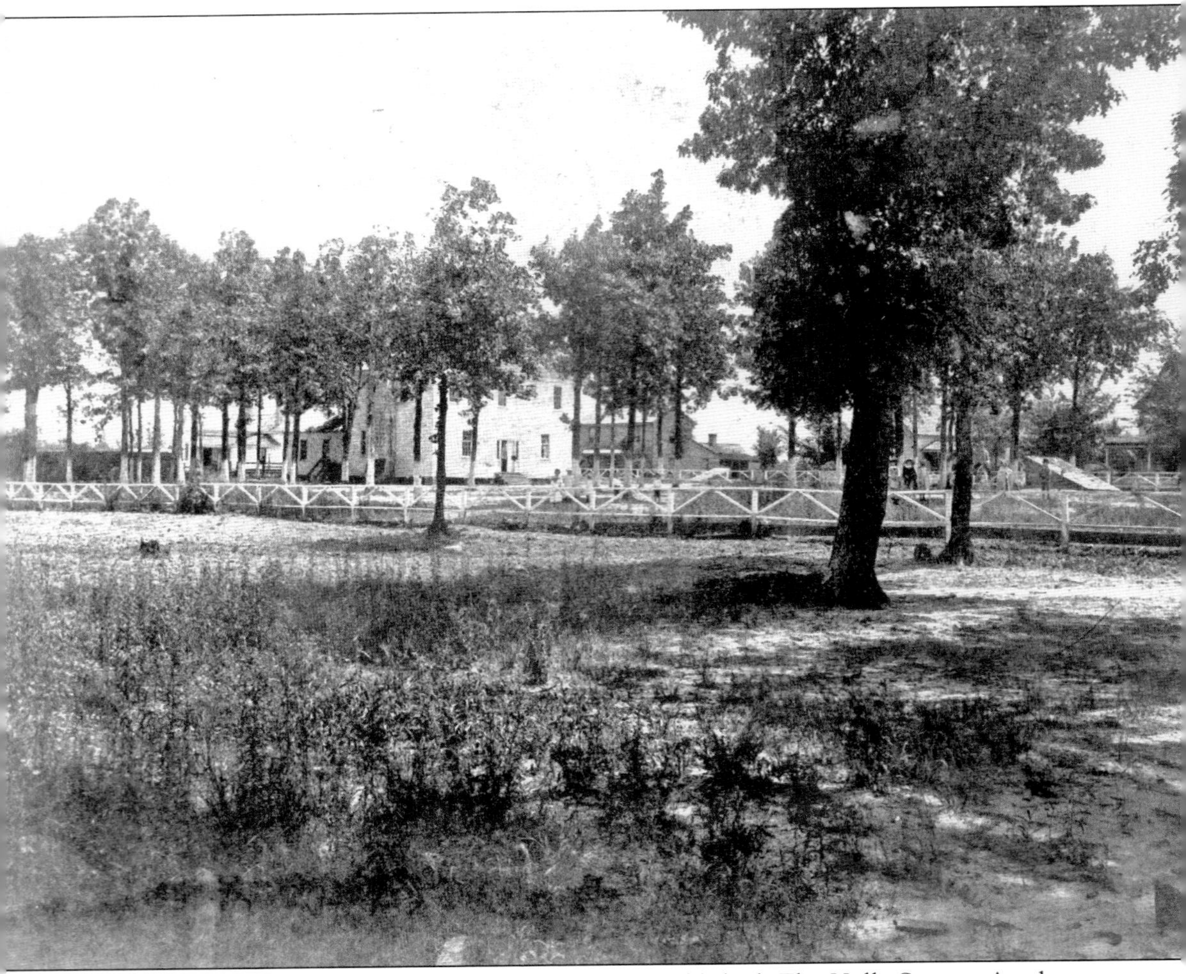

By 1854, the first school in the community was established. The Holly Springs Academy was an all-male school used as a preparatory school for Wake Forest University. At the outbreak of the Civil War, like nearly all Southern schools, this school was left without students or fathers to pay the tuition. After the war, the academy was reestablished and flourished, this time as a coeducational school. (Courtesy of North Carolina Archives.)

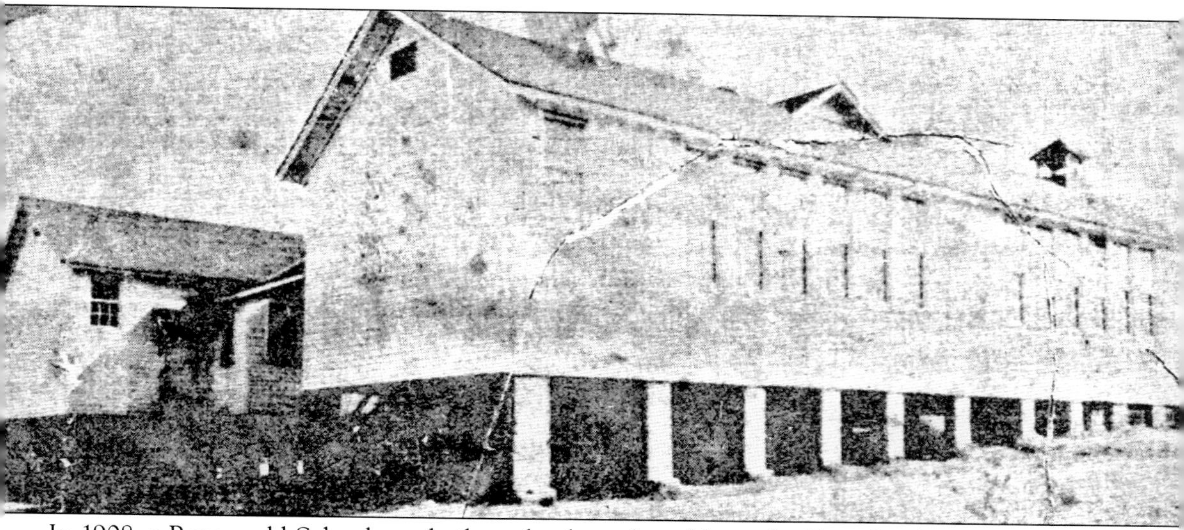

In 1908, a Rosenwald School was built on land purchased from the Earp family on the east side of what was then the old Fuquay Road. Known in the community as the "Plank School," it featured four classrooms and an auditorium that served as classrooms for the sixth and seventh grades. The school was heated by coal-burning heaters in each room, and students were sent to the woods to get light wood to start fires and were charged with filling coal scuttles to keep the fires burning. When it was torn down and rebuilt in 1923, classes were held in the Christian and Baptist churches during this renovation period. In 1951, at this same location, a modern brick structure was built, with additions in 1959. The building now serves as the town community center. The town named the center in honor of William E. Hunt, who served as a teacher at the school in 1943 and 1944 and as principal from 1945 until his death in 1959. Hunt, the beloved principal, who was known as a strict disciplinarian but also as a kind man, was ever interested in his school, his students, and the community. (Courtesy of Cora Lassiter.)

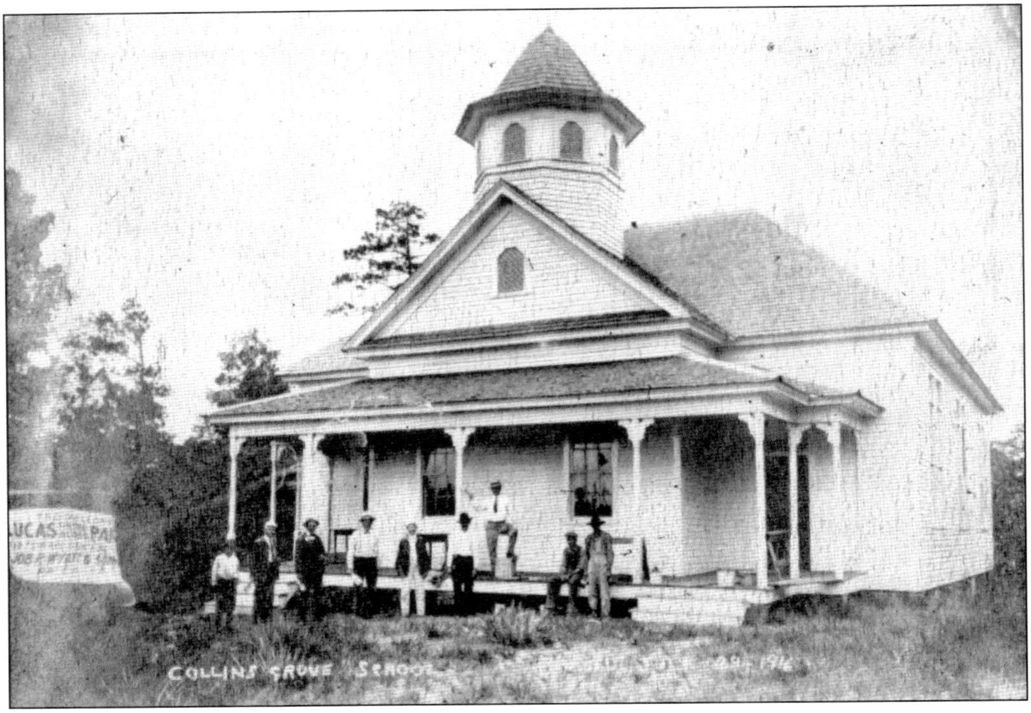


Shown above in a 1916 photograph, the Collins Grove School was one of the institutes of learning established in the early 1900s in the rural areas known as Collins and Holleman's Crossroads. (Both, courtesy of North Carolina Archives.)

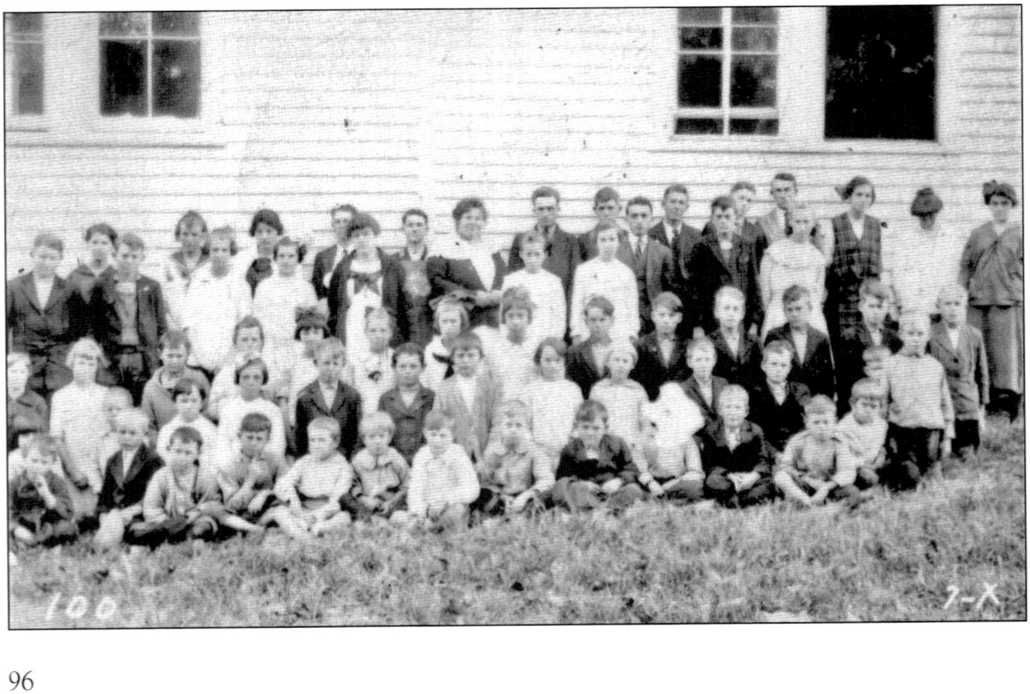

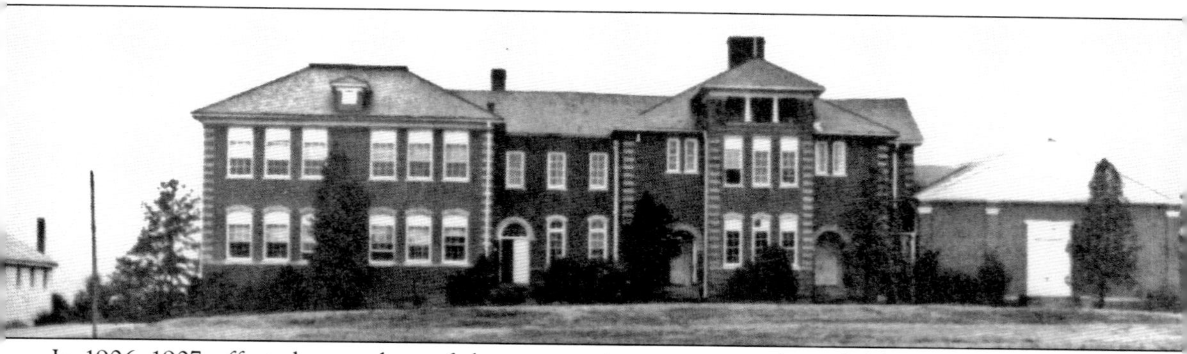

In 1906–1907, efforts by members of the community to improve their children's educational facilities were initiated. Ten acres of land were purchased near the springs. Four acres were planted with cotton, which was cultivated and harvested by the Holly Springs Woman's Betterment Association. These efforts among other fund-raisers won the group first prize from the county association, which was canvassing the county in an effort to secure a location for a high school. In 1908, the bell rang for Holly Springs' first public school, offering grades 1 through 11 for white children only. By 1914, an enlargement was made to accommodate the students wishing to attend this highly ranked school. The last graduating class was in 1946, after which grades 9 through 12 were bussed into Apex or Fuquay Springs. There was a detached gymnasium on the school campus where the children of the community recall roller-skating on Saturday afternoons. Their parents enjoyed attending lively square dances in the evening. Closed because of consolidation in 1958, the building was razed in 1978. (Sylvian Brooks collection.)

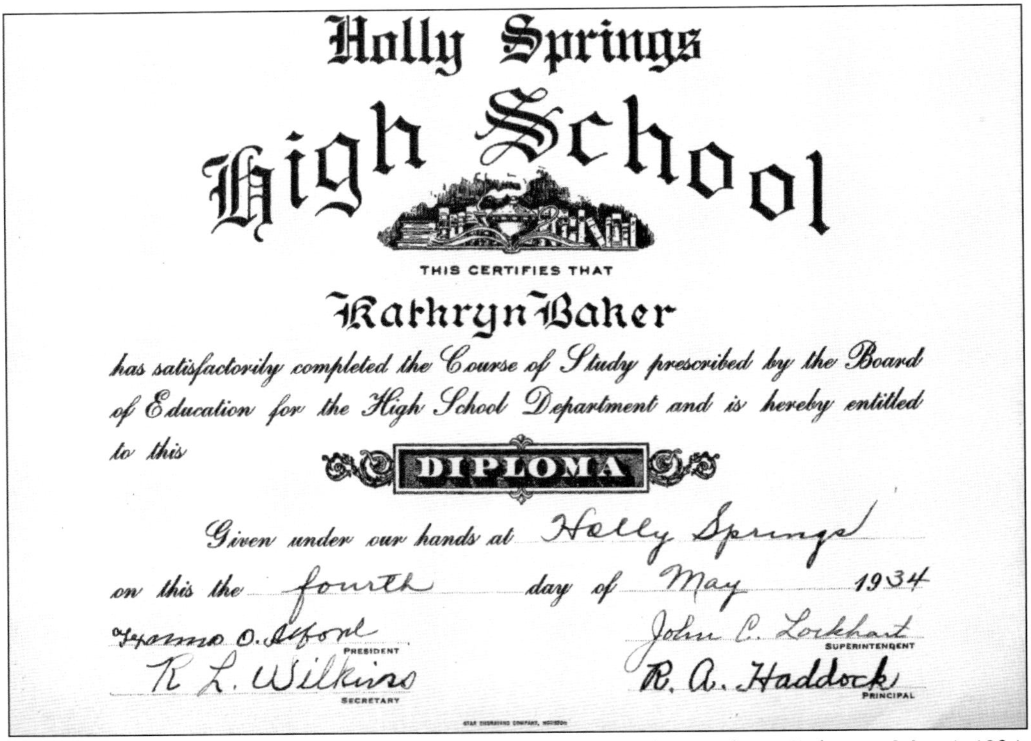

Holly Springs

High School

THIS CERTIFIES THAT

Kathryn Baker

*has satisfactorily completed the Course of Study prescribed by the Board of Education for the High School Department and is hereby entitled to this*

DIPLOMA

*Given under our hands at* Holly Springs

*on this the* fourth *day of* May 1934

Thomas O. Alford PRESIDENT John C. Lockhart SUPERINTENDENT

R. L. Wilkins SECRETARY R. A. Haddock PRINCIPAL

This diploma from Holly Springs High School was presented to Kathryn Baker on May 4, 1934, for her successful completion in the "Course of Study presented by the Board of Education." (Vada Fiegler collection.)

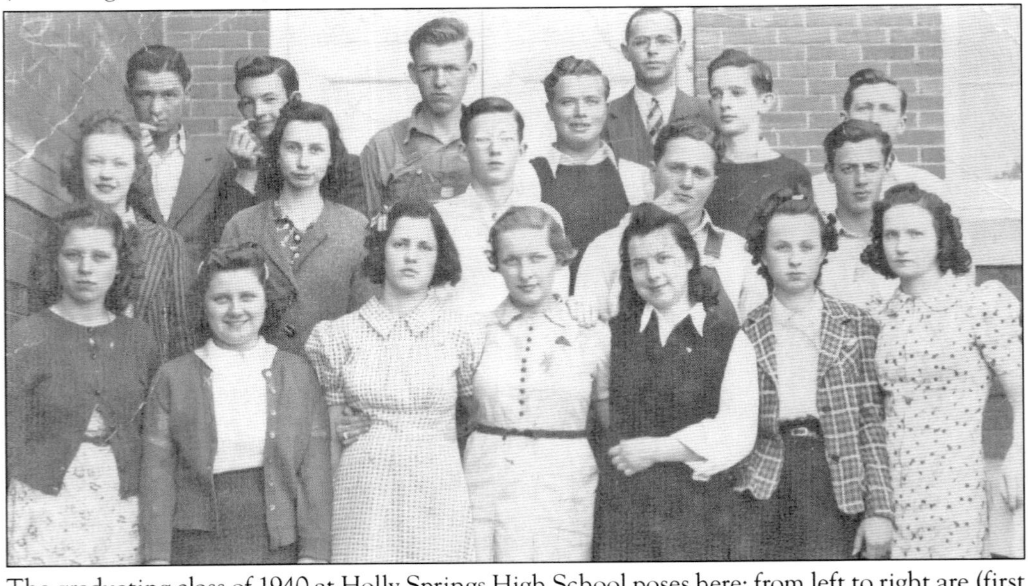

The graduating class of 1940 at Holly Springs High School poses here; from left to right are (first row) Agnes Slade, Alma Lee Bell, Ruby White, Sue Haley, Reba Matthews, Emma-Jean Matthews, and Arlie Holt; (second row) Mary Hare, Lydia Ragan, Jack Adams, Matthew Olen, and James Tutor; (third row) Coley Wilson, Stanley Goodwin, Howard Johnson, Carlyle Dean, George Cullipher (principal), Roy Collins, and Charles Cross. (Mary Macon collection.)

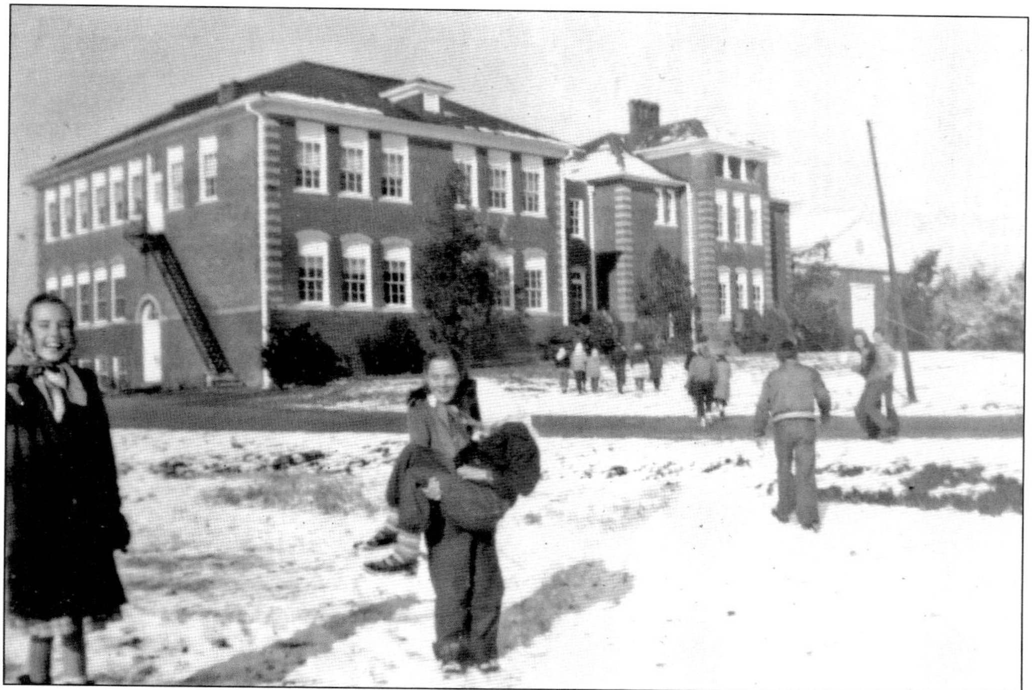

It's snowing in Holly Springs. These 1940s schoolchildren are surely making plans to meet after school to go sledding on Arbutus Hill, which was known to both young and old alike as the best snow sledding hill in town. (Sylvian Brooks collection.)

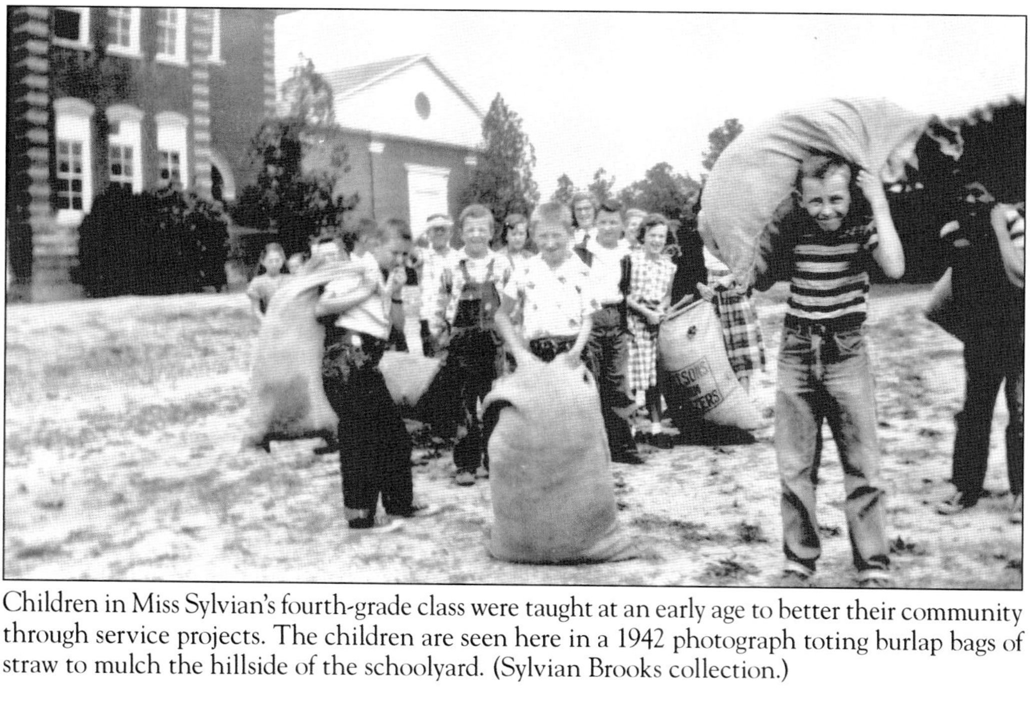

Children in Miss Sylvian's fourth-grade class were taught at an early age to better their community through service projects. The children are seen here in a 1942 photograph toting burlap bags of straw to mulch the hillside of the schoolyard. (Sylvian Brooks collection.)

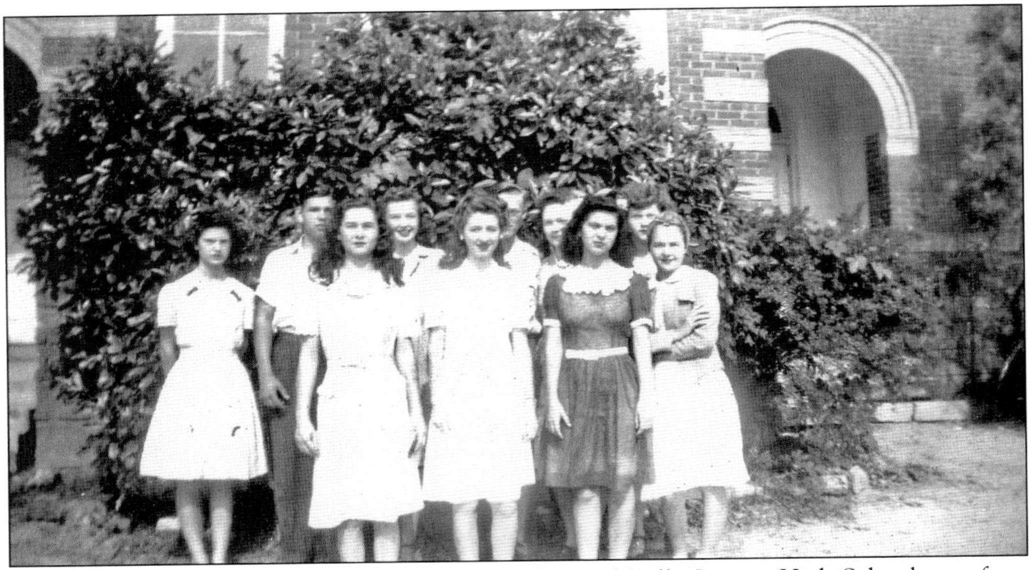

Having just completed the 10th grade, these students of Holly Springs High School pose for a picture on May 30, 1945. This class was the first to go to Apex High School to complete the 12th grade and graduate. Standing on the lawn are, from left to right, Pauline Whittington, Floyd Jones, Jean Hare, Martha Hare, Margaret Judd, Grover Honeycutt, Carolyn Hall, Gladys Whittington, Emma-Jean Nash, and Rubelle Campbell. (Nathan and Carolyn Williams collection.)

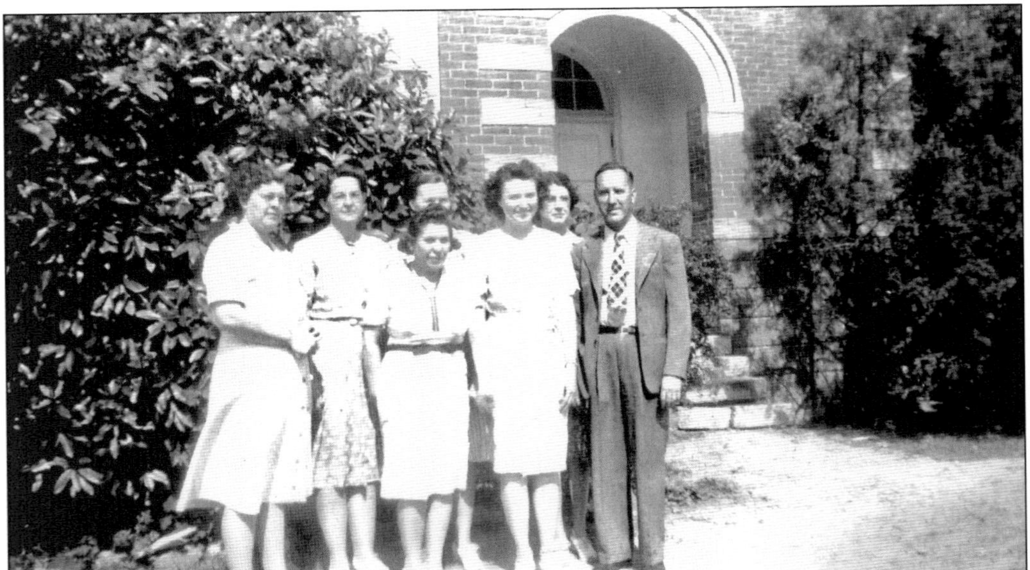

The teachers and principal of the Holly Springs High School pose for an end-of-year snapshot on May 30, 1945. Ready for the summer are, from left to right, teachers Lillian Hare, Mrs. George Rogers, Pearl Oldham, Ruth Walls, Katie Ragan, Margaret Wright, and principal Roy Shirlen. (Nathan and Carolyn Williams collection.)

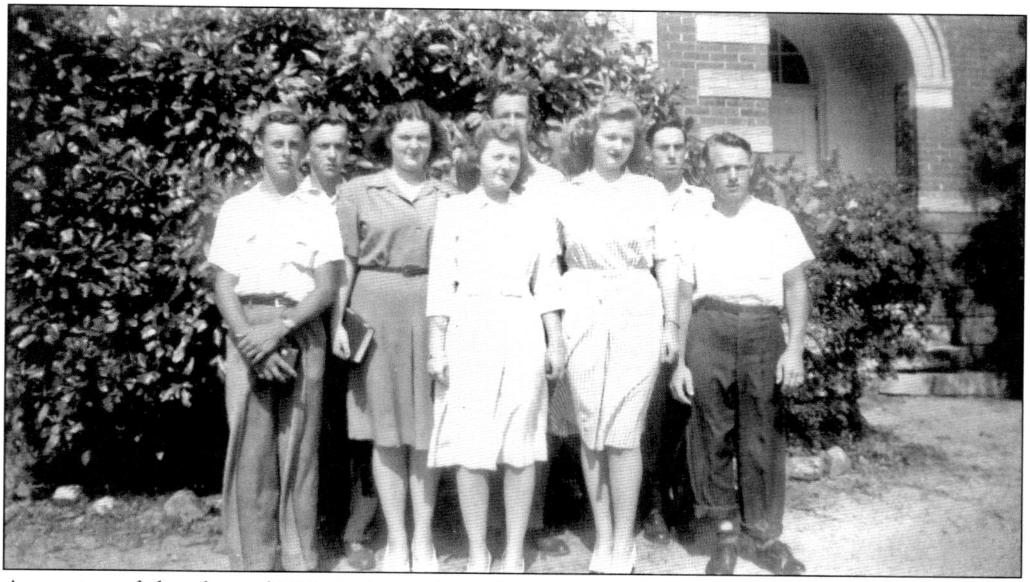

A portion of the class of 1945 is shown in a photograph taken on May 30, 1945. The students pictured here and the remainder of their classmates were the last class to graduate from this school. Standing here on the lawn are, from left to right, Billy Beaver, Truby Holt, Dorothy "Dot" Shaw, Dorothy "Dot" Brewer, Dewey Wade Johnson, Joyce Holleman, Bill Jones, and Leon Holt. (Nathan and Carolyn Williams collection.)

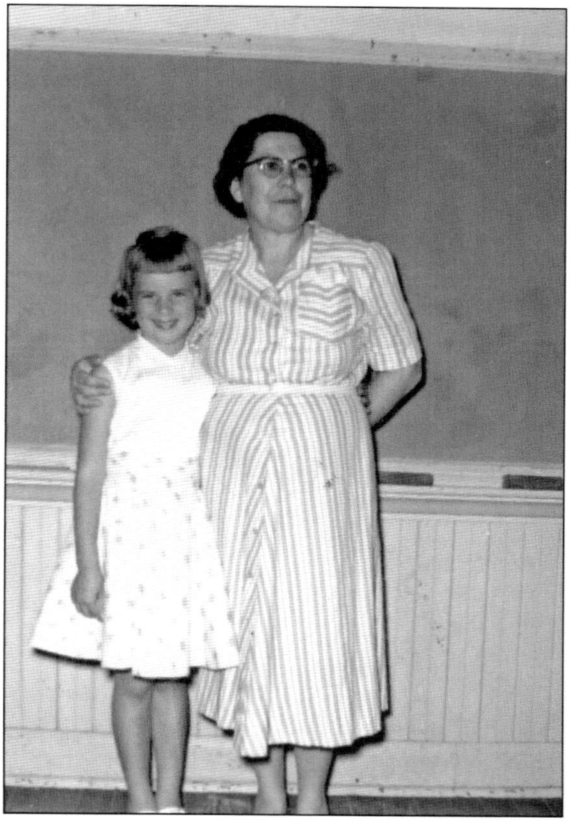

Jewell Dewar, the daughter of Bremen and Evelyn (Betts) Dewar, is shown here with one of her favorite teachers, Pearl Oldham-Jones, in June 1958. (Bremen and Evelyn Dewar collection.)

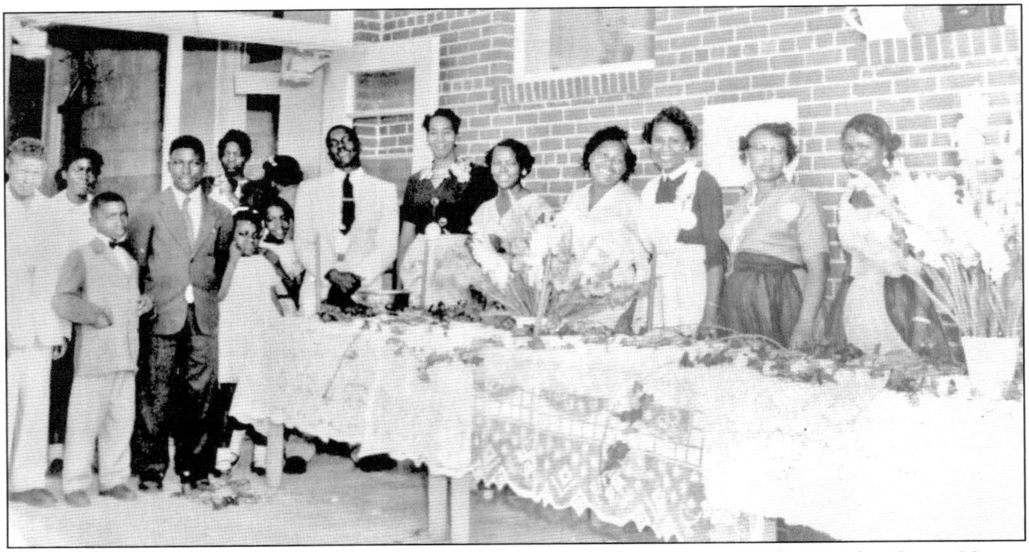

Students of Holly Springs School and their parents pose for a picture taken at the Open House Celebration in 1959. The school now featured a combination gymnasium/auditorium and modern kitchen with a sunny cafeteria. In the breezeway are, from left to right, unidentified, Flora (Kimble) Hawkins, George Kimble, Willie Kimble, Shirley (Beckwith) Woodard, Betty (Merritt) Lawrence, Catherine Robinson, McKiney Norris, Alechia Betts, Cora Mae Lassiter, Essie Jones, Annie (Jones) Beard, Elnora (Dewar) Robinson, and Dora (Beckwith) Jones. (Courtesy of Cora Lassiter.)

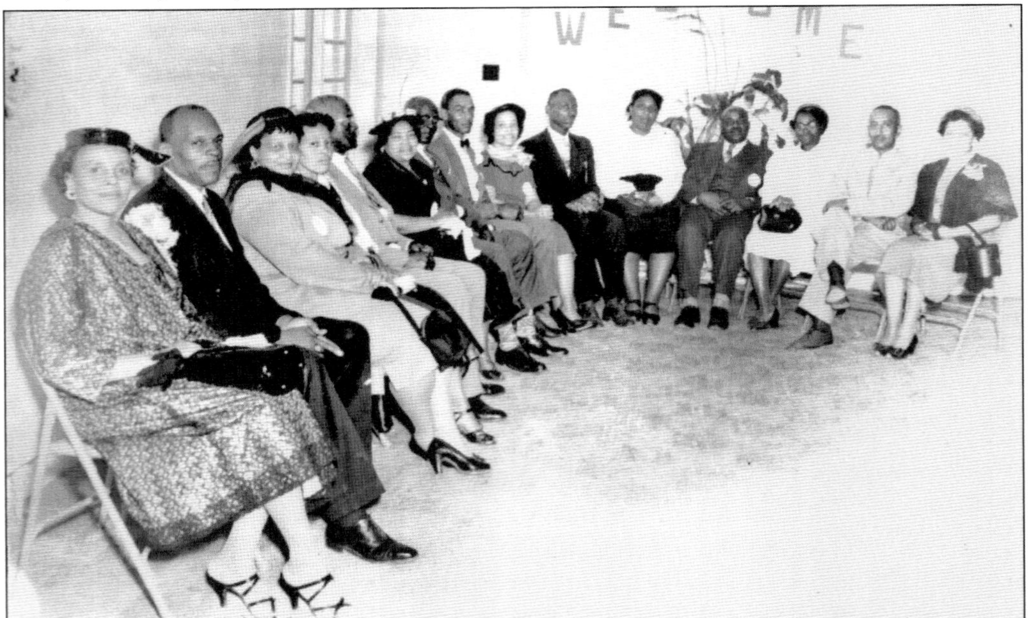

Parents, dignitaries, and local ministers are on hand at the open house of the newly constructed section of the Holly Springs School in 1959. Seated at the reception are, from left to right, Gladys (Stinson) Grigsby, William E. Hunt (principal), Carol Hunt, Emma Womble, Lattie Rogers, Dala Rogers, Dial Atkins, Ernest Betts, Georgia Betts, Rev. Jasper Johnson, Christine Johnson, Rev. James Merritt, Coretta Merritt, and teachers N. E. Toole and Mrs. Young. (Courtesy of Cora Lassiter.)

*Five*

# If Walls Could Talk

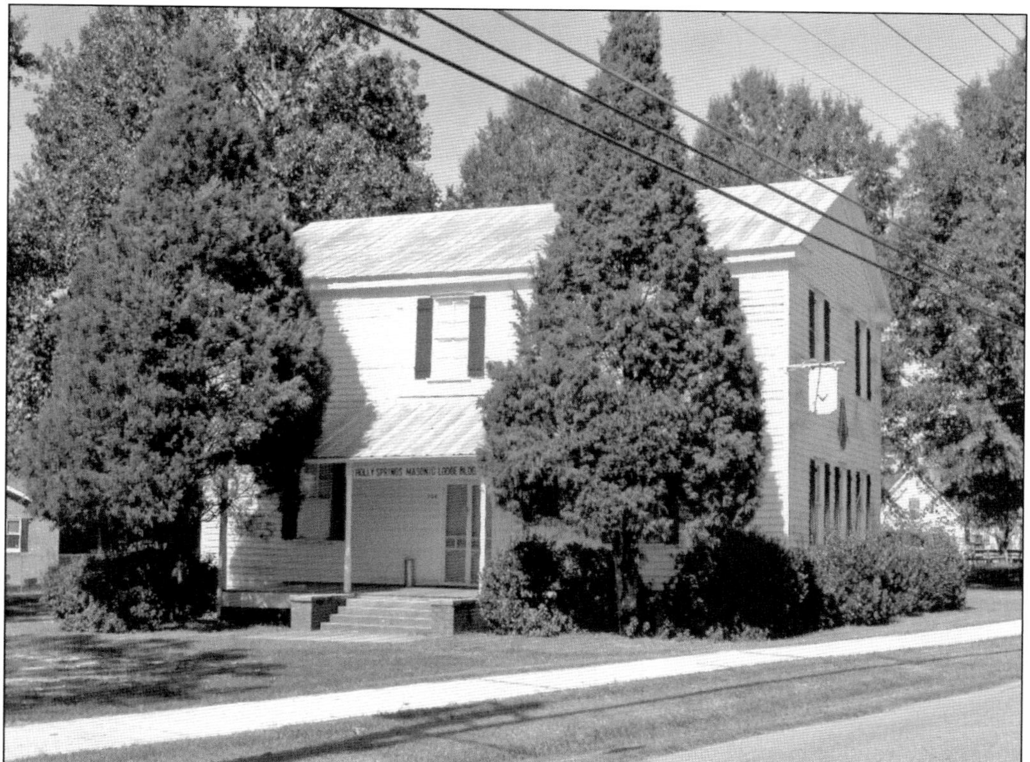


The Holly Springs Masonic Lodge No. 115 was organized and chartered in 1847, and the lodge building was constructed soon after. The Masons were active in the community, as evidenced by the number of dedicated cornerstones on buildings, which include the lodge itself, the Holly Springs United Methodist Church, and the Alford-Lashley-Dewar Store. The lodge is thought to be the oldest lodge and school building in Wake County. (Town Historical collection.)

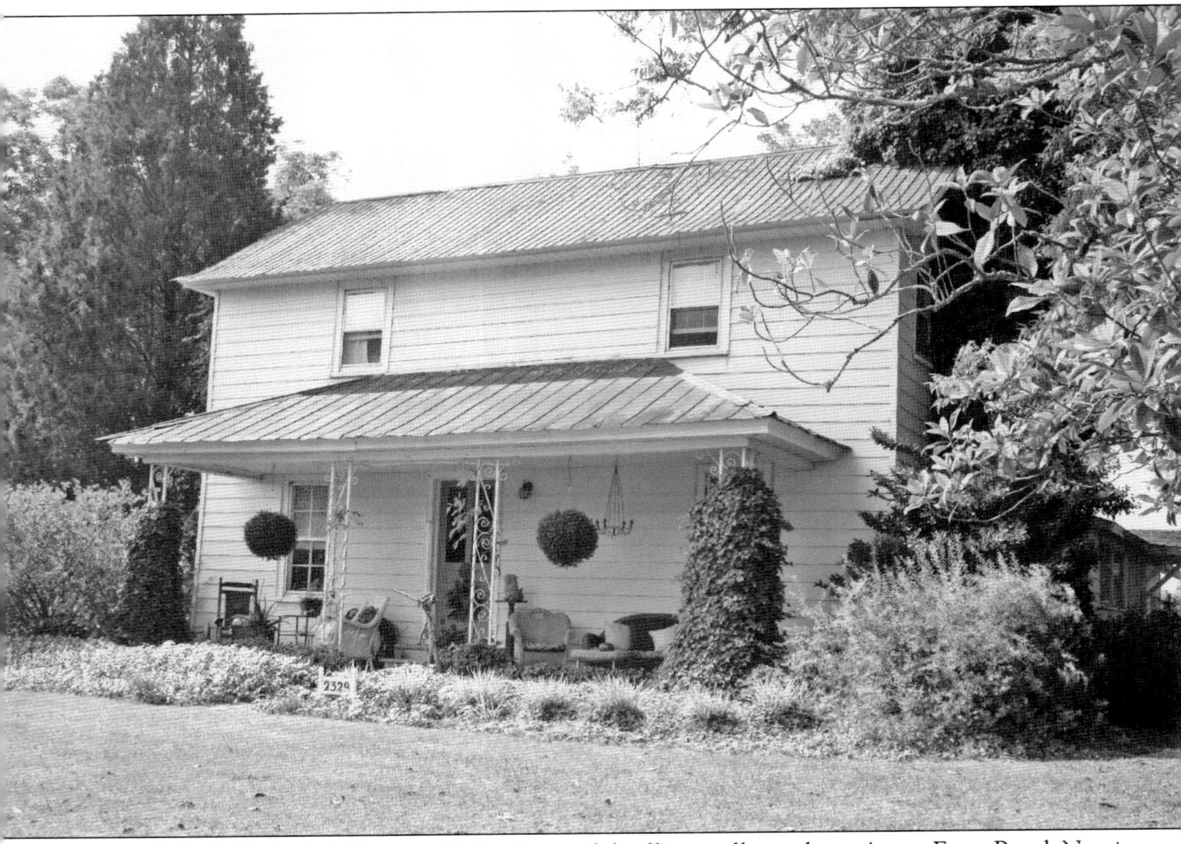

The Needham Norris House, a Federal-period dwelling, still stands on Avent Ferry Road. Norris was the son of Revolutionary War veteran John Norris Jr., whose service in that conflict is memorialized with a roadside marker nearby. Norris bequeathed his homestead and farm to nephew Simpson Washington Holland. Holland and his wife, Mary-Ann, continued to farm and rear their six children there until the events of the Civil War changed their lives. In September 1864, Holland left just one week after the birth of his youngest child to travel to Virginia in a quest to check on the welfare of his enlisted brother. Holland died in November 1864 while in Virginia. For a two-week period in April 1865, the Holland farm was encircled by the encampment area of soldiers from the 14th Union Corps. Mary-Ann and her children lived in the upper portion of the house while the lower floor was used as a field hospital. The house and surrounding farm remained in the Norris-Holland family until 2004. (Town Historical collection.)

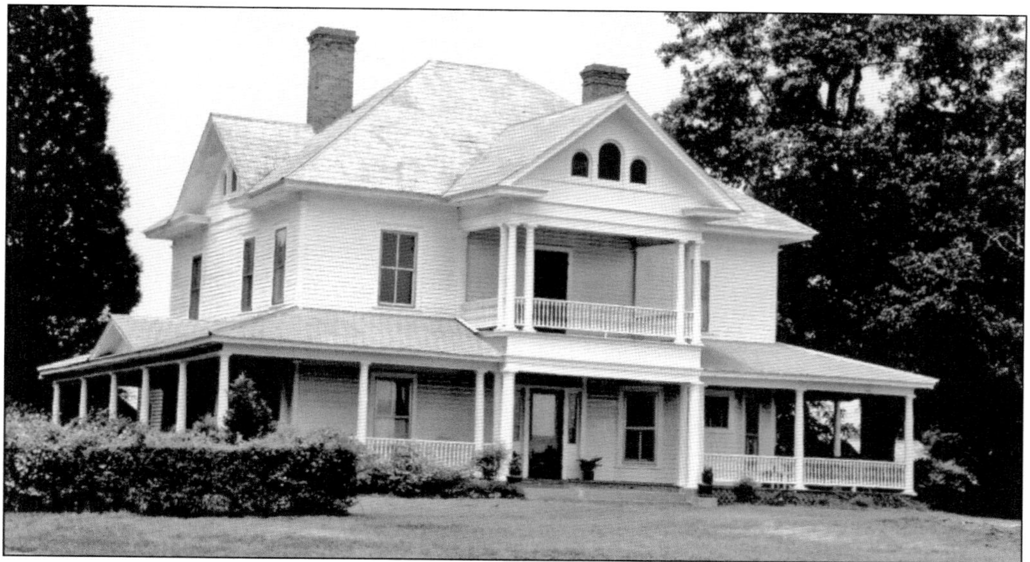

This home, known as the Samuel Bartley Holleman House and listed on the National Register of Historic Places, was built in the late 1890s in the area known first as Collins and later Enno before receiving its current name, Holleman's Crossroads. Around the beginning of the 20th century, the community supported several stores, including Samuel Holleman's cotton gin and store; the Enno Post Office, which was used 1881–1907; a school; and two churches, Bethel Christian and Collins Grove Baptist. (Town Historical collection.)

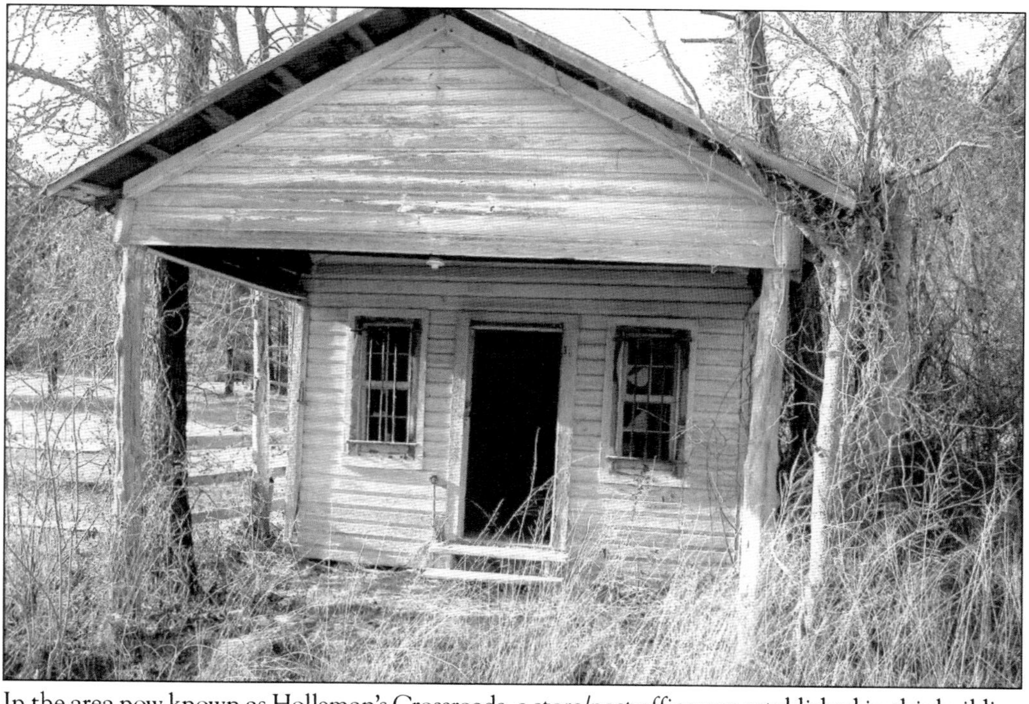

In the area now known as Holleman's Crossroads, a store/post office was established in this building in 1881. The area was first known as Collins, but shortly after, the name was changed to Enno, and it was referred to as this name until the post office was discontinued in 1907. (Courtesy of North Carolina Archives.)

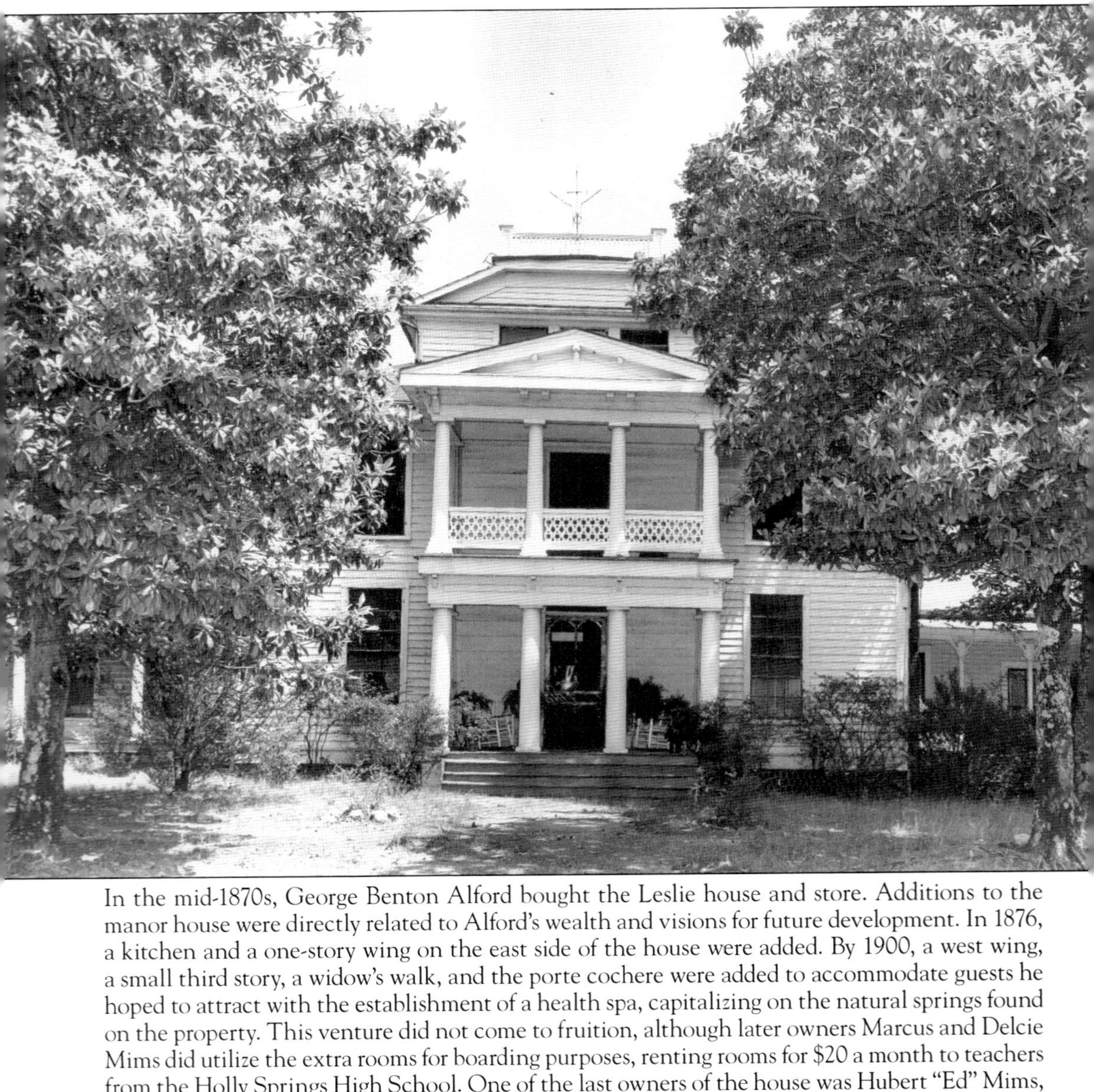

In the mid-1870s, George Benton Alford bought the Leslie house and store. Additions to the manor house were directly related to Alford's wealth and visions for future development. In 1876, a kitchen and a one-story wing on the east side of the house were added. By 1900, a west wing, a small third story, a widow's walk, and the porte cochere were added to accommodate guests he hoped to attract with the establishment of a health spa, capitalizing on the natural springs found on the property. This venture did not come to fruition, although later owners Marcus and Delcie Mims did utilize the extra rooms for boarding purposes, renting rooms for $20 a month to teachers from the Holly Springs High School. One of the last owners of the house was Hubert "Ed" Mims, who worked diligently to assist in the placement of this home, a true example of the grandeur of the Old South, on the National Register of Historic Places. (Wright collection.)

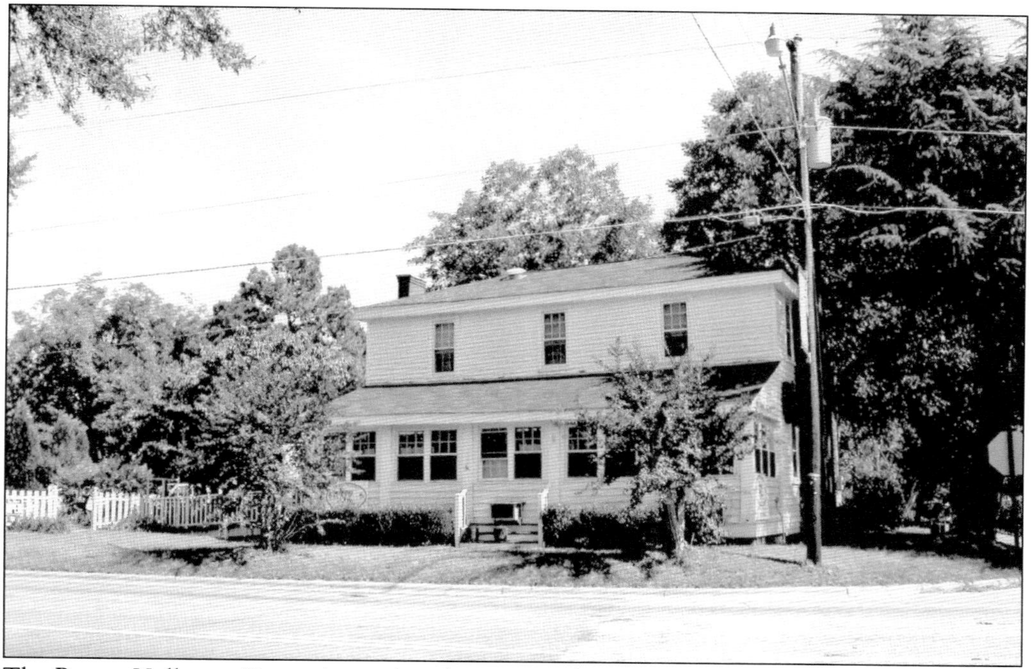

The Brown-Holloway House, located at the corner of Earp and Main Streets, was built around the 1840s by Dr. Brown, a physician in the New Hill area. In later years, the back room served as the post office, with the mail being passed out of a back window to residents. The front porch has been enclosed; however, other than that one alteration, the historical integrity of the home has remained the same. (Town Historical collection.)

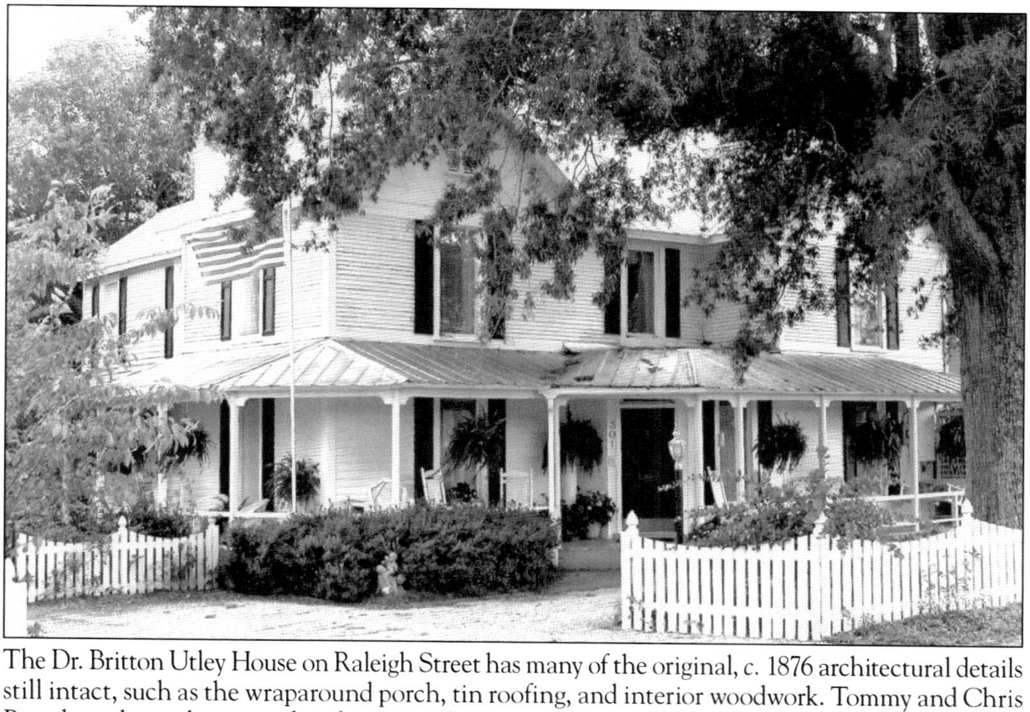

The Dr. Britton Utley House on Raleigh Street has many of the original, *c.* 1876 architectural details still intact, such as the wraparound porch, tin roofing, and interior woodwork. Tommy and Chris Pope have lovingly restored and preserved this stately home. (Town Historical collection.)

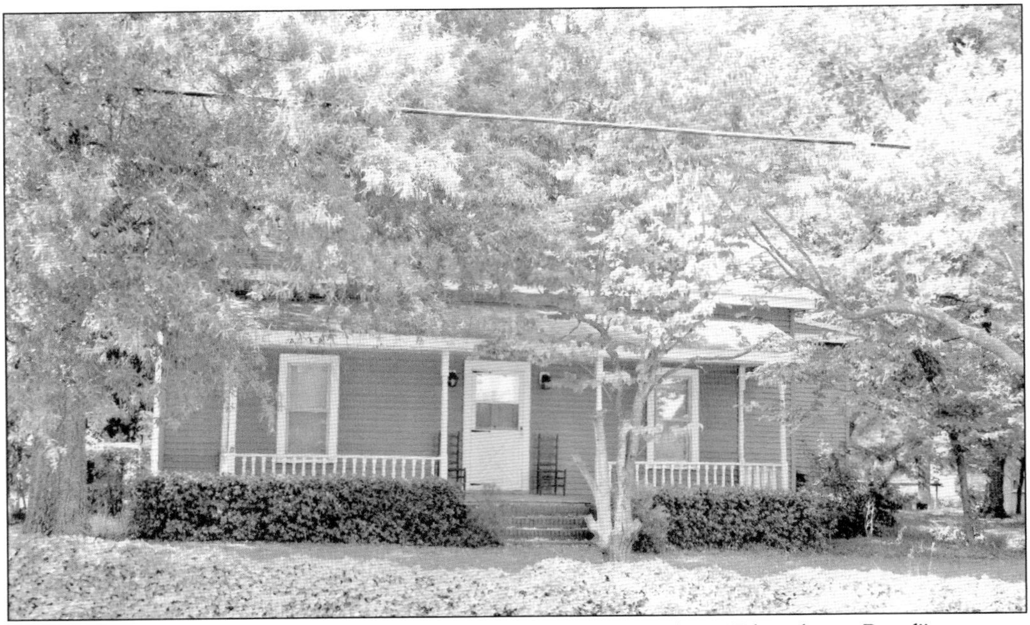

The Sebastian Scholl House is located on Holly Springs Road, or "Rhamkatte Road" as it was commonly referred to by the locals. St. Mary's Catholic Church was built in the early 1900s and sat next door on the corner of Raleigh Street and Rhamkatte Road. Sebastian Scholl's oldest son, William, was St. Mary's Catholic Church's first altar boy. (Town Historical collection.)

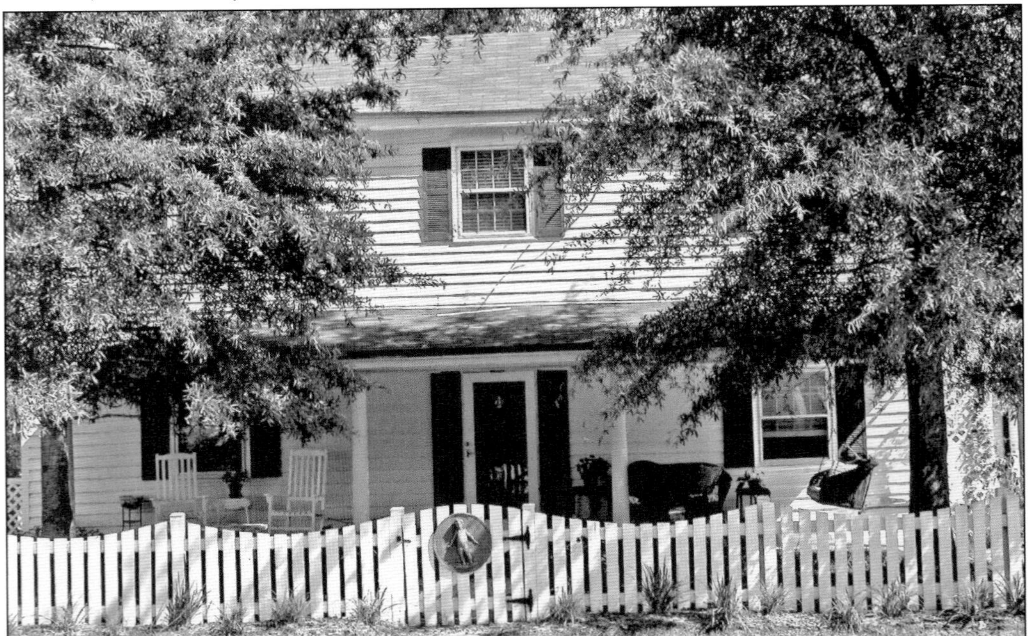

Built in 1899 by Peyton Norris, the Norris-Cross House on Raleigh Street was a popular boardinghouse for students attending the Holly Springs Academy, which was first housed in the Masonic Lodge directly across the street. The house retains its original staircase, plaster walls, woodwork, and functional hand-drawn well. The house is currently owned by Betty Deese. (Town Historical collection.)

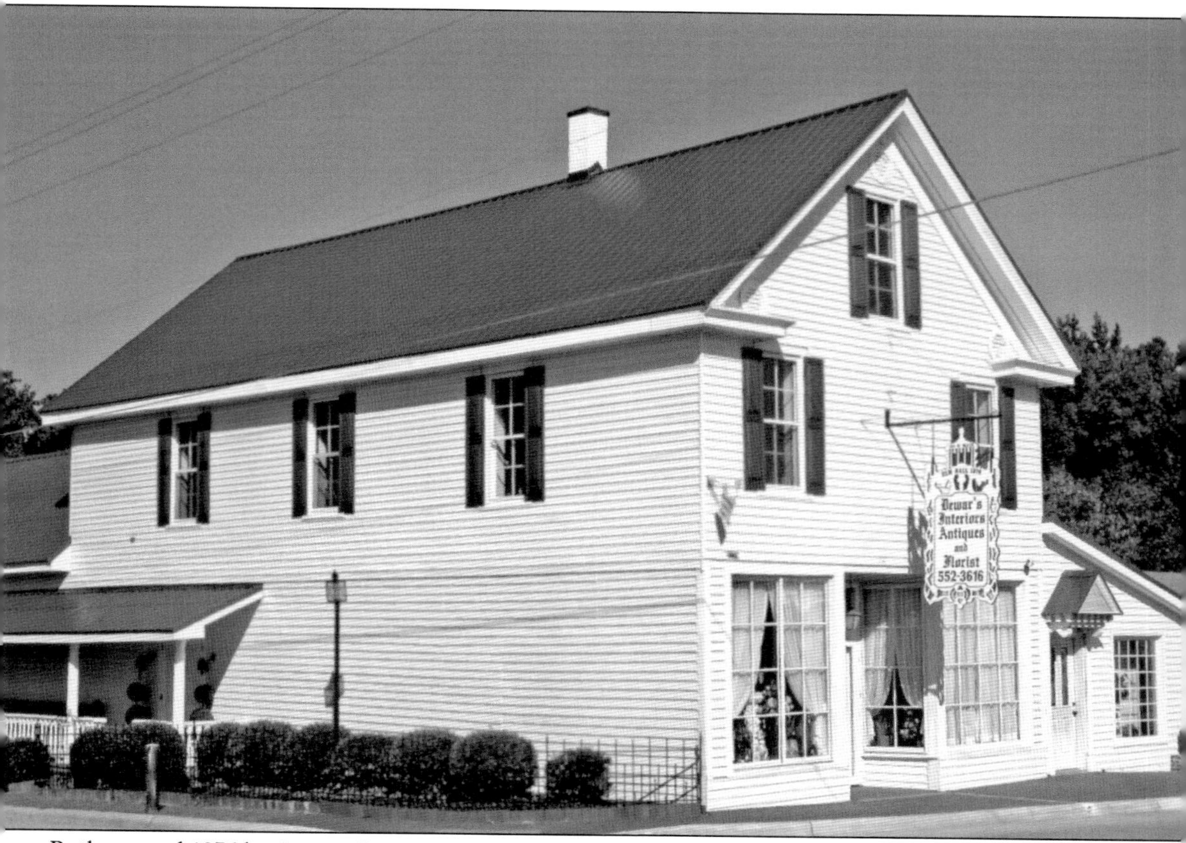


Built around 1876 by George Benton Alford, this general store located on Main Street also was a social gathering place for farmers to discuss crops or the weather or just play a game of checkers. After Alford's death in 1924, the store was acquired and run by Tom Lashley, or "Uncle Tommy" as he was known in the community. Lashley had a hoop cheese box filled with sand that was used as a spittoon. Near it was a sign that read, "If you spit on the floor at home, spit on it here; we want you to feel at home." By the early 1960s, new owner Rufus T. Bell used the store as a warehouse/office for his business, Bell's Heating and Sheet-Metal Shop. The building was in a sad state of disrepair when brothers Bobby and Larry Dewar acquired it in the mid-1970s. Lovingly restored, this building now is an antiques and floral shop. It is one of the oldest commercial buildings in Wake County. (Town Historical collection.)

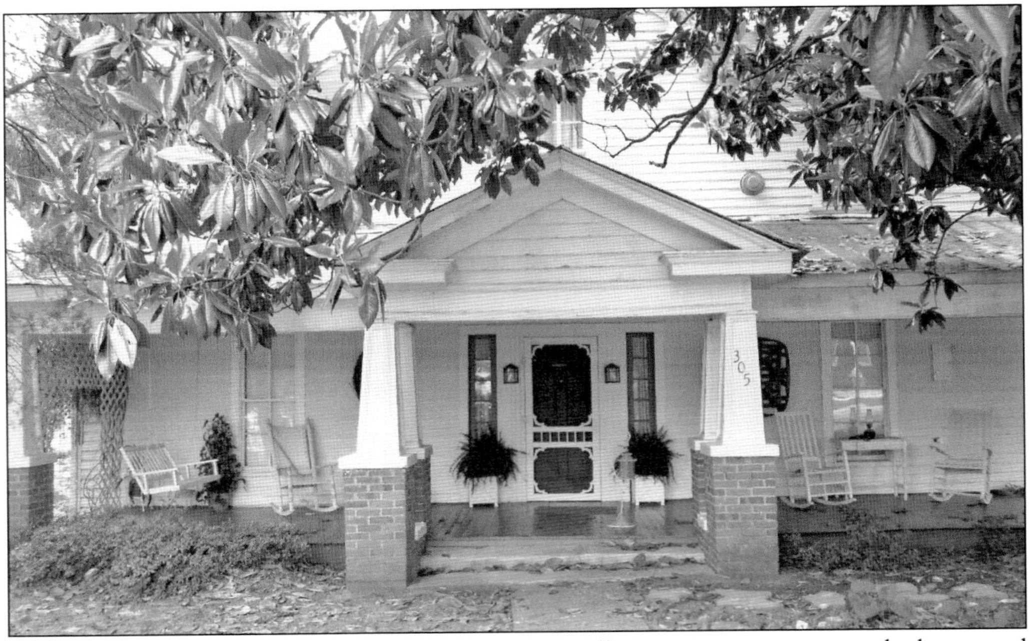


The Wood-Burt House on Raleigh Street was originally a one-story cottage with the second story added later. This once was the residence of Dr. Benjamin W. Burt. Current owners Kenny and Druscie Simpson enjoy the home, which retains its original transom window over the front door, heart-of-pine floors, four fireplaces, and bead-board ceilings on the second floor. (Town Historical collection.)

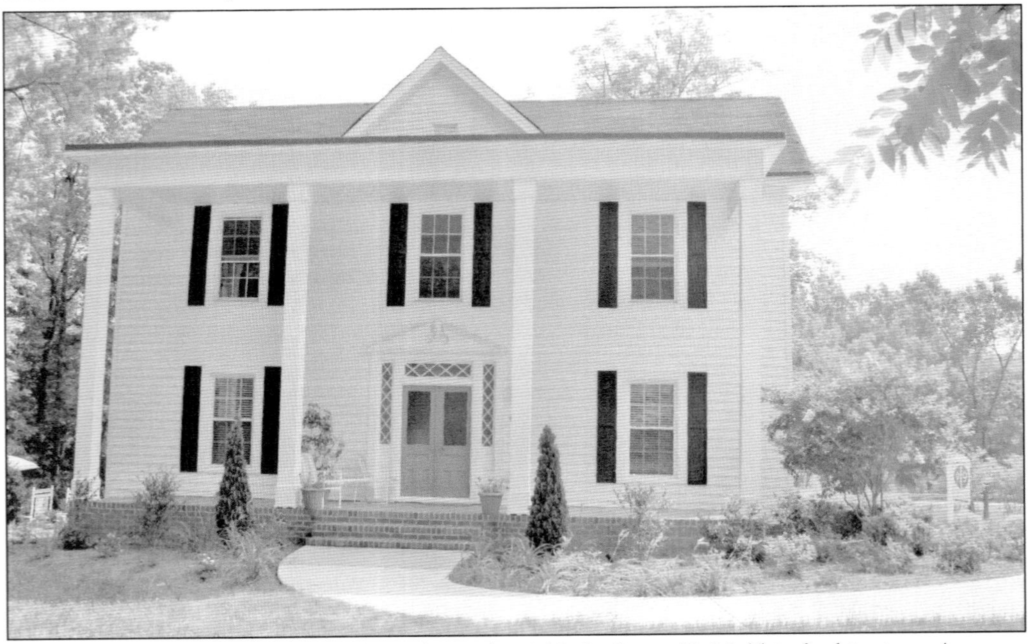

The Utley-Wright House was built in the early 1900s by Jason D. Hobbie for his sister Annette Utley. The present porch and columns were added later. Moved from Raleigh Street to make way for the Village Office Condos, the Utley-Wright House was relocated to its new site behind the Leslie-Alford-Mims House. (Town Historical collection.)

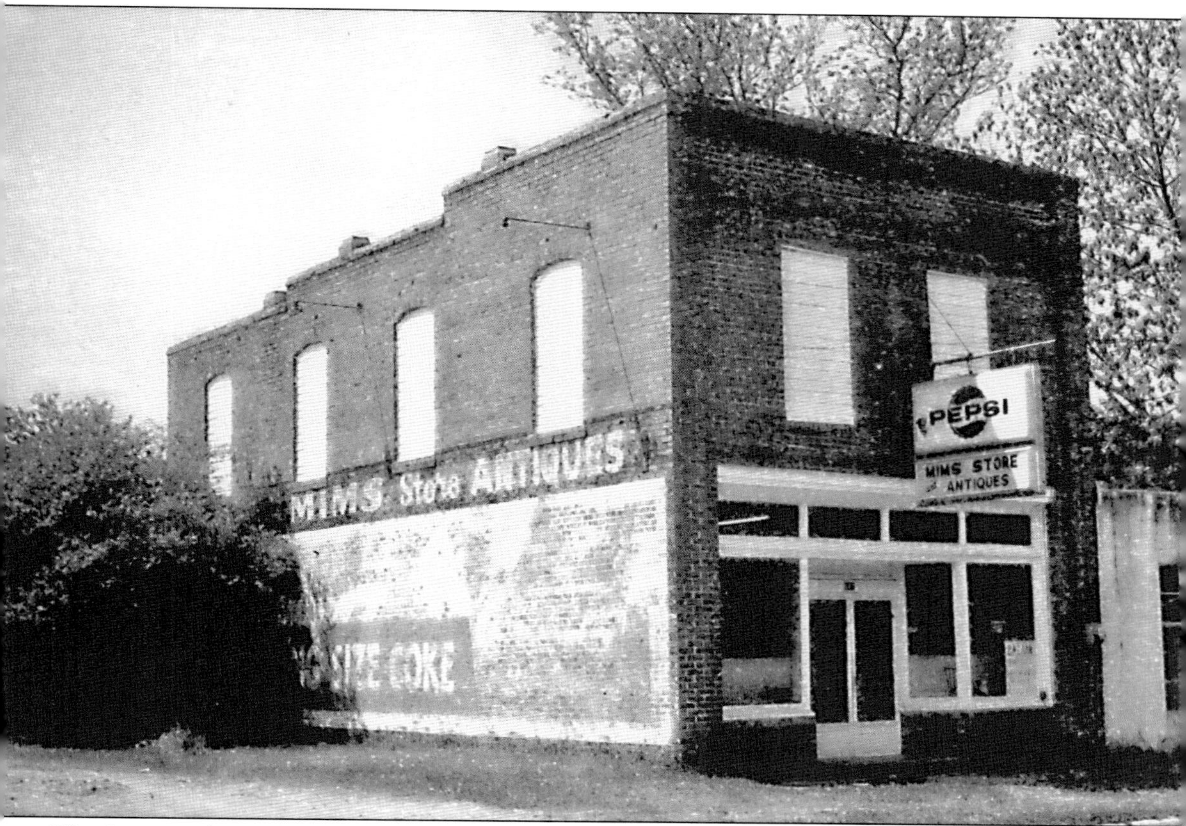


This business located at the corner of Avent Ferry Road and Center Street was known as the "Drug Store." Owned by William Lonnie "Father" Price, W. L. Price Manufacturing made most anything out of wood, its wares ranging from tobacco slides to caskets. Price's son-in-law, William Cecil Shaw, served as the druggist in the drugstore. Shaw, or "Shaw Boy" as he was referred to in the community, was beloved by all as a caring and compassionate man. Dr. Benjamin W. Burt had a small general practice that he ran from the second floor. In later years, the building was acquired by Ivan "Ike" Mims, who added general merchandise to the inventory. A soda fountain in the shop offered ice-cream sodas and was most definitely a favorite place on a hot summer day for many a Holly Springs youngster. At one point, in the small cinderblock building that abutted the drugstore, a hardware-type store was established as well as a post office for a short period of time. The last occupant was Hubert "Ed" Mims, brother of Ivan, who ran an antique shop until the building was razed in 2002 to make way for the Mims Towne Square. (Wright collection.)

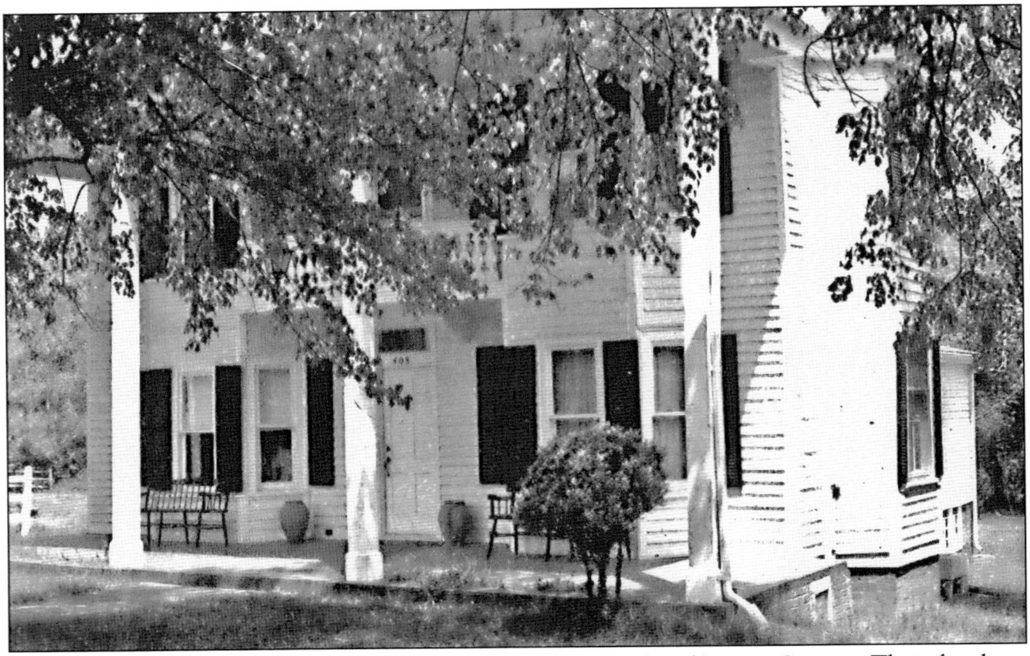

The Stinson-Grigsby House was the home of Alberta (McLean) and Lonnie Stinson. Their daughter, Gladys Natal, married George Talmadge Grigsby Sr., who was a professor and administrator for St. Paul's School in Lawrenceville, Virginia. The Grigsbys added the columns on the front porch and other alterations to the exterior. A wooden pole used to hitch horses is still located in the front yard of the home. (Town Historical collection.)

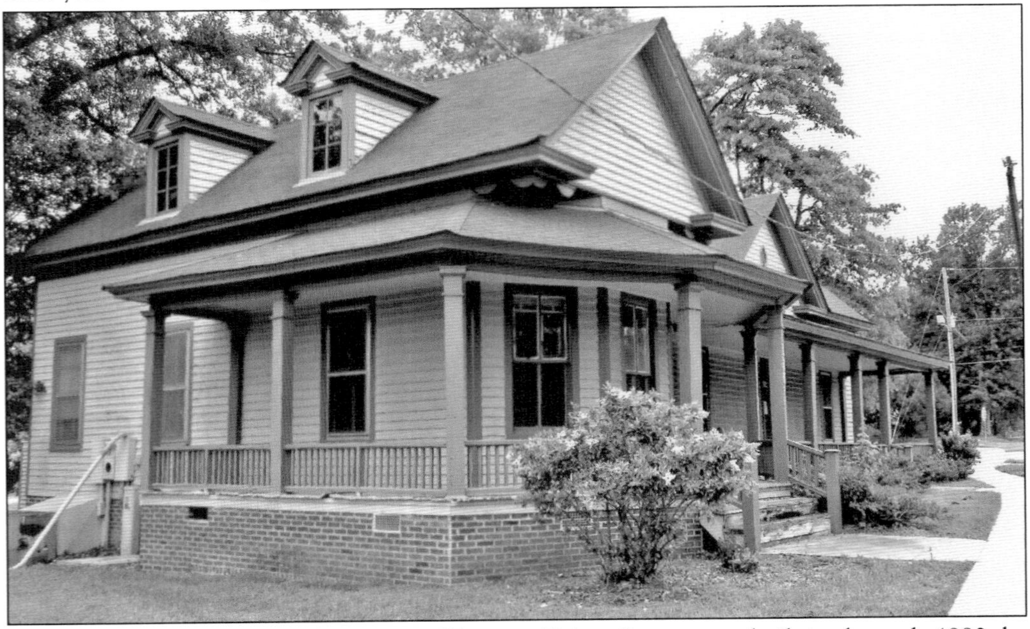

The Holt House, located at the corner of Earp and Main Streets, was built in the early 1880s by Thomas Benton Holt, who moved his mercantile business to the area at the urging of his good friend George Alford. The house remained in the family until sold to the town in the mid-1980s; it was used as the municipal offices and then the public safety office. (Town Historical collection.)

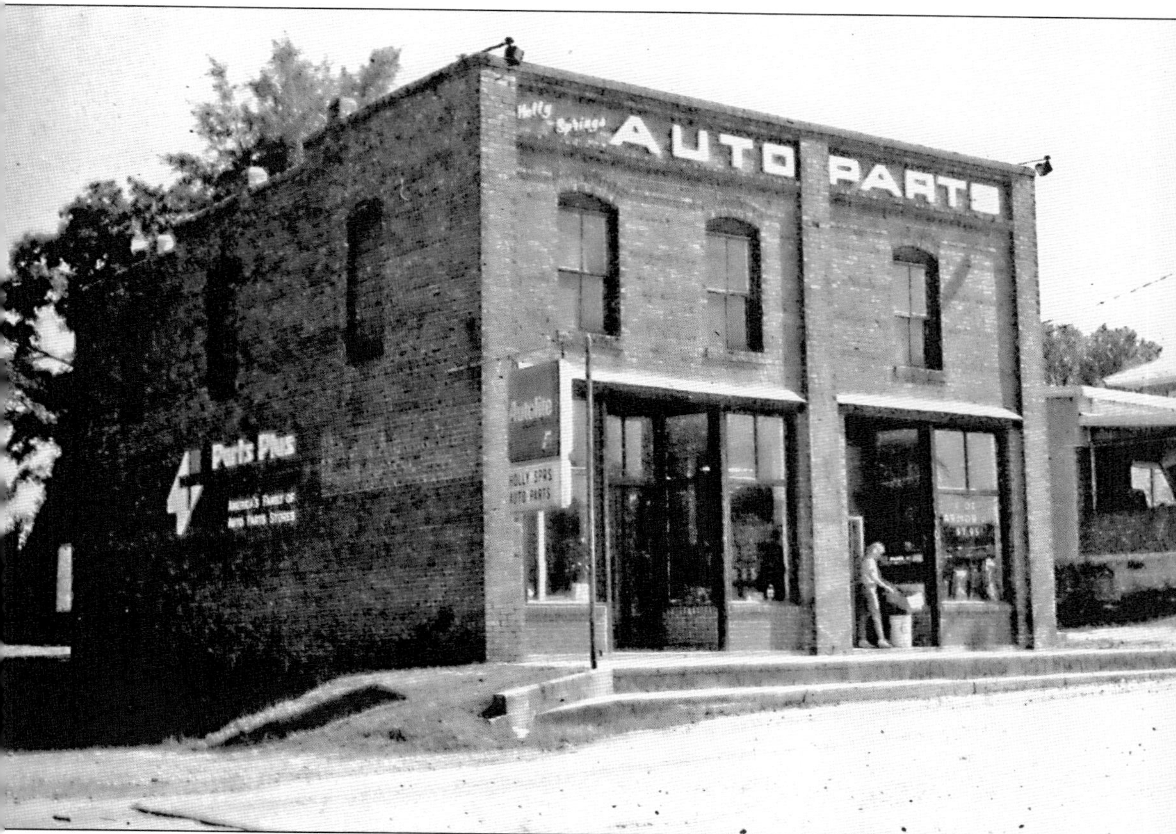


If the walls of the current police station could talk, they would tell a century's worth of stories. The building first saw service to the community as Seagraves Drug Store, run by Johnny and Mary Seagraves as a drug and sundries store, a post office for a short time, and a temporary train station. By 1946, the latest fashions from New York could be viewed there when Irma Gattman ran a dress/millinery shop in one half of the store as Claire and Sylvian Brooks ran a grocery store in the other half of the building. The building continued to serve the community, as Ernie Brewer ran a mercantile business in this building until failing health caused him to turn over his store to his brother Elmer and his sister-in-law Cleo in the mid-1960s. The last occupant was the Holly Springs Auto Parts store, run by Thad Tunstall from 1980 to 2000, prior to the acquisition by the town. The walls cannot talk. They do however, still stand, thanks to a careful, painstaking preservation project by the town to save the building. (Town Historical collection.)

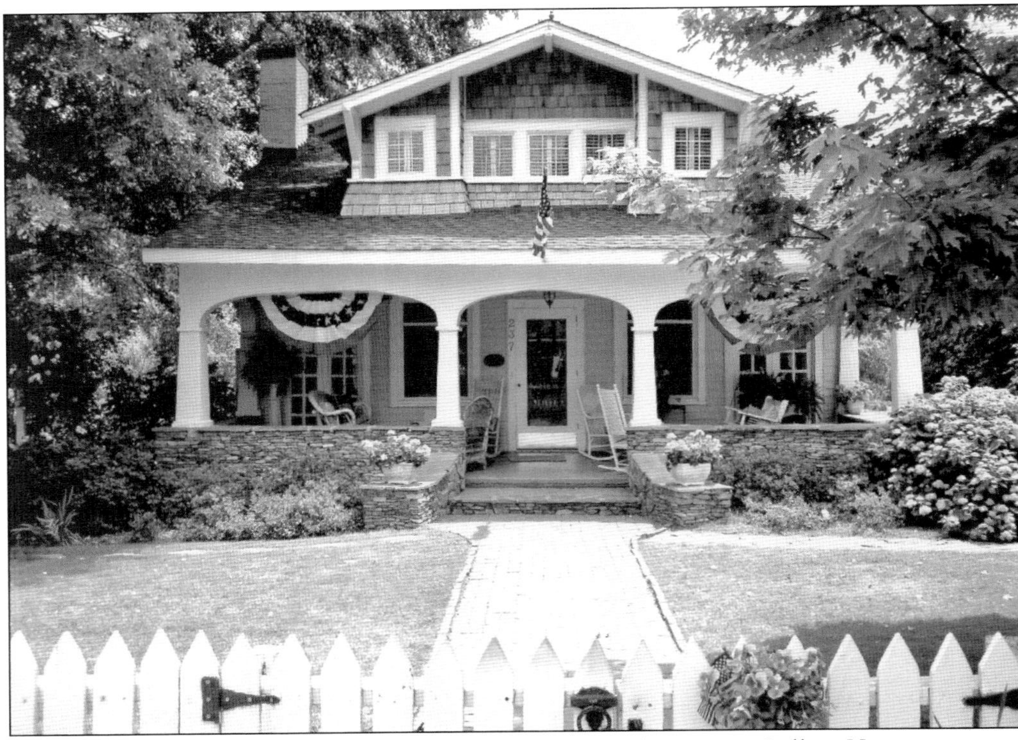

Commonly referred to as a "Sears and Roebuck House," the Martin Collins House came as a do-it-yourself kit, put together by an adventuresome homeowner in 1917. This Craftsman-style bungalow on Raleigh Street, currently the home of Stanley and Tina Rimmer, is one of the most photographed homes in the area with its extensive flower gardens and landscaping. (Town Historical collection.)

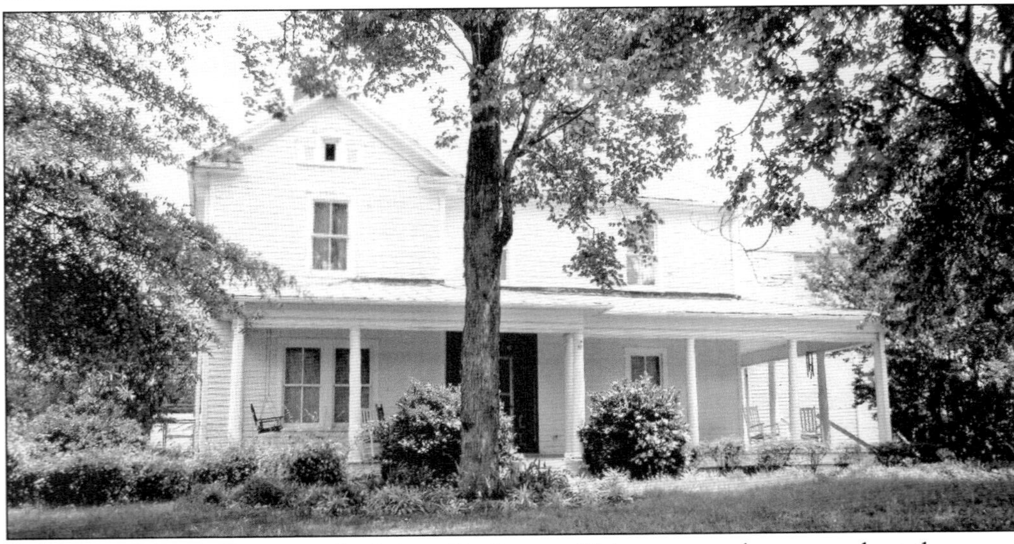

The Bryant-Brewer House was built by a Dr. Bryant. This two-story home stands at the corner of Grigsby Avenue and Raleigh Street. Later owners Willie Brewer and his wife, Pattie (Tucker), raised their 16 children in this house. Current owners Chip and Christine Kelly have added their own touches keeping with the architectural style of the house. (Town Historical collection.)

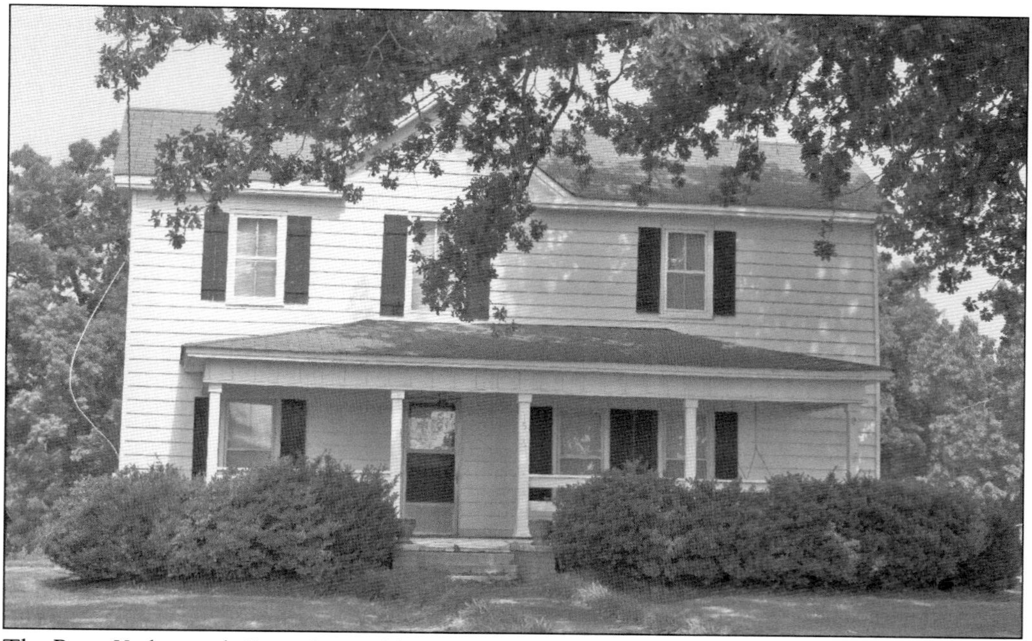

The Betts-Yarborough Farm, located behind the new Wal-Mart, was acquired by the Yarborough family around 1900 and is still owned by descendants. Outbuildings on the farm include a chicken house, several log tobacco curing barns, numerous barns and sheds, and a smokehouse. (Town Historical collection.)

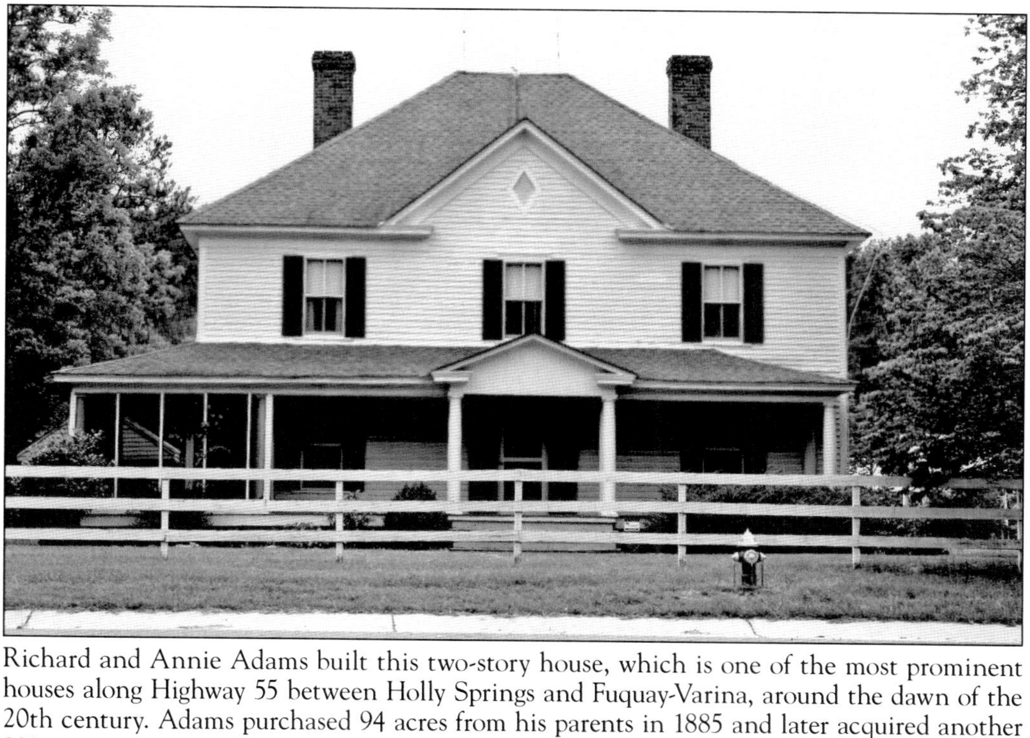

Richard and Annie Adams built this two-story house, which is one of the most prominent houses along Highway 55 between Holly Springs and Fuquay-Varina, around the dawn of the 20th century. Adams purchased 94 acres from his parents in 1885 and later acquired another 222 contiguous acres from other members of the family between the years 1899 and 1906. (Town Historical collection.)

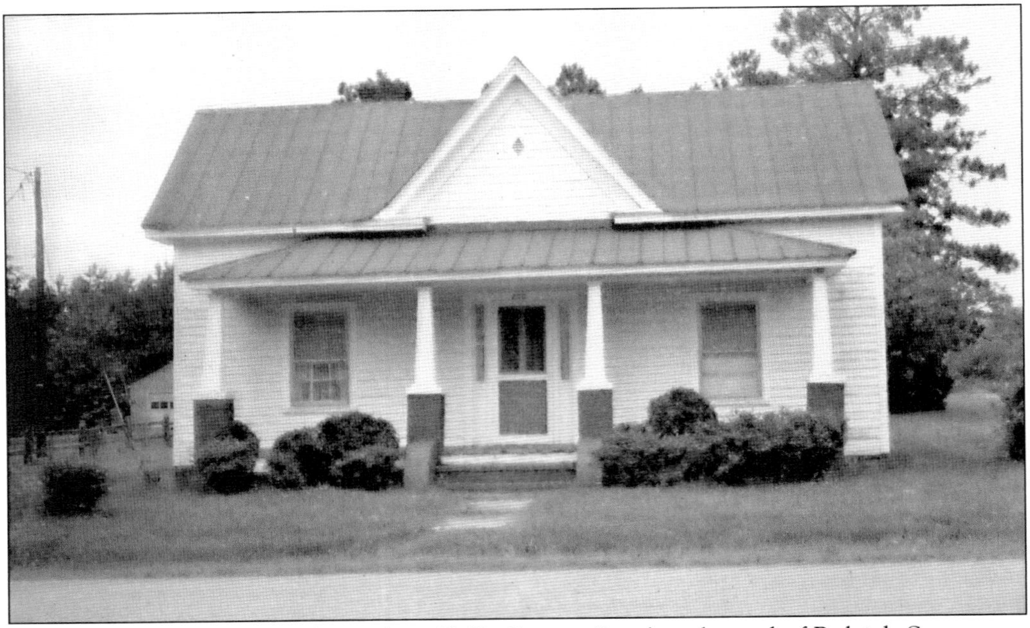

The William Jones House, located on Holly Springs Road at the end of Raleigh Street, was built around 1900, made from materials salvaged from a house built in the early 1800s. (Town Historical collection.)

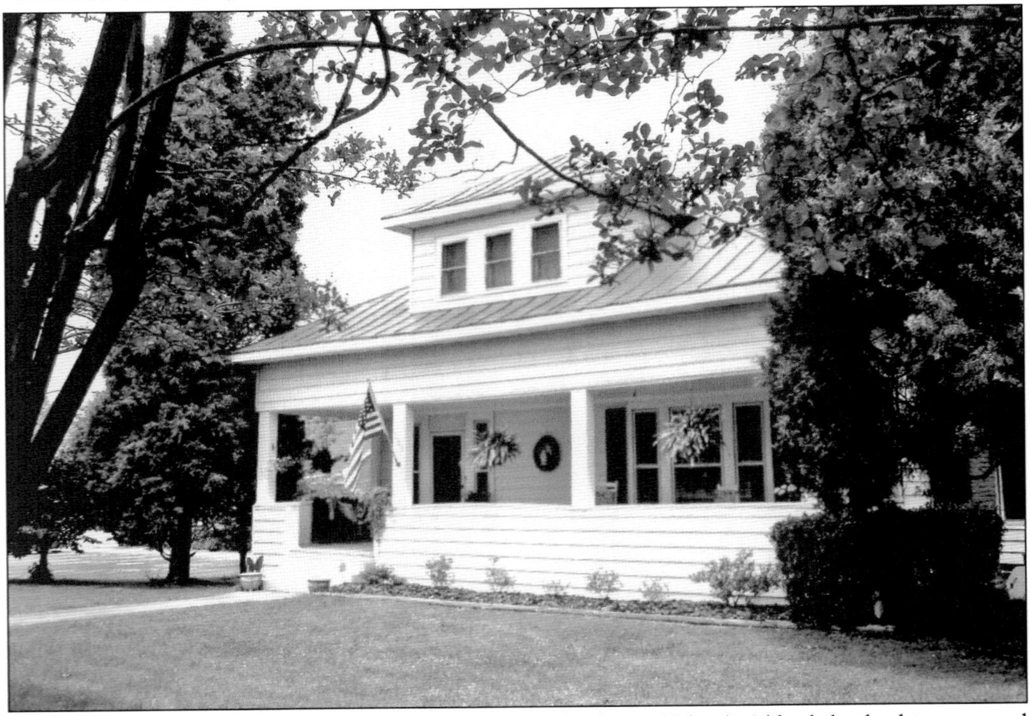

G. Haywood Alford, son of George Benton and Charlotte (Olive) Alford, built this arts and crafts–style bungalow house around 1915. Current owners Josef and Vada Fiegler have maintained the architectural integrity of the home and have preserved many of the period features so popular in that style of home. (Town Historical collection.)

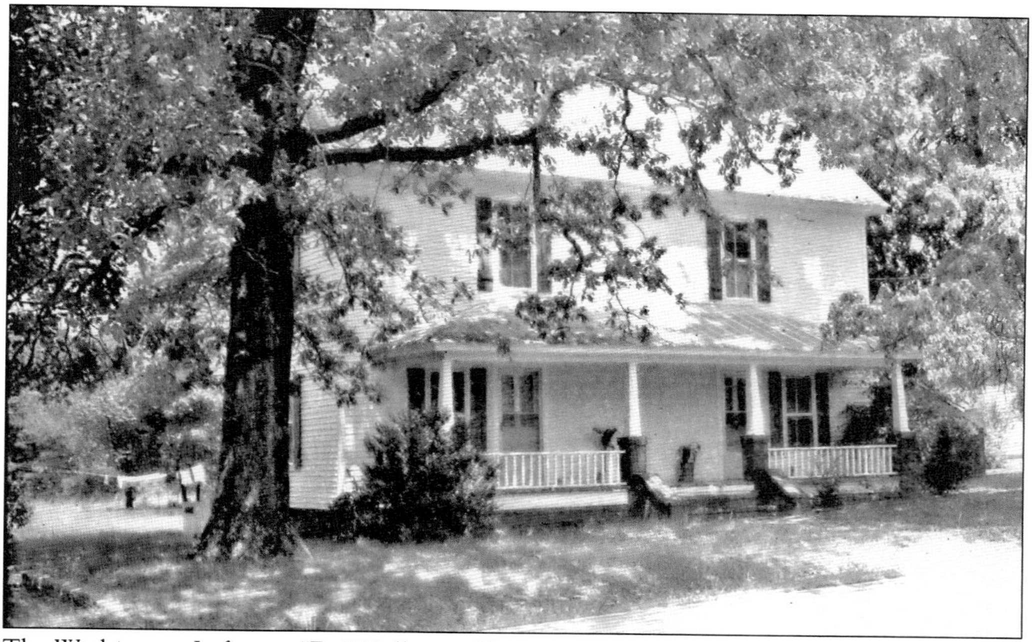

The Washington Lafayette "Fet" Holleman House originally was located across the street from the Scholl House on Holly Springs Road, but it was moved to its current location on South Main Street. Fet's wife was the former Elizabeth Ann Holland, daughter of Simpson Washington and Mary-Ann (Matthews) Holland. (Courtesy of North Carolina Archives.)

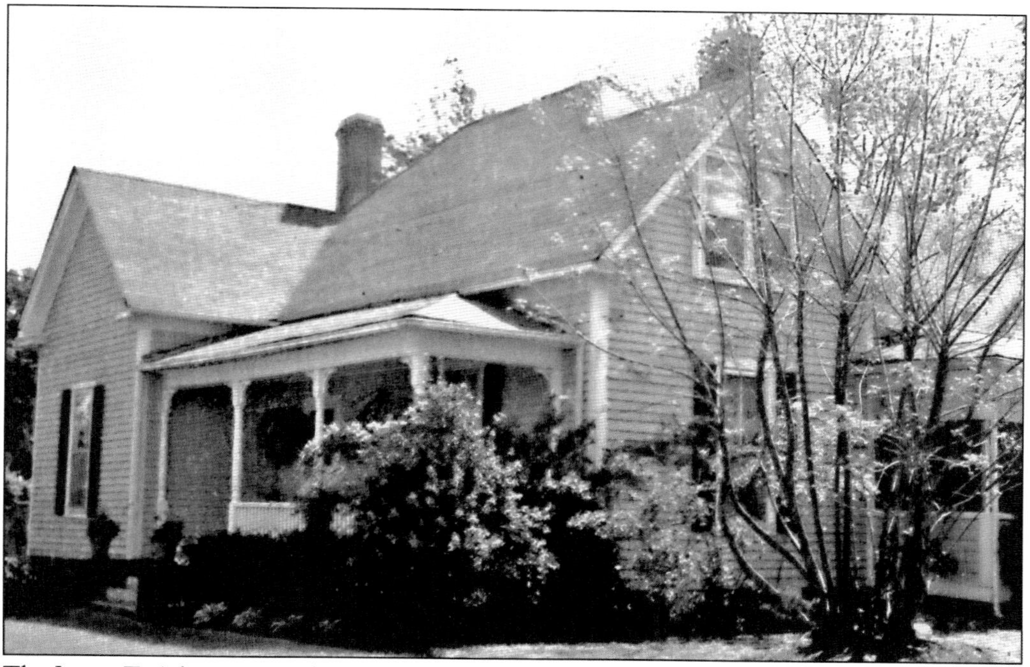

The James T. Adams House located on Avent Ferry Road near G. B. Alford Highway was built around 1908 by Confederate veteran James T. Adams. (Town Historical collection)

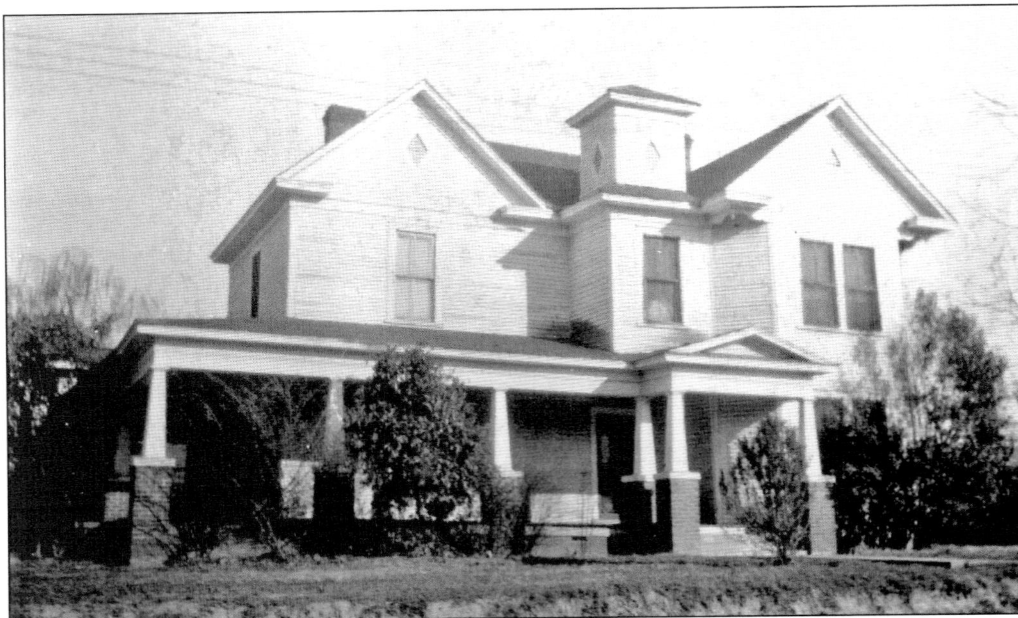

John Fabius and his wife, Helen Smitha Jones, owned this stately two-story home that once was located at the corner of Main and Center Streets, where the Holly Springs Baptist Church parking lot is now. Their grandchildren, Willie Eugene "Gene" and Cleo (Jones) Brewer, recall wonderful memories of this old house. (Doris Jones collection.)

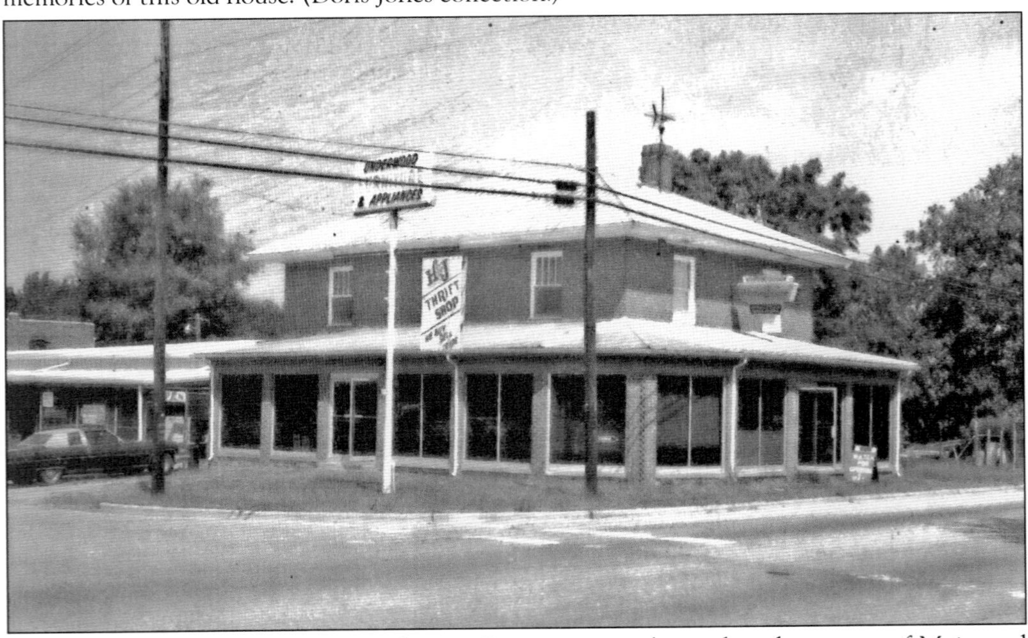


Seagraves Hotel, run by Johnny and Mary Seagraves, was located at the corner of Main and Ballentine Streets. It then became a private residence prior to reinventing itself as a commercial building. George Underwood added a metal warehouse/showroom to the building for his furniture business. The town purchased both buildings and used them as municipal offices until the buildings were razed in 2002 to make way for the existing town hall building. (Courtesy of Theresa Underwood.)

This monument was dedicated in 1923 through the efforts of George Benton Alford as a memorial for the valiant men of Holly Springs who answered the call of military service to their country in the Civil War, the Spanish American War, and World War I. It stands in the courtyard of the Leslie-Alford-Mims House and the Holly Springs United Methodist Church. (Town Historical collection.)

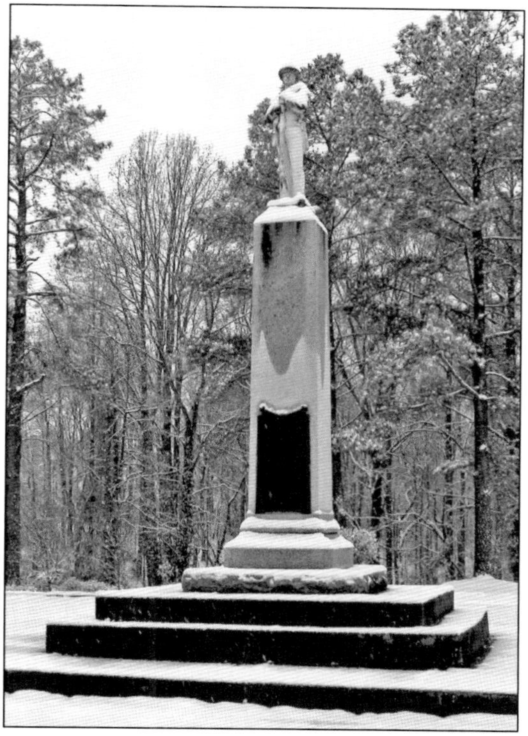

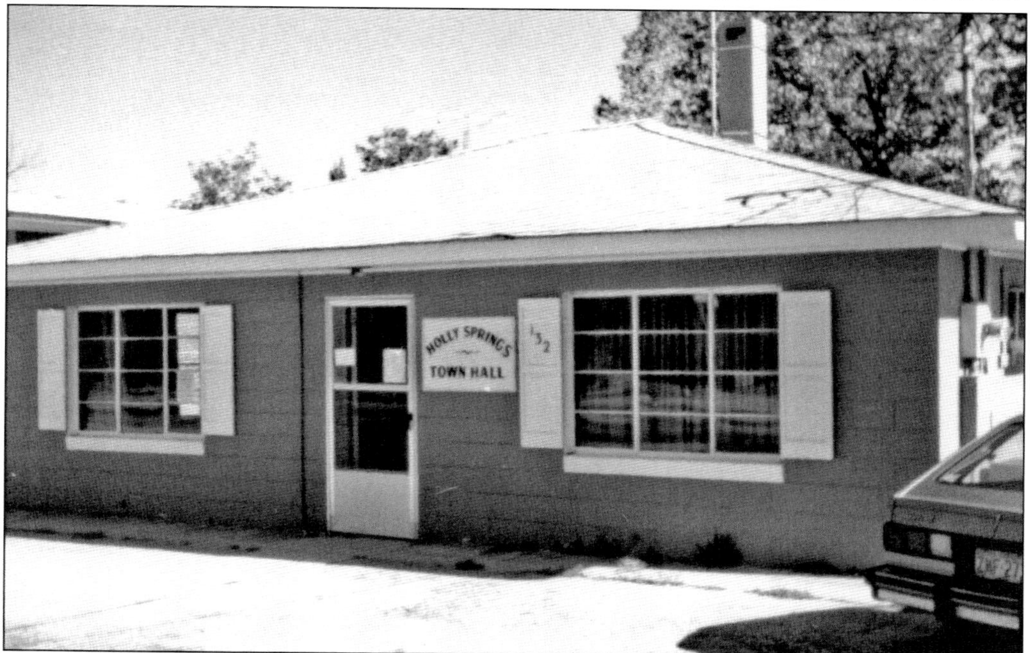


This cinderblock building served as the town hall from 1954 to the late 1980s. On this location once sat the Council No. 221 Junior Order of American Mechanics Lodge, which the town rented for $25 annually and eventually purchased in 1941 for $271.45. The old lodge building was razed in 1946, and soon residents would have their first brand-new town facility. (Nathan and Carolyn Williams collection.)

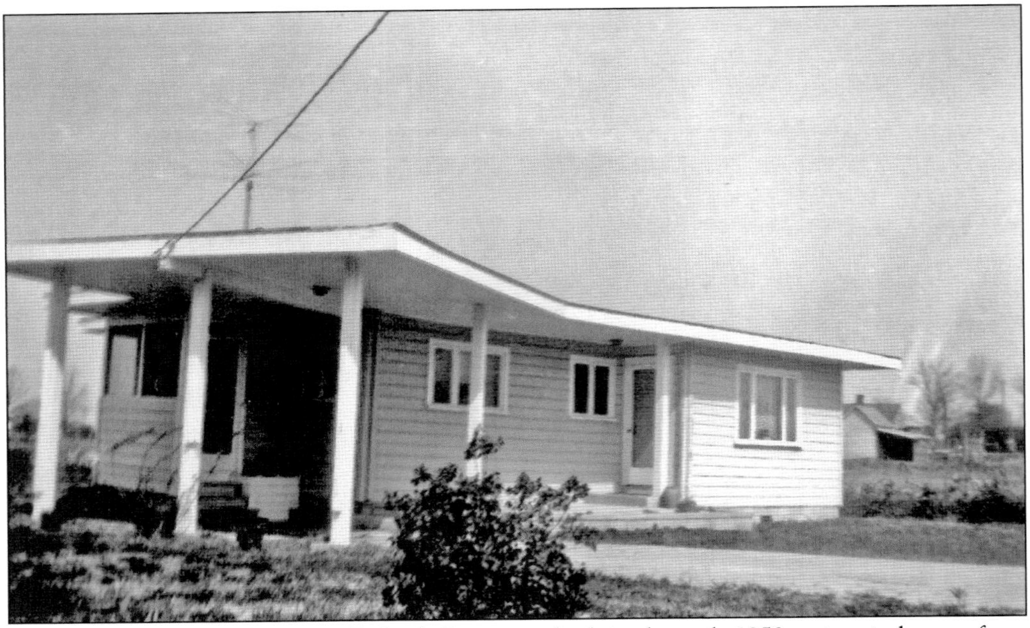

Ike and Rachel Mims's house on Raleigh Street was built in the early 1950s using timber cut from Rachel's father's land. The logs were loaded for transport, but the weight caused the truck to tip backward. Rachel sat on the hood of the truck to counter-balance the load! After construction, the house was painted pink, Rachel's favorite color. (Nathan and Carolyn Williams collection.)

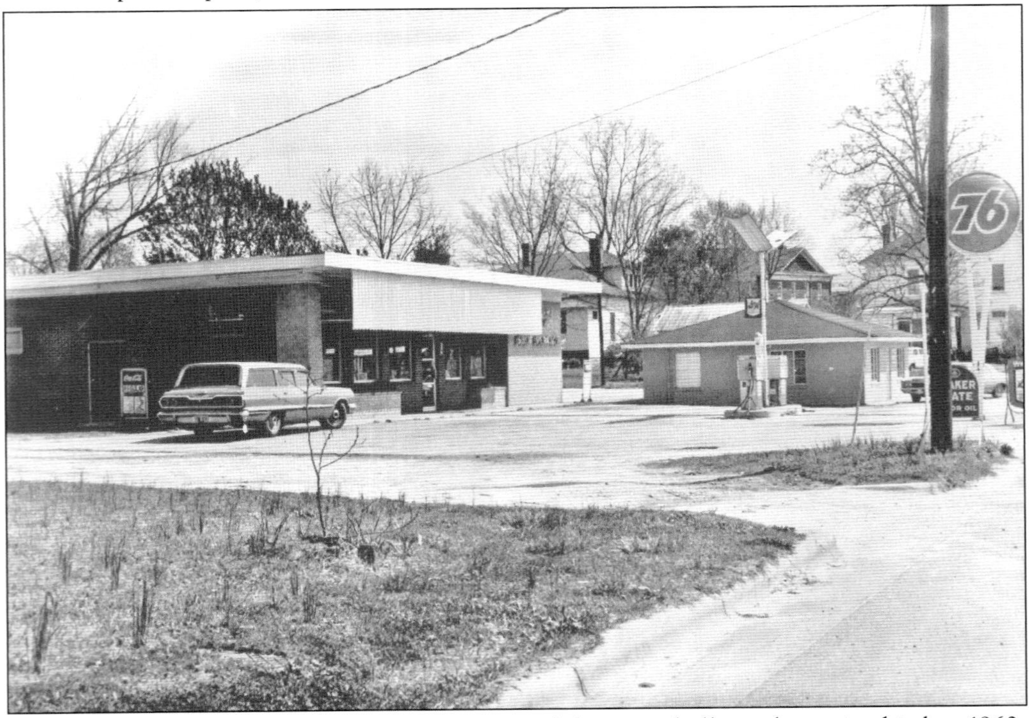


All new and improved, Paul Cummings's store and the town hall are shown in this late-1960s photograph. The original David Baker/Cummings' Store was razed when the town came through and widened the street and put in curbs and gutters. (Vada Fiegler collection.)

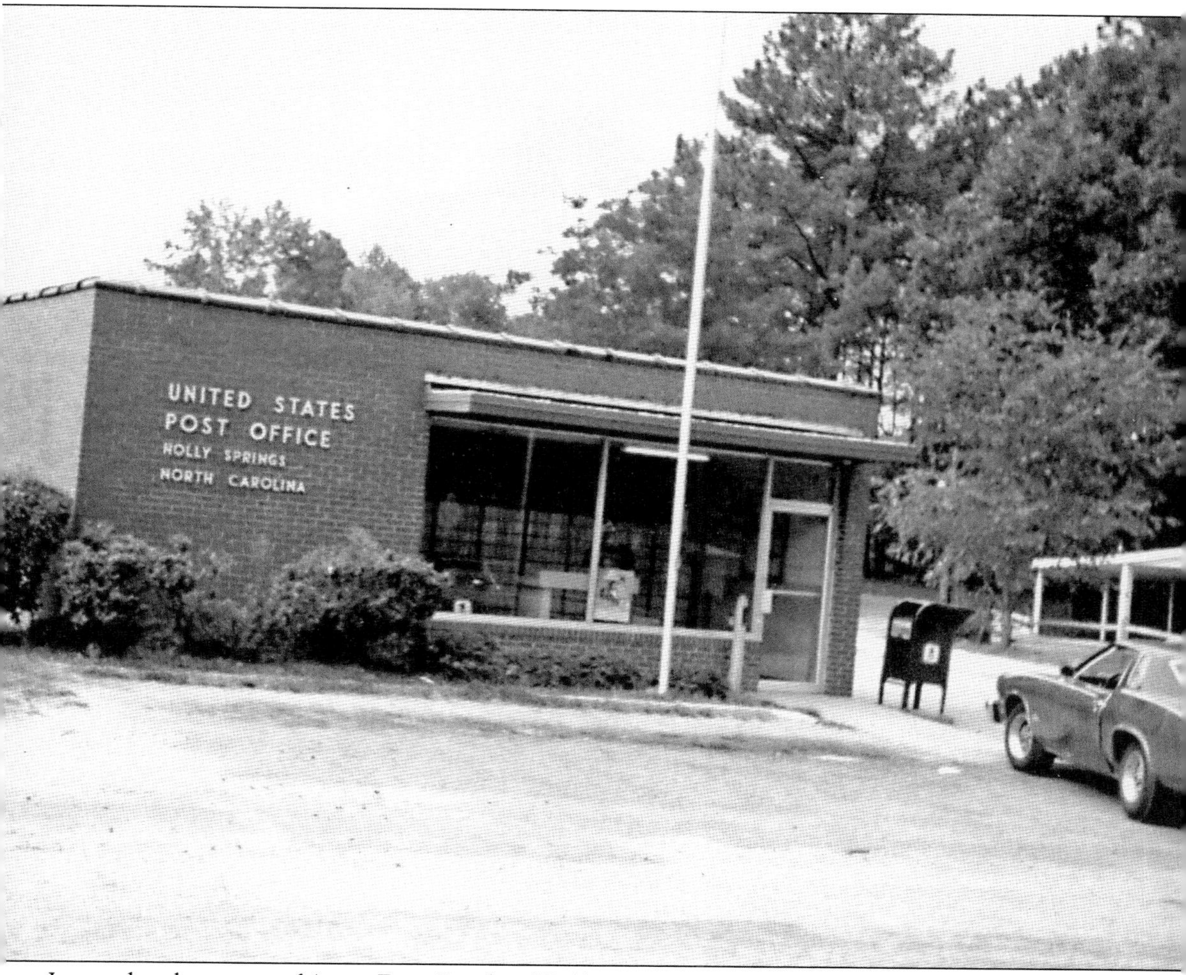


Located at the corner of Avent Ferry Road and Ballentine Street, a new, modern post office stood ready to serve the community. The dedication ceremony took place on Sunday, April 29, 1962. The ceremony was sponsored by the merchants of Holly Springs, and the master of ceremonies for the day was Charlie Woodhouse. The postmaster at the time was John F. Drake. (Nathan and Carolyn Williams collection.)

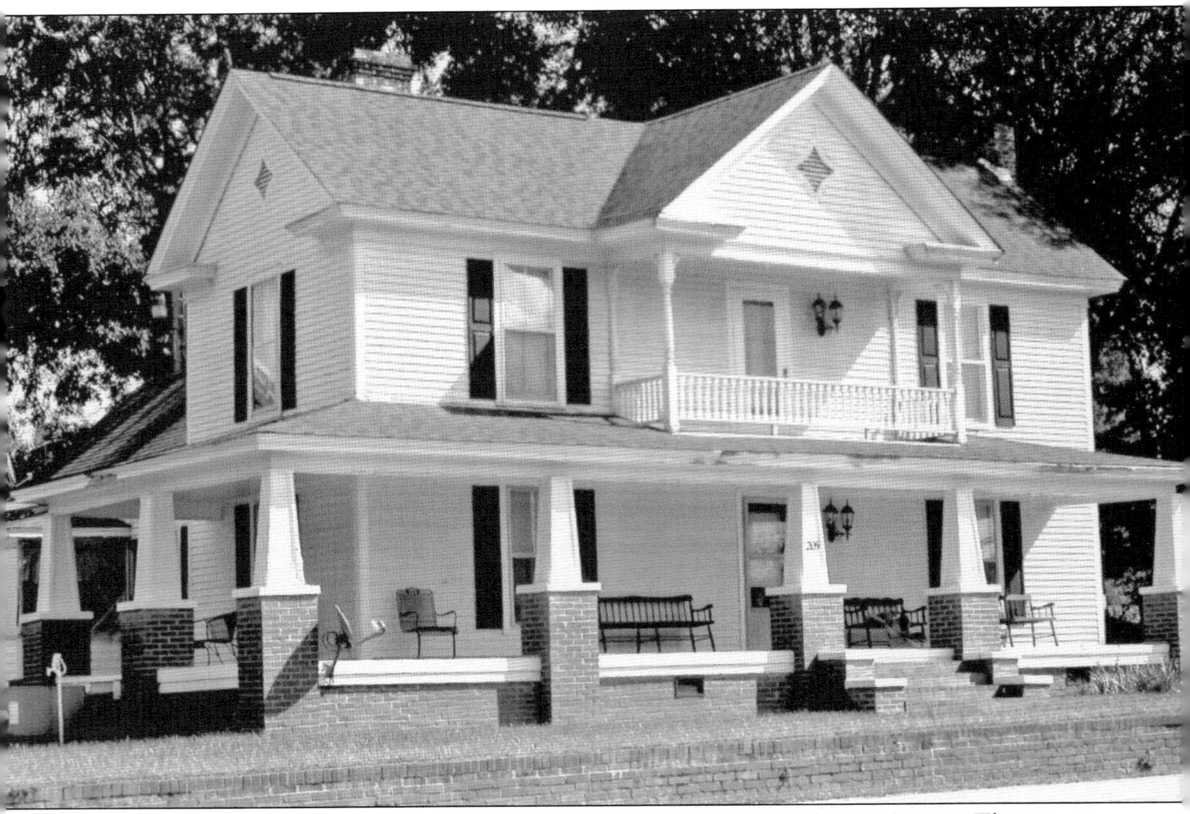

The Cross-Johnson House is situated at the corner of Raleigh and Earp Streets. This two-story white house with black shutters was built in 1910 by Davis Cross. It is now owned by Thomas Ragland; his grandmother was a Cross, and the family reacquired the house in 1968. Hurricane shutters grace the doors that lead out onto a small second-story balcony. Much of the original architectural features have been preserved, such as the woodwork and moldings, the main staircase to the second floor, and the front porch. (Town Historical collection.)

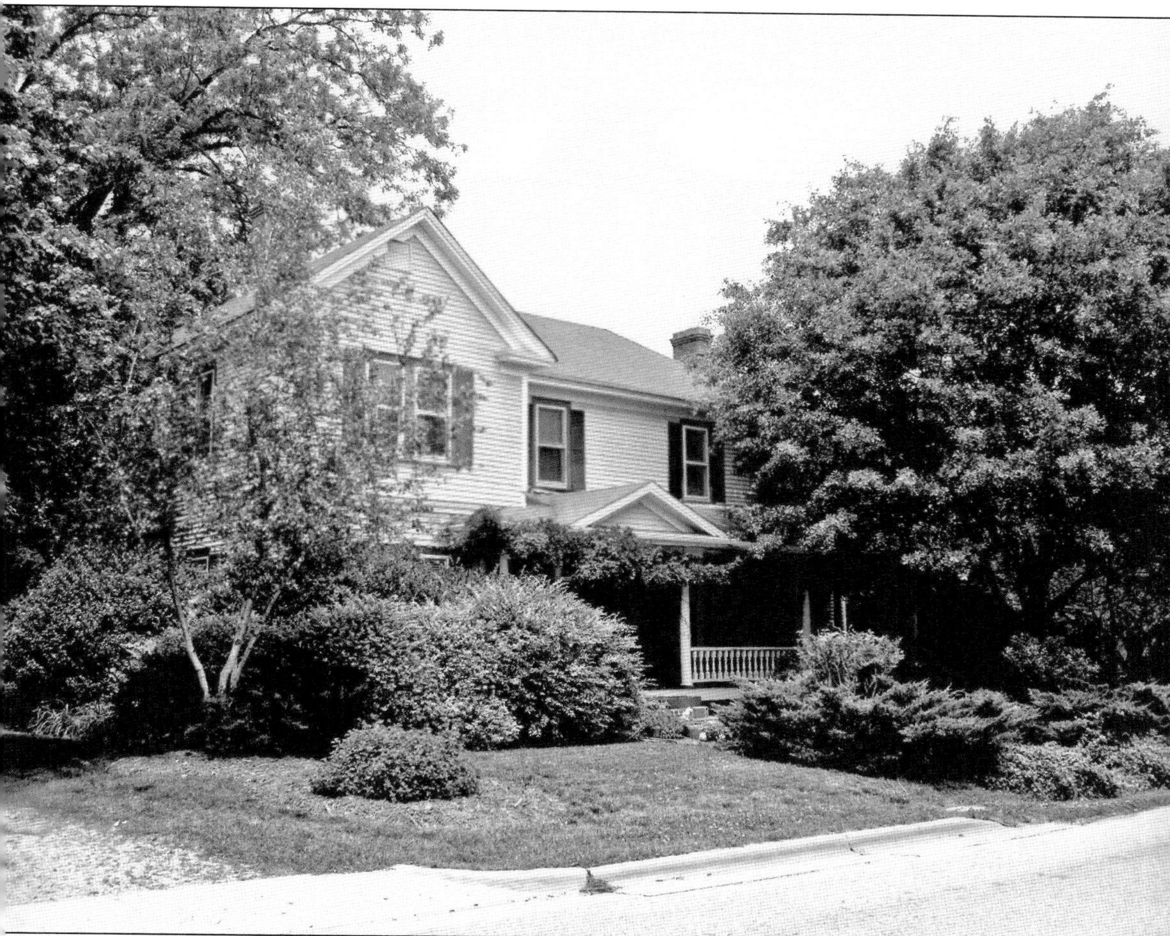

This house was built by Henry Norris around the 1880s and was expanded with an addition around 1900. Gerald Holleman recalls living here as a child and tells how he could lay on the floor and watch between the floorboards as the chickens scratched the dirt in the crawlspace. This home on Avent Ferry Road has been lovingly preserved and restored to its original glory by Jane and Ken Jarvis. (Town Historical collection.)

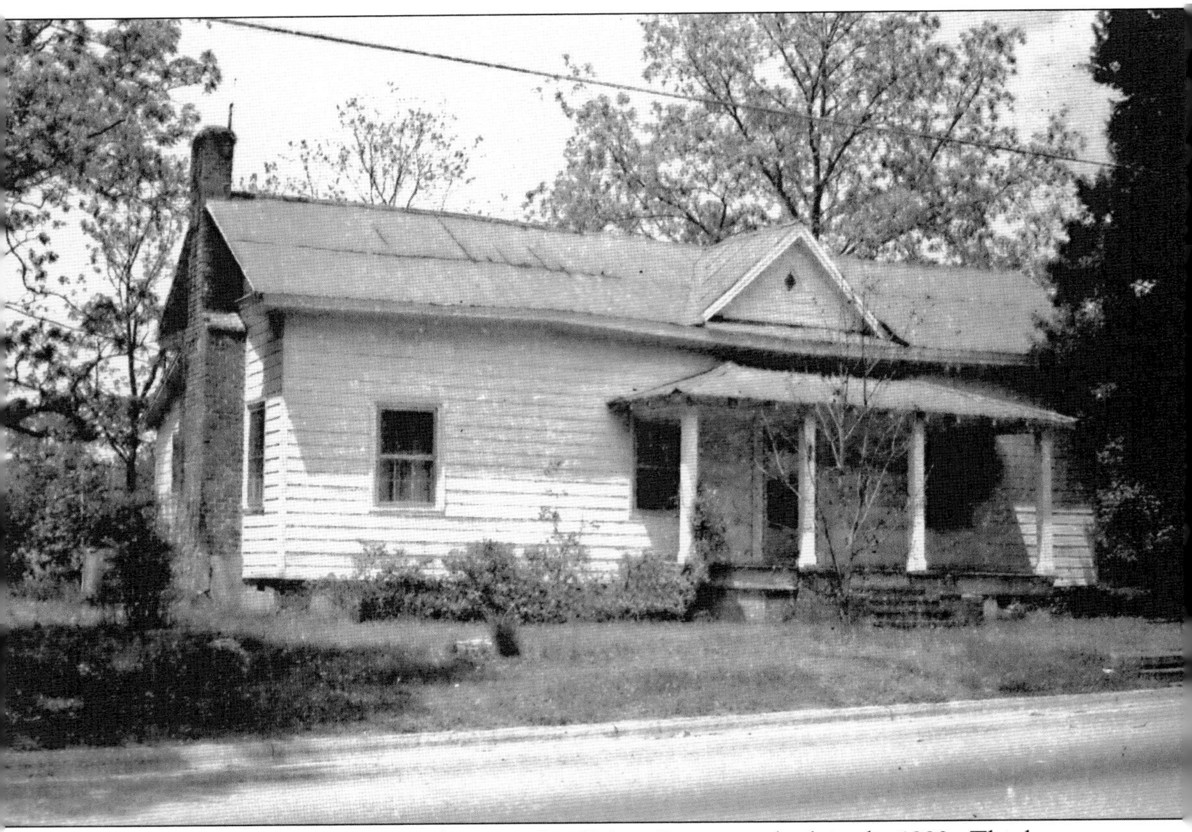

The Nathan Burns House, on the east side of Main Street, was built in the 1880s. This house was built on the site of an early dormitory for boys who were attending the Holly Springs Academy, housed on the first floor of the Masonic Lodge. (Courtesy of North Carolina Archives.)

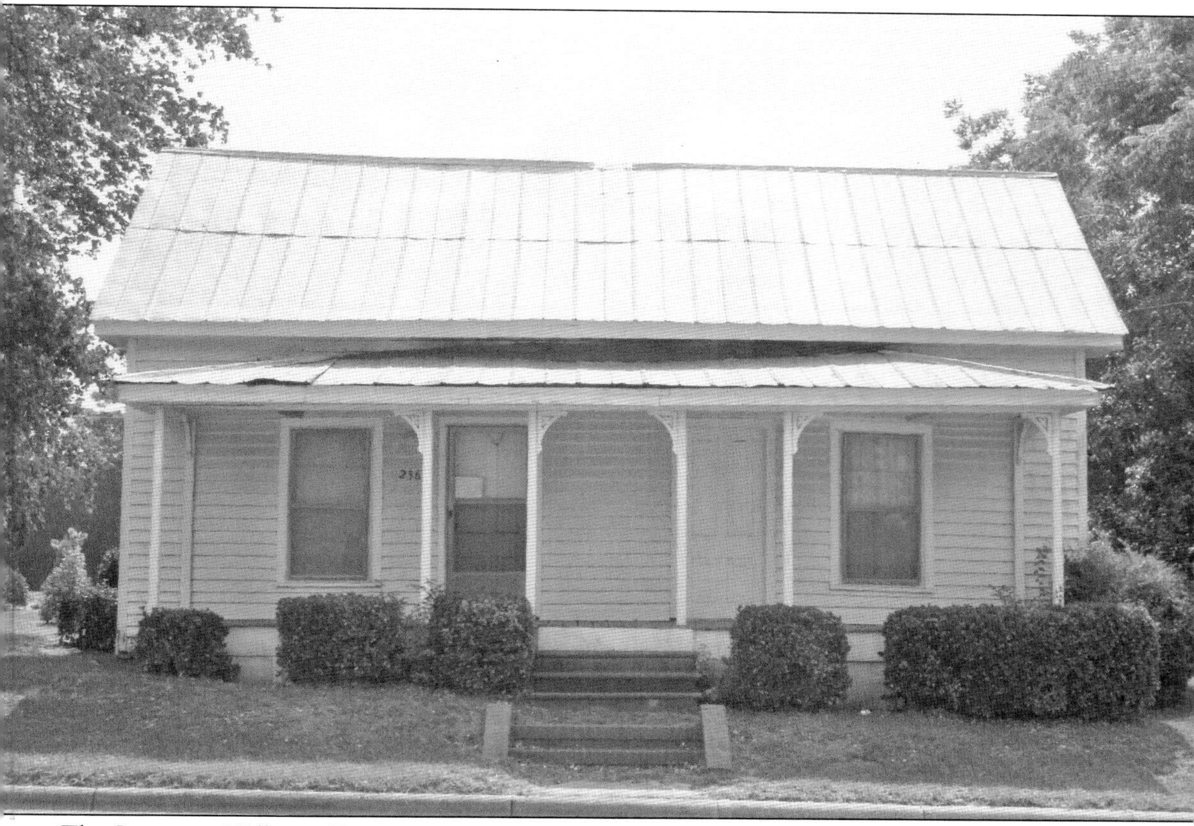

The Seagraves-Williams House on Main Street, put together with pegs, is said to be one of the oldest houses in town. The house is located between Shelly Lane Gift Shop and the Holly Springs Car Wash. (Town Historical collection.)

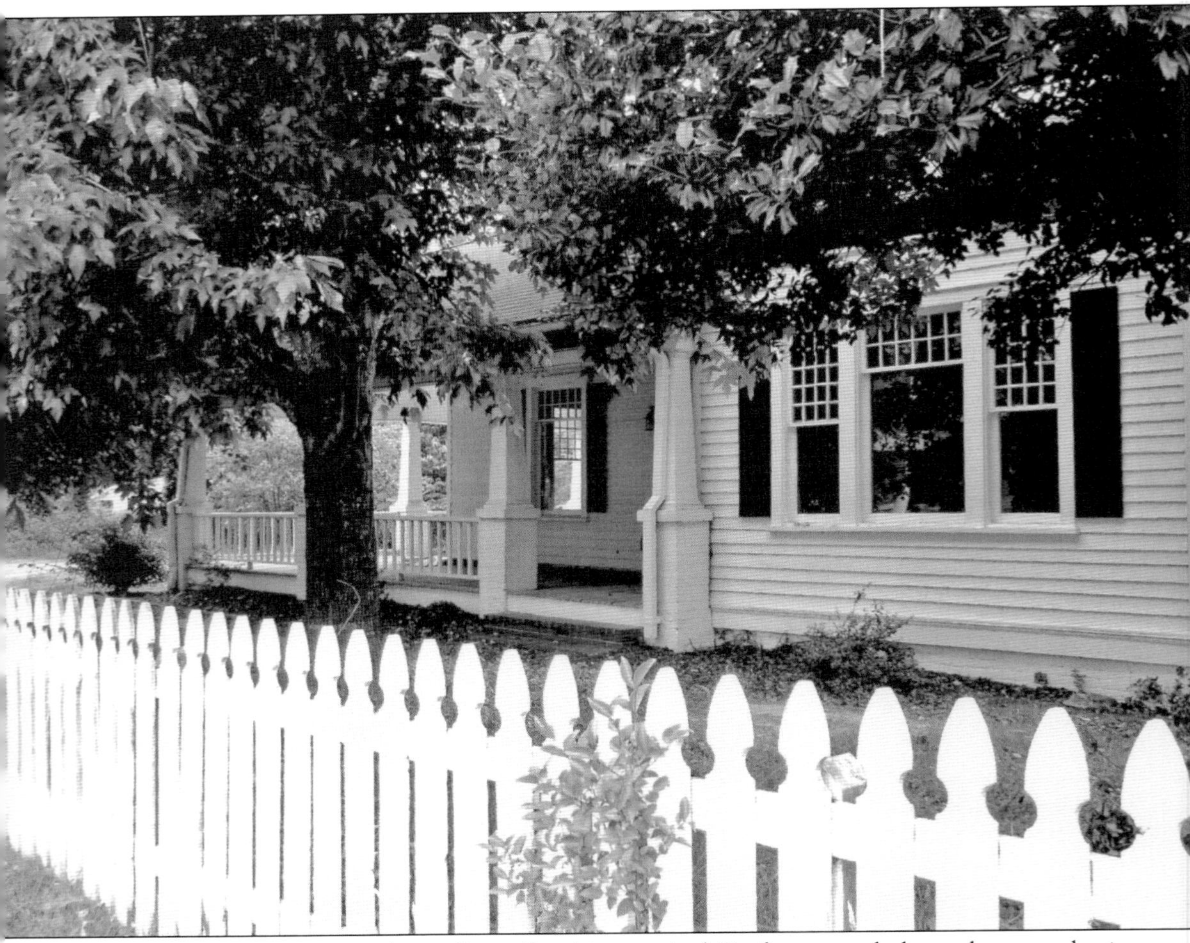

The Johnson House on Avent Ferry Road is a typical Craftsman-style bungalow popular in the 1910s–1930s. This home features interior pocket doors, oak woodwork, and plaster walls. A wraparound porch, white picket fence, and porte cochere add to the charm of this home. (Town Historical collection .)

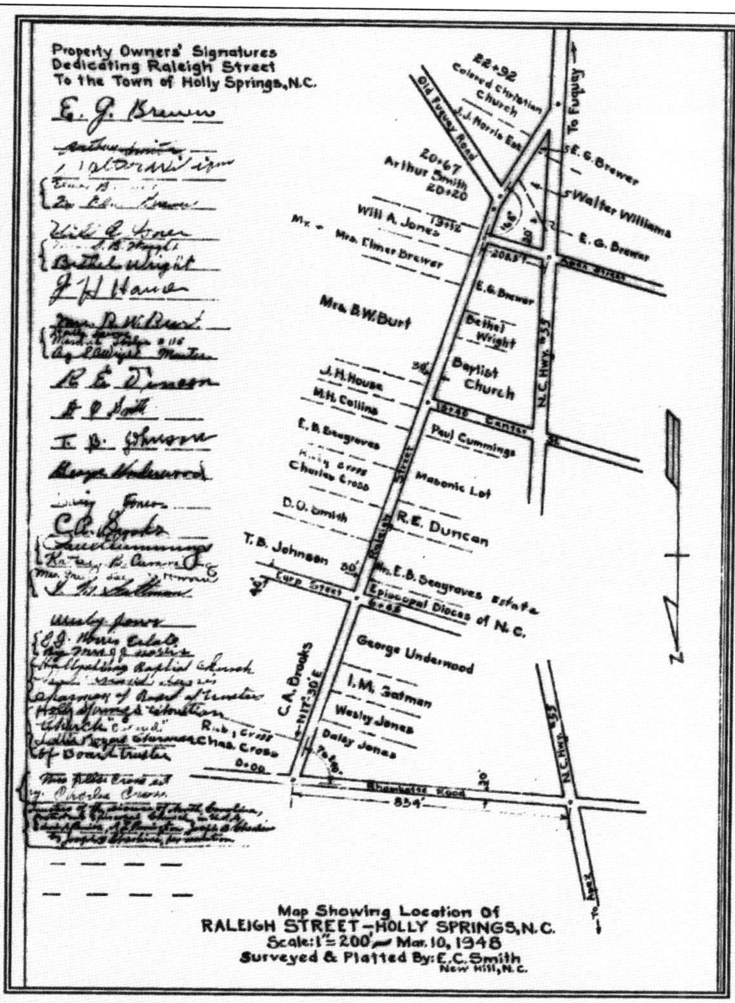


## The Beginnings of Raleigh Street

In 1948, property owners along Raleigh Street dedicated a public easement for the roadway. A map illustrating the names and signatures of those owners is below. Note that the bearing of the map is South, rather than North. Holly Springs Road today is what is labeled "Rhamkatte Road" on the map.

Here is an early map of Raleigh Street. (Town Historical collection.)